My Fair Lazy

OTHER TITLES BY *NEW YORK TIMES*
BESTSELLING AUTHOR JEN LANCASTER

. . . .

Bitter Is the New Black

Bright Lights, Big Ass

Such a Pretty Fat

Pretty in Plaid

My Fair Lazy

One Reality Television Addict's Attempt to Discover
If Not Being a Dumb Ass Is the New Black,
or a Culture-Up Manifesto

Jen Lancaster

 NEW AMERICAN LIBRARY

NEW AMERICAN LIBRARY
Published by New American Library, a division of
Penguin Group (USA) Inc., 375 Hudson Street, New York, New York 10014, USA
Penguin Group (Canada), 90 Eglinton Avenue East, Suite 700, Toronto,
Ontario M4P 2Y3, Canada (a division of Pearson Penguin Canada Inc.)
Penguin Books Ltd., 80 Strand, London WC2R 0RL, England
Penguin Ireland, 25 St. Stephen's Green, Dublin 2, Ireland
(a division of Penguin Books Ltd.)
Penguin Group (Australia), 250 Camberwell Road, Camberwell, Victoria 3124,
Australia (a division of Pearson Australia Group Pty. Ltd.)
Penguin Books India Pvt. Ltd., 11 Community Centre, Panchsheel Park,
New Delhi - 110 017, India
Penguin Group (NZ), 67 Apollo Drive, Rosedale, North Shore 0632, New Zealand
(a division of Pearson New Zealand Ltd.)
Penguin Books (South Africa) (Pty.) Ltd., 24 Sturdee Avenue, Rosebank, Johannesburg 2196,
South Africa

Penguin Books Ltd., Registered Offices:
80 Strand, London WC2R 0RL, England

First published by New American Library,
a division of Penguin Group (USA) Inc.

First Printing, May 2010
10   9   8   7   6   5   4   3   2   1

LIBRARY OF CONGRESS CATALOGING-IN-PUBLICATION DATA:

Lancaster, Jen, 1967–
   My fair lazy: one reality television addict's attempt to discover if not being a dumb ass is the new black, or a
culture-up manifesto/Jen Lancaster.
      p.   cm.
   ISBN 978-0-451-22986-1
   1. Lancaster, Jen, 1967–   2. Authors, American—21st century—Biography.   3. United States—Social life and
customs—21st century—Humor.   I. Title.
   PS3612.A54748Z46 2010
   814'.54—dc22   2009052760
   [B]

Set in Bulmer MT
Designed by Spring Hoteling

Printed in the United States of America

PUBLISHER'S NOTE

Penguin is committed to publishing works of quality and integrity. In that spirit, we are proud to offer this book to our readers; however, the story, the experiences, and the words are the author's alone.

   While the author has made every effort to provide accurate telephone numbers and Internet addresses at the time of publication, neither the publisher nor the author assumes any responsibility for errors, or for changes that occur after publication. Further, publisher does not have any control over and does not assume any responsibility for author or third-party Web sites or their content.

For Mary-Ellis Bunim and Jonathan Murray, who started it all.

For Stacey, who makes everything more fun.

C·O·N·T·E·N·T·S

Contents

Some characters have been combined for storytelling purposes. In addition, other names and identifying characteristics have been changed for privacy reasons with timelines compressed.

Progress isn't made by early risers. It's made by lazy men trying to find an easier way to do something.

—ROBERT HEINLEIN, *Time Enough for Love*

It is only the wisest and the stupidest that cannot change.

—CONFUCIUS

And as usual, what happens next is all Carrie Bradshaw's fault.

—JEN LANCASTER, *My Fair Lazy* BOOK PROPOSAL

P·R·O·L·O·G·U·E

*S*ipping wine out of a paper cup, I'm perched on a tall stool across from my literary idol, Candace Bushnell, who's interviewing me for her Sirius radio show.

This is the single greatest day of my life.

I've managed to keep myself together enough to avoid (a) bursting into creepy fan-girl tears, (b) asking if I can please, please braid her pretty, pretty hair, or (c) shrieking, "OMFG, you're the real Carrie Bradshaw!" but it hasn't been without heroic effort. I'm mostly holding my own in the interview until Candace tells me she's totally into Bow da Lair.

Beaux de l'air?

Botta-layer?

Baudelaire?

I have no idea what she's talking about. Baudelaire—what is that, a kind of sushi? Some superstretchy Pilates move? This season's must-have stiletto? I am without a single clue. Yet I quickly confirm that I'm *absolutely* into Baudelaire, too, and then change topics with the grace and dexterity of a veteran White House press secretary.[1]

....

[1] Or a Lohan family publicist.

As I try to keep myself from breaking into terror sweat, it occurs to me that I don't know who Baudelaire is because I've become a little bit dumb.

What prompts this epiphany isn't my dearth of knowledge of All Things Baudelaire. Plenty of smart people are unfamiliar with Baudelaire.[2]

What gives me pause is the ease with which I cover up my ignorance. I'm confident I used to be smart, but when I got laid off from an executive position post-9/11, I was no longer tasked to use my critical thinking skills. On top of that, while I searched in vain for a new job, reality television went from being an occasional guilty pleasure to a full-time source of solace. I mean, sure, I was unemployed and broke and I'd totally lost what defined me, but at least I wasn't one of those idiots attempting to get *Married by America*. And I never had to ask my friend Nicole Richie if Walmart was the place that sold walls. Reality television gave me an amazing feeling of moral and intellectual superiority without actually requiring any effort past moving the dogs to find the remote.

Although my life eventually improved,[3] I never weaned myself off of reality television once I started writing. And at this point I'm so used to not having much interest outside of what's happening with *The Real Housewives of Orange County* and in the *Rock of Love* mansion that I've become an expert in faking most other knowledge. Lying about what I don't know has become my lazy but elegant solution to not acquiring the basic facts in the first place. Because I no longer report to a boss, I never have to take on hard or boring tasks, thus traveling outside of my comfort zone is a rarity, and most likely involuntary.

Frankly, my steady diet of sloth and avoidance has served me well,

....

[2]Right?

[3]As evidenced by today's sit-down with Candace.

and I will see no reason to change things . . . until the unthinkable happens next week, and I inadvertently end up on the *New York Times* bestseller list.

Ten times.

Dude.

What gets me is the sneaking suspicion that I'd be a better writer if my first thought at this unexpected windfall wasn't *"Dude."* So I grudgingly admit that broadening my horizons is something I should work on, but I've got to get through this book tour first.

Anyway, our interview eventually draws to a close, and I leave the studio with no idea if Baudelaire is some kind of yogic breathing technique or French-Vietnamese cuisine.

But I do know if I want to be more like Candace Bushnell, perhaps I should make an effort to find out.

To: angie_at_home

From: jen_at_home

Subject: today's Jen-point quiz

It's late in the evening and you're just about to head upstairs, take a bath, and read a bit before bed when you hear a noise in the front yard. Upon drawing the curtains, you come face-to-face with a hipster who's using your lawn/the corner of your house as a urinal.

What do you do next?

(a) You smile and shake your head. Ah, the capriciousness of youth!

(b) You frown and shake your head. You don't like it, but you understand this kind of thing happens sometimes when you live in an urban environment.

(c) You call the police, knowing full well if they even bother to respond to your call, the hipster pisser will be halfway through his can of Pabst Blue Ribbon at the neighborhood watering hole before they arrive.

(d) You throw open the front door and scream profanities at the hipster, causing the stream of urine to soak his skinny jeans. And as he egresses at a brisk pace, you shout, "Doesn't matter if you run, motherfucker, because I know where you're going!"

(e) You spend the rest of the evening standing by your open front door, shaking your garden shovel at everyone who's unfortunate enough to park on your street.

(f) Answers D and E.

Scoring:

Award yourself zero points for Answers A–C, five points for Answers D–E, and ten points for Answer F.

Give yourself one bonus point if your shovel is rusty.

C·H·A·P·T·E·R O·N·E

The Rat World/Road Rules Challenge

(Three months earlier)

"**Y**ou are *not* watching that crap."

"No, no, I'm not." My eyes flick back to the screen.

I hear Fletch take a slow, deliberate breath before he says, "From where I'm standing, it would appear that you are."

Refusing to meet his eye, I counter, "Maybe you have a bad vantage point?"

Fletch is standing in the small hallway between our kitchen and living room, arms akimbo. From what I can see from the corner of my eye, it almost seems like he's glowering at me. "You're not *watching* that crap."

Breezily, I respond, "Nope, not me."

He repeats, "You are not watching that *crap*."

I peek up at him again. Oh, yes, there's distinct glowering. I try to hide my smile behind my hand.

"Does emphasizing a different word every time you say it somehow reinforce your message? Or finally make me understand?" I ask mildly.

To the layman, Fletch might seem angry, but I assure you he's not. My friend Gina says nothing makes Fletch happier than expressing righteous indignation about something trivial. Minor aggravations keep his blood flowing. And since almost nothing makes him more righteously indignant than fine, fine MTV reality programming, I figure I'll let this play out.

Fletch turns sideways to enter our tiny living room as if navigating between two closely parked cars. A while back I got new couches, and while they're the perfect size in both height and width, I kind of forgot to think about depth. So unless we want to do the Bump with the television stand, we scuttle in sideways when we enter and leave.[4]

Fletch eases in beside me on the couch. My odiferous pit bull, Maisy, is taking up most of the space on the other side of me. Fletch starts in again. "Maybe I'm saying this wrong. I guess what I mean is, *why* are you watching this crap?"

I press PAUSE and turn to face him. "Okay, number one, you sound like my dad, and number two, I'm not *watching*. I just happened to turn the channel and this was on."

He wipes his palm across his forehead and runs it down his cheek, his default gesture when he's frustrated. He's done it a lot in the fourteen years we've been together. But the way I see it, if I get him a little fired up

....

[4]The nice thing about having such a small living room is that the television looks HUGE!

over a nonissue, he'll sleep better at night. "That's what you said twenty minutes ago."

"Why do you care?" I shift away from him and toward Maisy. She returns my display of affection by violently thumping her tail against a pillow. With each stroke, dust motes float in the filtered winter sunlight and little puffs of her stink waft over me. "If there's something on you want to see, go watch it in the bedroom."

"That's not it. I just hate the idea of you wasting a perfectly good Saturday on this garbage." He turns and begins to scrutinize the action currently frozen on the set. I see a flash of recognition play across his features. "Wait, *I* know that girl. Considering I haven't watched this show in about twenty years, that would make her, what? Forty? Forty-five?"

"Something like that," I admit. "Although technically this isn't *The Real World*, which I totally don't even watch anymore. This is *The Real World/Road Rules Challenge*, a whole different beast. This isn't a *reality* show. This is a *game* show. Big difference." I unpause the program.

Fletch stands up and starts pacing in the limited space between me and the television. Every time he veers left, I veer right to make sure I don't miss any of the action. "But what's the deal? How can you possibly be invested in these idiots' lives? How is it they can always run off to some desert island to play tug-of-war? I mean, do they have jobs? Or bosses? Do they go to an office every day? Or are they professional reality show contestants? Are they all trapped in a state of perpetual adolescence? Does MTV cryogenically freeze them between appearances, or do they actually have lives with mortgages and husbands and wives and stuff?"

"They're usually not married because that way they can all hook up with each other once they get there." Then I reflect on other *Real World/ Road Rules Challenge*s for a moment. "A lot of times, though, they have boyfriends and girlfriends who they end up cheating on, like the first night, so that just adds to the drama."

He curls his lip in disgust. "Pathetic."

I give him a playful shove. "Oh, lighten up, Francis.[5] And besides, I'm only watching because I'm traumatized, and you can't argue with that."

To backtrack: a couple of months ago, we installed a home gym in our basement to supplement my ongoing fitness efforts. Because our rental house is more than a hundred years old, the entrance to the basement is a bit of a squeeze. You have to go down four steps and then duck as you walk under the far corner of the house before you can enter the wee little *Alice in Wonderland* door.

Bringing the boxes of exercise equipment in whole was impossible, so the deliverymen had to spend a solid hour disassembling the components in our garage and carrying them in, little by little. Once inside, the men had to navigate all the random floor joists scattered throughout the basement[6] while avoiding hitting their heads on the low ceiling beams. Every ten minutes we'd hear a loud metallic clang preceding an "Ooof!" and followed by what I assume was the world's longest string of Polish profanity.

Once they got the components inside, they had to reassemble the equipment in the spots I'd marked with tape. We had to place each item precisely between ceiling beams, or else we'd give ourselves a million concussions every time we used a machine. As it is, Fletch is too tall for the elliptical trainer and he can't incline the treadmill at all, unless he wants to hunch down. The one time he tried to run on a grade, he got all

....

[5]Wait. You don't go around quoting *Stripes* twenty-six years after its release?

[6]Apparently our house has a tendency to sink without proper support.

hunkered over with his back curled and his head jutting out. He looked like a gecko sprinting across the Australian outback.

From start to finish, Operation Home Gym lasted almost five hours. The delivery guys left the basement door propped open the entire time, as I imagine cursing the two Yuppie bastards upstairs is hot work.[7]

Here's where things got complicated. Our creepy old neighbors moved out around Christmas, leaving little in their wake save for the few Green Party presidential candidate stickers they couldn't unstick off the lamppost. When we watched them load up their U-Haul with stuff one normally doesn't pack—e.g., countertops, cabinet doors, floor tiles— Fletch remarked, "There's not going to be a wire, toilet seat, or lightbulb left in that place." They even took all the garbage bags that they'd been using for windowpanes on their back porch, thus giving all the neighborhood rats unfettered access to the indoors.

But then a developer bought the property and began to rehab it, displacing a colony of vermin. I imagine the rat packs standing on their haunches in the backyard, hurling rodent-sized rocks and bottles at the contractors, like tiny little Palestinians. I giggle every time I picture them wrapped up in tiny little kaffiyehs.

Now, because of all the comings and goings on the day of Operation Home Gym, I locked the cats in the guest bedroom and the dogs in the master. Eventually the dogs had to go outside, so I brought them out to do their business. Maisy's just as happy to go on a rug, but you know, standards of cleanliness and stuff.

Afterward, Maisy and I were sitting on the couch and Loki was positioned by the ottoman at my feet. Fletch was on a conference call, and I needed to talk to him before the dogs and I went back upstairs. As I

....

[7] Yes, we tipped them big. But they still hate us.

huffed, sighed, and generally made a nuisance out of myself while I waited, I saw movement out of the corner of my eye. I turned my head to get a better look, expecting to see one of the cats. Instead I saw something smaller skitter past. My initial reaction was *Oh, look, cute! Fuzzy! Pear-shaped!* until my brain fully engaged and. . . .

RAT!

IN MY HOUSE!

RAT IN MY HOUSE!

RATINMYHOUSE!!!!!

RATINMYHOUSE!!!!!!!

The rat, looking plump and robust from his two-month stay in the homeland next door, wandered around the corner from the kitchen with nary a care in the world. He'd strolled halfway to the living room before he caught my eye. Displaying zero sense of urgency, he made a U-turn and sauntered back into the kitchen while I sat paralyzed.

Did the pit bull—a *carnivore*, mind you—notice the rat five feet away?

No.

Did the German shepherd—*another carnivore*—notice the rat five feet away?

No.

Did any of the four cats upstairs, whose Spidey senses really *should* have been tingling so much that they were compelled to hurl themselves at the door, make any sort of noise?

No.

Anyway, when the rat and I locked eyes, I inhaled so quickly and deeply that I passed out for a moment.

When I came to, I very quietly informed Fletch there was a rat in the kitchen, in my house, in my house, IN MY HOUSE. Fletch went to inspect, and I mustered every bit of calm I could and dragged the dogs back upstairs before they noticed, as I didn't want the afternoon to turn into the squirrel scene from *Christmas Vacation*, with the addition of bloody entrails.

Fletch went into the kitchen, found nothing, shrugged, and went back to his conference call, mouthing that it was probably a mouse and more than likely found its way back outside.

Yeah, like I was going to take *that* chance.

Upstairs, I Googled "Chicago Rat Extermination" and began to make calls. The first place didn't believe me when I said my pit bull— part of the *terrier* family, meaning they instinctively go after things that are *terrestrial*—didn't notice the rat, who was practically whipping up a batch of ratatouille in front of her face. I eventually convinced them I wasn't (a) crazy or (b) living in complete squalor, but it didn't matter because they couldn't come until Thursday.

I left out the pit bull part when I called the second place. However, they kept blathering on about their patented no-kill collection process, which I'd normally be all about if the rats were, say, in my alley. Sure! Let them live! Take them to a nice farm in the country where they can run! But in my kitchen, the pristine place where pork chops are served? Not so much.

I talked to a guy at a third place and when I said, "Then he turned the corner and—" he interrupted me and said, "Hey, it could be a she."

Really? REALLY? I mean, yay for equal rights and all, but is now *the very best time* to play the politically correct pronoun game? Then he said something about HER being pregnant, and I may have passed out again.

Fletch enjoys being contradictory, so he refused to believe that it was a rat. Because we were dealing with mice (in his opinion), he said we should simply handle the extermination ourselves. We got a ton of traps from Home Depot, set them everywhere, and installed those electronic rodent repellants.

We caught nothing, save for head colds from our repeated home-improvement-warehouse trips in the dead of winter.

A few days passed, and in a brilliant stroke of irony, Fletch was in the middle of lecturing me about how there was no way a rat could be in our house, when something ran across his foot and under the stove.

Seriously, I despise rats but I've got to give the old boy[8] props for timing.

We stepped up our trapping efforts for a while, until Fletch again claimed we were tilting at windmills.[9] He said there was no way any rodent would still be here, what with the six hungry carnivores we keep. He promised me that nothing could survive the killing fields of our house and that the second the guys caught the scent of vermin, their instincts would kick in, and it would be over. Dogs and cats would work together to circle and trap their prey, snapping and tearing and rending flesh before going all *Lord of the Flies*, putting the tiny rat/mouse head on a stake as a warning to any others who dared cross their path.

Fletch *sounded* convincing, yet when I looked at the five furry mass murderers, all snoozing comfortably together on the guest bed, I had my doubts.[10]

A couple of weeks ago, Fletch needed to access a plug in his little back-porch office. I heard him moving furniture to get to the outlet be-

....

[8]Or gal.

[9]What is he, on the rats' payroll or something?

[10]FYI, the sixth killer was in the closet, curled up on my cashmere sweaters.

fore poking his head into the kitchen to ask me, "Hey, why do you think there are a hundred pieces of dog food behind the couch?"

"Hmm," I replied, "I guess maybe because the ratinmyhouse you promised had left? Didn't."

That was when my rat-based nightmares started. I saw them everywhere—swimming in the toilet, helping themselves to blocks of cheese in my fridge, hiding in my car, et cetera. I took to tucking my pants into my socks for fear of one running up my leg.

This goddamned creature turned me into Carl Spackler from *Caddyshack* as I tried to get him with nontraditional means, and by nontraditional means, let's just say there was more running around the kitchen banging pot lids together than I care to mention.

I decided the reason we weren't able to flush him[11] out was because we didn't know where he was hiding. So, I came up with yet another cunning plan. I spread flour in front of all the places I thought he might be. I figured that he'd walk in the flour and leave little powdery footprints behind him, and I could ambush him in his home.

Again, did I mention the cunning part?

Yeah.

And . . . here are the lessons I learned from this little *CSI: Martha Stewart* exercise:

(a) Although they will leave a slash where their tail trails (thus confirming their continued presence and prompting me to spray my counters with more bleach) rat feet are too small to pick up enough flour to leave tracks.

....
[11]I refuse to acknowledge the possibility of it being a female.

(b) Cat feet, however, are not. Would you like a detailed account of every place each of my extraordinarily busy cats walked the night of the experiment? Because I can give you one.

(c) Stupid pit bulls named Maisy believe raw flour is the most delicious treat imaginable and will lap that shit up until the combination of flour and saliva glues her jaw shut.

(d) Flour, particularly when combined with pit bull saliva, will never, ever completely come out of hardwood. Or leather. Or wool.

(e) This is somewhat unrelated to the experiment, but watching *Ratatouille* will actually not prevent me from being squicked out by the idea of vermin and may[12] actually cause a minor panic attack whenever congregating rats are shown. And suddenly, my nightmares are sponsored by Pixar.

Anyway, we'd seen neither hide nor hair of any rodent for a couple of weeks, so today I'd let my guard down.

Oh, wait, I have another rat-related lesson:

(f) Never let your guard down.

After a rigorous basement workout of scouring litter boxes, I took my garbage bag of doody out the basement door. I walked through the backyard and into the garage, where I opened the door to the alley. I lifted the lid on the big black garbage can the city provides to control the rat population. And it was at this point that I happened upon something

---

[12] Read: will.

gray and furry, snout buried in an old cat food tin, residing in the one apparatus in this trash-strewn alley meant to *deter* rats.

In his surprise at having been happened upon, said vermin then *lunged directly at my head, exactly like they do in my nightmares,* before dashing from the alley, through the garage and backyard, down the stairs, and I can only assume, into my basement. Fortunately, my sheer terror provided me with enough of an adrenaline boost to launch a vertical leap worthy of Michael Jordan or a *Matrix* special effects artist, so the rodent hit me in the parka instead of the puss.

I shudder at the thought of what might have happened if that stupid rat had better aim. "Hey," I say to Fletch, gently moving him out of the way of the television, "I almost had a rat *in my mouth* an hour ago. If that doesn't give me license to watch a little bit of crap TV, then truly, the terrorists have won."

To: stacey_at_home

From: jen_at_home

Subject: Can't come over

Hey, we can't get together tonight because I accidentally made myself sick when I drank an iced latte that had been sitting out for five hours after I forgot to bring it with me to the suburbs. I took a sip and thought, "Hmm, this is warm. Maybe I'll just add ice. Genius!"

Guess what.

Not genius.

Because *milk spoils.*

Wish I'd figured that out before I had to spend the evening crying on the toilet.

Later,
Jen

To: barbie_at_work

From: jen_at_home

Subject: Canceling personal training session

Listen, I've got to bail on our session today. I had a banana for breakfast like you suggested—26 grams of good carbs!—but it was apparently really old and now my small intestine feels all stabby.

I may have banana poisoning.

See you on Thursday?

Thanks,
Jen

To: stacey_at_home

From: jen_at_home

Subject: oops, I did it again

Guess what I did this weekend. Yes, that's right: I poisoned myself 1.5 times!

The half was the half an omelet I ate before Fletch found out the cream cheese I used expired six weeks ago. (I guess it's a good thing I told him that it had started to taste "tingly.")

The whole was when I wanted a BLT but didn't feel like going out to buy fresh produce, so I just cut off the moldy bit of the one tomato we had. I guess the "bad" kind of went all the way through.

Later!

Jen

P.S. I have grave doubts about the antique bacon, too.

To: jen_at_home

From: fletch_at_work

Subject: Re: my tummy hurts

If you e-mail me at the office every time you poison yourself, I'm never going to get any work done.

(Not My) High School Reunion

*B*eyond the gracious picture windows, snow falls gently, glistening in the halogen glow of the streetlights. We've reached the point in winter when city snowdrifts turn grimy and sharp, held together primarily by a strata of dirt and salt and crumbled asphalt. But tonight, perhaps in honor of the author's special event, big, airy flakes drift down, forming a thick buttercream blanket that softens the edges of Halsted Street one story below.

This is the perfect place from which to witness the gathering storm. The windows reach from floor to ceiling, but the room is warmed by incandescent lighting and plush rugs. Rough wooden beams span the ceiling and the walls are exposed brick, providing an elegant contrast to the minimalist animal-print chairs and sleek, low tables. Artfully scattered candles twinkle around the room.

Inside the party the guests are equally radiant, as many are glitterati in their own right. The private event is full of important people, most of whom seem to have stepped out of the pages of *Chicago Social Magazine* to gather in celebration of the author's newest tome.

Some of the men have come straight from the office and wear finely tailored suits in muted shades of black and gray. Other guys, perhaps the more artistically minded in the crowd, sport high-concept shirts and jeans by designers like Dolce and Gabbana, topped with beautifully battered leather coats.

As for the women, their looks vary—they run the gamut from couture cocktail wear to bohemian chic. The author herself oozes glamour in a crimson wrap dress that appears to be both couture *and* vintage. And despite the absolute certainty that all the women here will have to trudge through snowy streets later, their shoes are of the open, strappy, and impossibly high variety.

The thing is, tonight isn't just an event for people who *look* beautiful. The author's invited revelers are decidedly academic. Their repartee sparkles just as much as the weighty diamonds on the women's necks, wrists, ears, and hands.

Throughout the room, snatches of Important Conversation can be heard on a variety of highbrow topics: this season at the Lyric Opera; a new piece of surrealist art by someone named Claude; and the best vintage of Mouton Rothschild. Guests discuss amending sections of Chicago's municipal code and the risks commercial paper carries because there's no collateral behind it. The author holds court in the corner by the bar, detailing the ways in which the Italian legal system differs from our own.

At this point, it should be fairly obvious that I'm not the author in question, and this isn't *my* event. I mean, my last book release party was held around my tiny kitchen table and in my microscopic living room with everyone drinking Two Buck Chuck, eating bricks of cheese from Aldi, listening to the GoGos, and playing Scattergories.[13] At some point in the evening, I went upstairs and changed into my lightest pair of pajama pants because I got sweaty.

So this here? This tonight? Is *so* not my scene. My friend Stacey, another writer (but not the host), invited me. She keeps encouraging me to mingle so I'm not bored while she says hello to other guests. Unfortunately, small talk is not my forte, unless it involves my hair or a solid rehashing of that time Pumkin spit on Miss New York in the first season of *Flavor of Love*. (My academic summation? Them bitches be crazy and shit!)

I quietly slurp my Diet Coke and contemplate what I'll say if I'm asked a direct question about any of the topics floating around in here. I get superanxious when I'm put on the spot about subjects I don't know much about. What am I supposed to say about municipal code? It's good? It's bad? It's Dan Brown's new book? I have no freaking clue.

As for opera, the extent of my familiarity comes from Dan Aykroyd in *Trading Places* saying, "*La Bohème*—it's an op-er-a." Perhaps I should interrupt the surrealist conversation dudes to let them in on my theory that all contemporary art is a huge scam? I mean, last time I went to a museum, there was a barbell sculpted out of Vaseline. Seriously. You think a piece like that's going to make the curators at the Louvre go all, "*Ooh, let's put the greasy barbell next to the* Venus de Milo! *Maybe we can even build out her stumps with Vaseline!*" Right.

I notice Stacey nodding encouragingly at me from across the room, so I steel myself. I'm determined to at least try . . . so then I can quit

....

[13]It was awesome!

legitimately. I start grinning awkwardly at the people around me, attempting to catch their eyes and be invited into a conversation. But no one bites because I'm pretty sure I come across as desperate and freaky as the chicks at an open-casting call for *Rock of Love*, minus the boob job and inflamed downstairs lady parts.

This would be so much easier if I were drinking. A little social lubricant would go a long way to make me feel more at ease. But Fletch is joining us later tonight, and I lost the rock-paper-scissors on who'd be the designated driver. Why do I perpetually remember too late that the bastard *always* throws scissors?

I'm on my third lap around the party[14] when I hear a couple of professor-looking guys talking about *Syriana*.

Hey! Here's my opening!

I saw that movie!

I can join in!

Look at me go!

So . . . apparently when two men wearing tweedy jackets with leather elbow patches are discussing the geopolitical ramifications of the creation of an artificial state, à la Iraq, they aren't looking for someone to interject, *"I totally saw that movie! And if you ask me, Clooney really needs to lay off the pie!"* They stared at me as though I was insane, and I slunk off back to the safety of Stacey's side.

I tried, it was hard, I quit, the end. Story of my life.

This deal tonight could be classified as less of a party and more of a

---

[14] And fourth Diet Coke.

soiree.[15] Boring fusion jazz, which I despise, plays in the background. If I want to hear metallic clattering, I'll wrongly install my pot rack again. I hate jazz so much that I won't even go to brunch most places. Thanks a lot, Miles Davis. You've totally ruined waffles for me.

Waiters circulate with shiny silver trays covered with something yellow and trendy and lovely served on a bed of something green and crisp. Is it a cube of cheddar? Because I'm all about cube cheese! I glom onto a toothpick as the waiter cruises by and stuff the contents in my mouth when I hear someone exclaim, *"Ooh, fois gras!"* Then I promptly hawk it back up into my napkin and hide the whole thing in a potted plant.

I'm pretty sure no one saw me.

Scratch that: Stacey saw me.

Fortunately, she just laughs.

Even though we get along famously, I suspect I wasn't her first choice of companion for this evening. She says I'm a bad wingman because whenever we're together in public and someone weird corners her with something like four thousand handwritten pages about the history of masonry, I run and hide in the bathroom, giggling until the coast is clear, while a good wingman would swoop in and explain to the bricklaying scribe that our publishers don't let us read unsolicited work. Fortunately, this is a private event, and the only one liable to create a socially uncomfortable situation is me.

Stacey's having an animated conversation with one of the clever, pretty people about Chef Grant Achatz. She had the twenty-course tasting menu at Alinea in Old Town recently and tried to explain it to me, but I didn't quite understand all the fuss.

....

[15]I don't actually know the difference, but I'm guessing a soiree includes cheese made by someone other than the Kraft Corporation.

"Molecular gastronomy is foams, like what Marcel kept using on that season of *Top Chef*, right?" I asked. "Did you eat a whole meal made of foam? Because that sounds gross. What, were they all, *'Hey! Have some Caesar salad. It's foam! Would you like a steak? A thick, juicy, foamy steak?' How about some pie? It's foam-tastic. Finish up with a cappuccino. (No foam.)*"

Patiently, Stacey explained, "There may have been one dish with foam, but that's it. You know, Jen, molecular gastronomy's more than just food infused with air. It's really about changing the chemical makeup. For example, it can take a solid and turn it a liquid."

"I can do that with a blender," I countered.

"No, you can *puree* something, but you can't change its physical properties. Each of the tiny bits is still a solid. Chefs use liquid nitrogen to make liquids into solids—"

"I can do that in my freezer."

"—solids into gases, et cetera. For example, one of the dishes was 'the soup course,' which was a tiny bubble filled with tomato water. You put it in your mouth, and the second it hits your tongue, it transforms into a liquid."

I can do that with my teeth—it's called chewing—but I suspect Stacey is not so interested in my editorial commentary. Instead, I said, "Like the juice on your cutting board after you slice a tomato?"

Stacey considered this for a moment. "Kind of, only condensed and amplified."

"And you just get one bite? Wouldn't you rather have a whole bowl of delicious soup?" I asked.

"I might not be explaining this right. Another course was a lozenge made out of pineapple and bacon. What looked like a tiny piece of candy turned out to be an explosive mouthful of flavor."

I simply shook my head. "I understand the words you're saying individually, but together as a concept? No."[16]

"Try it sometime and you'll get it."

"Sure," I agreed. But, honestly, why would I spend four hundred dollars for a bacon cough drop when I can get a beautiful, nonexplode-y steak dinner for two at Morton's for a quarter of the price? No, thanks.

While I shift awkwardly and mainline my Diet Coke, Stacey's conversation partner eventually drifts away. She turns back to me expectantly, so I lean in to ask her the one question that's been plaguing me all night.

"Hey, can you smell my feet through these boots?"

Food snobbery aside, she's still a great friend. She leans closer and inhales. "Nope, you're good."

"Excellent. I was worried because the only boots I could find to fit over my stupid calves are pleather, and they usually reek after I stand around in them for a while. I'm just hoping their funk doesn't permeate the room."

Stacey gives me a wry smile. "No worries."

"Although I'm probably one of the only ones in here who won't lose a toe to frostbite tonight." Then I suddenly remember why we came in the first place. "Hey! Where's your boyfriend?"

She stands on the balls of her feet and scans the crowd. "Not here yet." Stacey recently reconnected with a high school crush via Facebook, and it turns out they're both friends with our hostess. Stacey hasn't seen Crush in twenty years, but still remembers how she'd swoon every time he walked into geometry class. Having transferred schools and lost credits, Crush found himself the only senior in a roomful of freshmen, of which

....
[16]Also, "explodes in your mouth" is not really a selling point.

Stacey was one. She says she spent the entire semester gazing at him the same way Samantha Baker stared at Jake Ryan in *Sixteen Candles*.

"I have no idea if I'd even *want* him as a boyfriend. Adult Stacey may have very different taste than Young Stacey. I'm not wearing Love's Baby Soft anymore. I'm also not into slap bracelets or white Ray-Bans or asymmetrical haircuts." Stacey shrugs and looks around the room again. "It'll just be fun to see him again, though. Hey, wait—there he is!" Crush spots Stacey and jogs over, practically picking her up with the force of his hug.

This? This guy is Jake Ryan? But where are his plaid shirt and work boots and forward-brushed haircut? Is his Porsche out front? And what of his sweater vest? I mean, this dude's a perfectly normal-looking forty-year-old guy. I suppose he's handsome enough, but nobody's heart is exactly going to skip a beat at the prospect of sharing a birthday cake with him on a glass-top table.[17]

Stacey introduces us. Interestingly, Crush shares a name with a famous department store. While we shake hands, Stacey briefs me on Crush's life and various accomplishments. I learn about his advanced degrees and his big-deal job in human rights law and how he leads a weekly discussion group in an upscale gastro pub about the various ills befalling our fair city, to which I reply, "Your blueberry muffins *kick ass*."

His expression is guarded. Maybe it's a lawyer thing? "Heh. Yeah. You must have grown up on the East Coast."

"I lived there till I was ten!" I exclaim. "Anyway, are you any relation?"

....

[17]Speaking of glass tables, ever notice that all the tables in the Ryan household were glass? Weird.

He gives me a crinkly smile that may have been what fueled Stacey's crush twenty years ago. "Afraid not."

"Bummer. I bet you'd get all the blueberry muffins you could eat if you were a department store scion."

Except I don't think I said "scion."

I might have said "cyclops."

He and Stacey give me odd looks and begin to chat when I'm struck by another thought. "Hey," I bark, "how funny would it be if your name were Marshall Field? Wouldn't that be hilarious? You could get all the Frango Mints you want! HA!"

They politely nod and begin to reminisce about high school. Since this is a reunion of sorts, I find it's the perfect time to recount my favorite scenes from the WB's series *High School Reunion*, but neither of them saw it, so no one laughs when I shout K.K.'s famous line, *"I want to peel my skin off!"*

Damn.

They continue to chat, occasionally grinning in my direction—whether out of genuine pleasure for my company or an underlying desire that I keep my piehole closed, I can't be sure. I stay really quiet for fear of saying the wrong thing. My Achilles' heel has always been my mouth. I'm the person who *says* every single thing she thinks, sometimes to others' amusement, and almost always to my detriment.

Before I was a writer, I had slightly more control of my mouth, at least in important professional settings. To keep myself from blurting out whatever crossed my mind in crucial client meetings, I'd make cheat sheets. I'd prepare myself for the social-niceties portion of the gathering by researching the company and their top brass. Whenever possible, I forced myself to say ingratiating stuff like, *"I noticed the Mapplethorpe photos in the hallway! What a great collection!"* and *"Congratulations on making* Crain's *Forty Under Forty List!"* instead of what I was thinking, which was, *"Does your receptionist* not *totally smell like cabbage? What's up with that?"* I turned into my usual abrasive self once back in the office, but on the road, I was golden, and I eked out a successful niche for myself.

The problem is that in regular social conversation, there's no opportunity for cheat sheets. I'm flying without instruments. Plus, if there's any kind of spark between these two, I don't want to derail a potential romance with a comment about how I'm considering Botox injections to keep my feet from sweating. Best to just lock my lips.

Stacey leans conspiratorially into Crush and admits, "You know, you were my Jake Ryan in high school."

Crush is confused. "Your *Jake Ryan* . . . what does that mean?"

"From *Sixteen Candles*? Jake Ryan was the senior in some of Molly Ringwald's classes, and she had such a thing for him even though he had no clue she existed," Stacey informs him.

"Huh. Never saw it."

Yes!! Here's my opening! I've been waiting for this all night! I mean, I can't tell you shit about opera or art or law, but I pretty much have a Ph.D. in John Hughes.[18] We've hit upon one of the few subjects in which I excel, so I unclamp my lips. "You never saw *Sixteen Candles*?" I blurt. "How is that possible? How could you practically go to high school in John Hughes's backyard and not see *Sixteen Candles*?"

Crush flashes a nervous grin while he runs his hand across his stubbly chin. "I don't know. I just didn't."

I continue on my tirade. "Anthony Michael Hall as Farmer Ted?

---

[18]RIP, sir. And thank you for making the kind of films that defined my entire generation.

Trapped under a glass coffee table, screaming, '*JAAAAKE!*' Ring any bells?"

Crush shakes his head. "I'm sorry, no."

"Come on!" I insist. "*Sixteen Candles* is a classic coming-of-age film. You weren't allowed to leave the eighties without seeing it."

"Apparently I was." He glances over to Stacey for help but she just shrugs. Wonder if she wishes he was talking about masonry right about now?

"No! Wrong! Think harder! You must have seen it! John Cusack's first role? The beginning of the Brat Pack? Molly Ringwald as Samantha Baker? And the scene where her grandmother felt her up because she 'got her boobies'? Nothing?"

"I'm sorry, no."

"'*Dong, where is my automobile?' 'We have seventy dollars and a pair of girl's underpants. We're as safe as kittens.' 'Now we're BOTH on the pill!*' Anything?"

"Nope."

"'*I can't believe it; they fucking forgot my birthday.*'" I wait for his flash of recognition, but it never comes. "Seriously, nothing? I mean, come on! EVERYONE has seen *Sixteen Candles*, so everyone knows who Jake Ryan is."

Crush takes a series of small, deliberate steps back from me.[19] "If I say yes, will you stop shouting at me?"

I weigh his request. "Well, *no*. I can't understand how you're unfamiliar with the cultural touchstone that Jake Ryan was for our generation."

He remains steadfast. "And I maintain that it's an esoteric reference."

Okay, seriously?

----

[19]Yeah, there's accidental spittle.

Them's fightin' words.

I fling my purse off my shoulder and whip out my wallet, which is adorned with a giant Paul Frank monkey.[20] "Listen, I have"—I count—"eight dollars. I have eight dollars that say you are flat-freaking wrong. I'm willing to wager these eight dollars that every single woman in this room between the ages of thirty and forty-five knows exactly who Jake Ryan is. Are you in? Or are you a tremendous pussy?"

He pauses. "I'm not a tremendous pussy."

"Ergo, you're in. Scoot." I give him a helpful shove in the direction of the stunning girls who'd previously been discussing some guy they kept calling Proost. Not more than ten seconds into the conversation, I hear the lone male in the group squeal, "JAAAAAKE!" Crush catches my eye and I mouth, *"I told you so!"*

Stacey and I watch as he hops from group to group, and I congratulate myself each time he shoots me a sheepish thumbs-up. Embattled cries of "JAAAAAKE!" occasionally puncture the otherwise civilized din of the party.

Crush works his way around the room, and we spy him chatting up a particularly beautiful girl in a raspberry beret.

Oh, honey, Prince called—he wants his cliché back.

Crush lingers there for a while. "Huh," I remark. "I wonder what they're talking about. We already got the Jake thumbs-up, which means I am totally eight dollars richer. I wonder why he's not coming back?" Raspberry Cliché giggles at something Crush says, and they put their heads closer together. Her hair brushes his face, and he casually smoothes it back for her. "So, whaddaya think, Stace, you like him or not?"

....
[20]Hi, I'm forty years old. (Ask me about my Barbie collection, too.)

Stacey purses her lips. "Definitely as a friend, but I can't tell if there's any electricity or not."

"Really? How come? I mean, he was your Jake Ryan, for crying out loud." I gesture so grandly that half my Diet Coke sloshes out onto my boot.

Stacey swipes at a stray curl on her forehead and levels her gaze. "Um, because before we got a chance to connect, you and your eight-dollar bet sent him off to talk to every single attractive girl in this place."

This? Right here? Is exactly why you can't take me anyplace nice.

"Oh, no! I'm SO sorry!" I gasp. "It never occurred to me that I just provided your crush with the world's greatest opening line!"

Stacey pats me on the shoulder. "Jen, it's fine. I'm not mad; it's funny. But you really are the worst wingman ever."

I've got to make this right. "Want me to help you meet someone else here?" My mind begins spinning. Maybe I can get one of the elbow-patch academic guys to talk to her? I know Stacey saw *Syriana* because she's the one who had to explain it to me.

I take a bracing sip of my Diet Coke. Okay, here's what I'll do. I'll find the tweedy blazer guys, and I'll tell them that Stacey's not only cute but totally smart because she wasn't all distracted by Clooney's child-bearing hips and double chin in *Syriana*, and she's actually able to see him as a serious actor and doesn't just think of him as the guy who starred on the later seasons of *The Facts of Life* and had that stupid mullet and—

She quickly throws her hands up into the universal symbol for stop. "NO! No. Thank you. I'm okay on my own." At this point Fletch arrives. He's shaking the snow out of his hair, and his face breaks into a sweet smile when he spots us.

He kisses me, then gives Stacey a hug. "Hey, sorry I'm late. I had a client issue that took forever to resolve. What'd I miss?"

"I just made an eight-dollar bet with Stacey's high school crush and, in so doing, accidentally sent him out to talk to every woman at this party."

Somehow Fletch doesn't seem surprised by this news. He tells Stacey, "She's truly the world's worst wingman."

"Agreed." Stacey nods.

"What are you drinking?" he asks me.

"I've had, like, nine Diet Cokes," I admit.

Fletch turns ashen. "Stacey, you can't let her have that much soda. Ever. You think she's a handful when she drinks? That doesn't hold a candle to her with a caffeine buzz."

But I'm pretty sure she already figured that out.

Crush eventually joins us again,[21] and while the grown-ups discuss the mayor's latest budgetary follies, I discuss this week's follies on the first-ever winter edition of *Big Brother*. As they debate the merits of a flat tax, I debate how flat the top ten female semifinalists were on *American Idol*. While they grouse about their jobs, I grouse about who was just fired on *Celebrity Apprentice*.

At some point I interrupt my own personal version of *Talk Soup* to mention the delicious brisket I had at lunch. Turns out Crush hates brisket, and I argue that it's *impossible* to hate brisket and that EVERYONE loves brisket and that I now have sixteen dollars[22] to prove it, and before you know it, I manage to turn the argument into a chance for Stacey to cook him brisket.

....

[21] After getting Raspberry Cliché's number. D'oh!

[22] WINNAH!!

We hang out for a little while longer until Fletch notices I'm practically levitating after too much soda and not enough protein. The four of us decide to grab some grilled cheeses at Four Moon Tavern, which is now a bonus date for Stacey on top of the brisket date.

See? I'm NOT the worst wingman ever.

We make our way through the crowd to say our good-byes, and I can't help but notice how almost every conversation in the room now revolves around either reality television or John Hughes movies. I even hear Patches and Tweedy grudgingly admit how much they identified with the boys in *Weird Science*.

As we head into the snow, I begin to wonder how the evening might have gone if I'd been there with my pre-9/11 brain. Maybe I couldn't have kept up with everything, but I definitely wouldn't have brought an entire room down to my level.

On the one hand, it's funny that everyone got dumber by having been around me.

On the other, it's a bit of a hollow victory.

Dear Alderman,

Yesterday I said good-bye to my husband and made my way upstairs to get dressed so I could work. But before I got a chance to sit down at the computer, something caught my eye. I noticed chunks of snow and ice flying . . . almost as if they'd been hurled. I heard the rev of an engine, over and over, growing more insistent. And, despite the room's triple-paned glass, I heard obscenities.

Oh, so many obscenities.

Four-letter words filled the air in capital letters, with exclamation points, like one of the fight scenes from *Batman*, the Adam West era.

Our alley had claimed another victim.

I threw a fleece on over my flannel nightgown, stepped into my woolly Crocs, grabbed my coat, and headed outside, where Fletch was in a state of what can only be described as "bitch-panic." Fletch had gotten his car stuck in an eight-inch-deep ice valley, formed in the perfect storm of snowing, hailing, melting, refreezing, and non-storm-drain-cleaning-despite-having-asked-your-office-twenty-times-to-please-please-please-do-something.

Unfortunately, I was the one tasked with rocking the vehicle rather than the more desirable job of steering, what with my propensity to hit the side of the garage even when the pavement is dry and clear. Pajama-clad, I spent the next forty-five minutes throwing my weight against the trunk while the useless back tires sprayed me with a mixture of road salt, ice, and liquefied kitty litter.

Finally, he stopped swearing long enough to remember we had roadside assistance—a service not only included in the purchase price of the car, but also the main argument he'd used to convince me it was fine to get the rear-wheel-drive model—and the nice folks at BMW quickly dispatched Sherpas bearing crullers, hot brandy, and a tow truck. OK, they didn't bring liquor or donuts, but they did arrive promptly and free of charge.

Later, my husband brought home a big box of pastry to apologize for being all shout-y.

So I guess what I'm saying is, the alley drain that you promised was fixed?

Isn't.

As I see it, you have two options. You can use your position as Alderman to pressure the city water department to actually do what they said they did, or you can supply me with a nice box of éclairs so I don't go all Dick Cheney in your office at the next ward meeting.

Your choice.

Best,
Jen Lancaster

C·H·A·P·T·E·R   T·H·R·E·E

So You Think They Can Dance?

"**W**hat's the problem?'"

I'm here getting therapy, or at least my version of it, perched on the couch in Stacey's living room in front of her flat screen. For the past few years, ever since we met on a book event panel and discovered we may well be the same person,[23] we have a standing date on Wednesday nights to watch whatever's on Bravo. At the moment we're onto *Top Chef 4* but we've done multiple seasons of *Project Runway*. Last year we even tuned in to *Shear Genius*, a hair-cutting competition. That's right: a show about *haircuts* and we're not *hairdressers*. Apparently I *will* watch whatever Bravo tells me to.

I drove over here tonight with the windows open. Winter's finally

....

[23]Together we are Stennifer.

over and spring's arrived. I'm feeling somewhat melancholy about the change of seasons. Winter's my favorite time of year because it's the one time when I'm not all wrapped up in deadlines. Early spring is spent getting ready to promote whatever new book I've written, and in late spring, I tour and do publicity. Summer's when I write and fall's all about the edit.

After I finally put *Such a Pretty Fat* to bed this last November, my friend Angie asked me what I was going to do with all my free time. Would I travel? Spend some time enjoying all the cultural offerings of my city? Start working for charity? No.

My response? "I'm going to watch so much television!"

And I have. This winter's been nothing but an endless stream of *American Idol, America's Next Top Model, The Biggest Loser, Supernanny, Wife Swap, Beauty and the Geek 5, The Apprentice, The Bachelor, My Super Sweet Sixteen, The Real Housewives of Orange County, The Real Housewives of New York, The Ultimate Coyote Ugly Search 3, Bad Girls Club 2, Rock of Love, Make Me a Supermodel, The Gauntlet III, Big Brother 9, Survivor: Micronesia, Step It Up and Dance, The Janice Dickenson Modeling Agency, Crowned: The Mother of All Pageants, Millionaire Matchmaker, Paradise Hotel,*[24] *Randy Jackson Presents: America's Next Dance Crew, A Shot of Love with Tila Tequila 2, Gene Simmons Family Jewels, I Know My Kid's a Star, My Fair Brady . . . Maybe Baby?,* and, of course, *Scott Baio Is 46 . . . and Pregnant.*

I don't watch *Keeping Up with the Kardashians*, though.

I do have some standards.

Anyway, at this very moment, I'm not paying attention to one of my

---

[24]Which is far inferior to its previous iteration.

favorite reality programs and am instead having a panic attack about going on book tour.

I take a big breath, and when I exhale, it comes out sounding ragged. "I'm not worried about the *tour*, per se." Right now my problem isn't some abstruse struggle about poise and self-assurance in unfamiliar or urbane circumstances. My issue is a little more pedestrian. "I don't have good luggage. I had to sell all my adorable, matchy-matchy Kate Spade pieces years ago to pay rent when we were broke. What I've got is a packing dilemma, and no one seems to want to help me figure it out."

Stacey, always sagacious and sweet, won't let me struggle alone. "*I'll* help you. What you want is a Travelpro bag. I've got the platinum series and it was worth every dime."

"Yeah," I agree, "but . . ." I scratch at the faint chocolate stain I left on Stacey's couch cushion last year when I accidentally sat on a Raisinette.

"Too expensive? Average out the price versus times you use it, and I guarantee you'll make up the cost over the bag's life span." She grabs a scratch pad, ready to do the math, but I wave her off.

"Well . . . it's just that I saw these really cute suitcases in a catalog and they're flowered and striped and all the colors in them would match my polo shirts. They're dreamy! My favorite one comes covered in big pink polka dots on a chocolate background, but I also like the one with grosgrain ribbons and a monogram, and I could totally see Elle Woods carrying . . ."

Stacey's indulgent grin slowly fades into the kind of confused expression Loki gives us when he hears another dog bark on television. "Um, *wow*," I observe, "you should see the look on your face. What are you, like, the Henry Ford of luggage or something? You can have any color you want as long as it's black?"

"No . . . no, not at all," she finally responds unconvincingly. "I'm curious, though. What catalog was it?"

"Well . . . when I got it, I didn't notice the company name on the cover. I was just thumbing through it, looking at the furniture and linens and decorating items, and I was all, *'This stuff is so the real me!'* Turns out it was a Pottery Barn TEEN catalog." I pause to consider the implications. "Meaning I have the design aesthetic of a twelve-year-old girl."

Stacey nods and adds, "From the suburbs. Yet I say if that's what you want, get it. However, if you decide you want to carry the kind of luggage *not* favored by seventh graders and Girl Scouts, I can send you to where I get mine. Or I can come along and lend a hand. Your choice."

"Thank you. No one ever wants to help."

"Does that abate some of your worries?" she asks.

"A little, but then I'm still freaking out about all the mechanics of the tour—like, I don't sleep well in hotels."

Stacey suggests, "Try not to sleep on the plane because that'll wreak havoc on you later when you try to go to bed in the hotel."

I snort. "*Pfft,* I never *sleep* on the plane. I have to be awake and using my mind power to keep it in the air."

"I . . . see." Stacey hesitates for a second because it's clear she does not see. Gamely, she presses on. "Your best bet is to not drink on the plane because you're already going to be dehydrated, and flying's going to make it worse. Probably mess with your circadian rhythms, too. Oh, and be as comfortable as you can—maybe wear yoga pants and a hoodie."

"No, no, I have to drink or I get too nervous. Also, whenever I fly, I try to wear a black Lacoste shirt. I find they best mask Bloody Mary spills."

"Of course . . . I'm curious, though—the drinking doesn't interfere with your, um, what is it you said, *mind power?*"

I shake my head. "I steer the plane better drunk."

Stacey clears her throat and quickly switches topics. "What are you going to wear to your events?"

"Hopefully it'll be warm and I can wear my standard summer uniform of black or khaki shorts and a pastel polo shirt. But what do I do if it's cold?" I wonder.

"Maybe you could bring a little trench?"

"If I wore a trench over shorts, I'd look like a flasher."

"Then bring some capris."

"I want to wear my shorts so everyone can see that I have nice calf muscles."

Stacey tries hard to not sigh. "Um, fine, then why don't you pack a cute jean jacket?"

"Sure . . . I could do that. Of course I'd have to go back to 1985 to get one. Bah! BAH HA HA HA HA!"

Stacey waits for me to finish. When she thinks I'm done, she continues. "Ahem, right. Then how about—"

I start howling with laughter again. "BAH HA HA HA! 1985! HA!"

"Maybe you could—"

"HA! JEAN JACKET! GET IT? NO ONE'S WORN ONE SINCE 1985! GET IT? HA HA HA!!"

Stacey gives my brilliant humor a small nod and then tries to move on, unsuccessfully. "So . . ."

"HA! HAA!! 1985! I'D BETTER PACK EVERYTHING IN MY TRAVELPRO TIME MACHINE! HA!!"

After five full minutes of side-clenching laughter—all of it exclusively on my part—I finally compose myself and meet Stacey's gaze. I notice her pinched lips and lowered brow. "Wait, this is why no one ever wants to help me with anything, isn't it?"

I buy a bunch of cute Empire-waist sundresses and matching cardigans so that whole wardrobe thing is now under control. Plus, I go to Stacey's luggage store and find a great bag. I'm vaguely disappointed that it's black, so I pick up a fluorescent pink-and-green luggage tag to add a touch of my personality.

Also? I find a jean jacket. When I put it on, it reminds me of the one I used to love but then abandoned back in 1985 after learning too late that one does not wear a jean jacket to a sorority rush.

And FYI, the Kappas can suck it if they don't like it because it looks hot.

"Stop holding out on me!" Barbie shouts.

"I'm not!" I grunt.

"You can keep going!"

"Pretty sure (*gasp*) I can't."

"Breathe!" Breathe? She wants me to breathe? My lungs feel like I'm trying to suck a bowling ball through a garden hose. Trust me, if I could draw breath right now, I would.

I'm at the gym getting in my second-to-last workout with my personal trainer before I leave to go on tour next week.

I wrote the book because I figured the best way to shake off all my baby (back rib) weight was to challenge myself to write about the process.[25] Somewhere between the Atkins and Zone diets, I accidentally stumbled upon what's been at the root of my weight problem—my refusal to behave like an adult. By mocking the birthday cake Nazis at Weight Watchers and quietly selecting/competing against various nemeses at the gym, I inadvertently began to grow up, improving my well-being in the process.

Even though I'm not yet thin, I'm healthier both physically and spiritually.[26]

Unfortunately, all my effort will be for naught if Barbie kills me on this goddamned treadmill.

For our final session, Barbie decides we're going to do yoga. Ugh. Yoga. I've done this before and it's never gone well. I normally forget the effect gravity has on loose T-shirts and end up smothering myself. Today I've at least had the foresight to tuck my shirt into my shorts, Urkel-style.

I admire the muscle definition yoga enthusiasts sport. They aren't gross like the professional yogis—their arms are nicely defined and not too ropy or stringy. Strong muscles are beautiful. Visible tendons? Not so much.[27]

---

[25] Technically, I gained a lot of weight while unemployed after the dot-com crash and not because I had children. (Besides, with the amount of burgers, steaks, and barbecue I used to eat, I'd have birthed a calf, not a kid.)

[26] I've yet to make any great strides intellectually, which will become evident when I meet Candace Bushnell for the first time a few weeks from now.

[27] Ahem, Madonna, I'm talking to you.

Since it's gorgeous and sunny, Barbie says we should exercise on the patio that separates the gym from the office building next door. That would not be my first choice, but we're just coming out of eleventy thousand straight months of winter, so fresh air's a powerful draw.

The stretching feels good, but between my smaller-but-still-present girth, shorts pulled up to my armpits, and total lack of grace, I fear I may look like Chris Farley in that old *SNL* Chippendales skit. Sure, he had the same moves as Patrick Swayze[28]—unfortunately, certain parts of his body *kept* moving when he stopped dancing. I'm giving myself a real bowlful of jelly vibe here.

That's when I notice office workers watching us from the building next door. Hopefully they're leering at the cute blond trainer and not laughing themselves into an asthma attack over the human Weeble. I tell Barbie, "If this ends up on YouTube, you die."

I'm sweaty and covered in concrete dust from the patio after our session, but Barbie hugs me good-bye anyway. After a year of working out together three times a week, I'll miss not seeing her every couple of days. I'm going to spend the better part of the next two months on the road, sometimes only coming home overnight. I probably won't have a chance to do my laundry when I get home, let alone squeeze in a training session.

I'm delighted with the level of strength I've achieved, but I worry about keeping up my regimen while I'm on the road. Who knows if I'll even have a minute to hit the hotel gym between all the travel, media, and events? There'd be a great irony in me getting fatter on tour for a book about dieting, no?

....

[28] RIP, Johnny Castle. Also, can everyone good please stop dying while I write this book? Thanks.

The tour's over and summer's officially begun, which means I'm working on the next book. My deadline's looming, so naturally I feel the best use of my day is to head to Stacey's family's weekend place for swimming and grilling and gossiping—basically doing anything *but* writing. I'm en route, happily singing along to my Fergie CD, when the accident happens.

A few minutes before, I noticed the red pickup truck in front of me with a bunch of new furniture loaded into the back. Since the pickup was laden with a queen-sized mattress and a variety of other household items stacked on top of it, I wisely checked my speed and changed lanes, partially because I'm careful and partially because Fletch urged me to keep his precious, precious car safe. Too bad for him that before he mentioned how important my safety was, he told me not to get the car sticky . . . so I obviously had to get the messiest burger I could to eat en route.[29]

When I left the house, the skies couldn't have been more blue or cloudless. I opened the sunroof and windows, delighted to feel the sun on my skin and wind in my hair. I spent the better part of the last two months in airports and hotels breathing recycled air, so I'm loving the breeze blowing through the front seat, even if it means being pelted in the teeth by the occasional grasshopper.

The closer I get to my destination, the more the azure sky darkens and begins to look as though it's bruised. Having lived in a particularly tornado-y part of Indiana, I recognize these conditions, so I pump the

----

[29]Whopper with cheese, holla!

gas a little harder, inching my speed up to a full fifty-eight miles per hour in a fifty-five zone.[30]

I notice I have to put both hands on the wheel to control the car as winds begin to whip. I close the windows and sunroof when powerful currents begin to blow around roadside trash and kick up loose bits of soil.

As I tool along, I wonder if that bitch Mother Nature's going to ruin my first official pool day of the year. Seriously, it's like forces are conspiring against my getting a tan this year. Whenever I've had time to catch some rays, it's rained. Sometimes I'll use self-tanner, but the end result is always disastrous because self-tanning only seems like a good idea after I've cocktailed Xanax and Ambien.

(Sidebar: Even though my doctor says I *can* take them at the same time doesn't mean I *should*. And FYI for you amateur med mixologists, please note that one glass of wine plus one Ambien almost always equals shameful online shopping sprees. My Barbie Fashion Fever styling head and I urge you to trust us on this.)

While I contemplate exactly how pasty I am, a strong gust of wind sweeps one of the boxes off the back of the truck and drops it onto the two-lane highway fifty yards ahead of me. I'm far enough back that it doesn't come crashing through my windshield, but there's so much traffic in the right lane that I have nowhere to go but forward.

I'm down to about twenty miles an hour when I plow into the box, which I'm hoping is filled with something light, like Styrofoam peanuts or popcorn or maybe paper plates. Perhaps it's filled with piñatas, and when I hit it, fun-sized packages of Snickers and Sweet Tarts and Twizzlers will rain down on me and voilà! Impromptu fiesta!

....

[30]Scofflaw!

No such luck.

I'm pretty sure I just smashed into an anvil or bag of cement or perhaps some depleted plutonium. The impact isn't enough to deploy the airbags, but it *is* enough to deploy the fresh thirty-two-ounce Burger King Diet Coke out of my cup holder. The soda explodes and splashes the windshield and sunroof before raining brown liquid and ice chips all over the dashboard, the front seat, my hair, face, and lap.

I pull over on the grassy shoulder and blot my sunglasses with the edge of my T-shirt while shaking chipped ice out of my hair. Then I leap out of the car to inspect the damage. There's only a small nick in the bumper, but after the unpleasantness with this same bumper and the side of the garage earlier this spring (and, let's be honest, the lipstick and the side mirror), I happen to know that it's going to cost at least a grand to replace it, and damn it, *this time* someone else's insurance can cover repairs.

Soda streaming down my legs, I stomp down to where the pickup truck driver has stopped his car. He's an older man with an oiled black pompadour, Civil War–worthy sideburns, blue eyes, and skinny legs supporting a big gut. He sports some enormous white teeth—dentures?— that he arranges into a scary grin when he sees me coming.

Well, hot damn—Elvis isn't dead; he's just delivering mattresses in Northern Illinois now.

The King steps out of his truck, saying, "Oh, thank you, thank you ver' much for stopping! That's really ver' kind a you."

"I stopped because I hit your stupid box!" I snap. I'm taking a deep breath in preparation to yell like I've never yelled before when the Memphis Flash holds out a callused hand and says, "I'm Reverend Smith."

That shuts me down completely. While I wouldn't say I'm incapable of evil (as evidenced by much of my sorority career), I simply cannot shout at the Lord's emissary. Or the reincarnation of Elvis the Pelvis.

While he gets back into his car to call the police,[31] I'm stuck muttering to myself about Reverend TossyBox from the Church of the Flying Furniture. I make my way over to the cardboard to see what I hit, and when I get there, I shake my head. Un-frigging-believable.

I return to my car, open the trunk, and pull out my beach towel to sop up as much of the mess as I can. I toss handfuls of ice on the side of the road and sweep out a tidal wave of sugar-free soda. Fortunately, with all the bending and stretching, I find the few stray fries and lettuce shreds that had fallen under the seat. Fletch's going to be upset enough about the chipped paint—no need to bait the bear with Burger King, too.

While I wait for the cops to take an accident report, I figure I'd better call Stacey.

"Yeah, hey, it's me. I'm running a little late. Why? Because I just got into a head-on collision *with an Adirondack chair.*"

"Dude, what's up with the frogs?" I ask. "This is, like, biblical."

"The frogs aren't coming from the sky. This isn't biblical. This is just annoying," Stacey counters. Despite positively ominous skies, Stacey and I are in the pool. The second we see lightning, we'll get out, but until then, we swim, damn it. Plus, I have all that soda to rinse off.

"Well, if they're not a plague, then where are they coming from?"

"You've got me. We get a couple of them in the pool every year, but

---

[31]Or maybe Colonel Tom.

this is bizarre. Maybe they hopped in from the woods because of the storm." As we wallow in waist-deep water, we attempt to scoop out the dozens of dime-sized frogs swimming around us. They'd be cute—like, so cute they could be manufactured by Sanrio, actually—if only they'd keep their distance. I had one work its way into my hair a couple of minutes ago, and now my throat hurts from all the screaming.

I brush a wee amphibian off my arm. "What's going on with you? How's your book[32] coming?"

"Great! I've spent the week entering recipe contests."

Stacey isn't working on a cookbook, but this statement makes perfect sense to me. Any writer will tell you the best part of being a writer is not writing. Oh, the random, unimportant things you can accomplish when you owe someone a manuscript! In the past two weeks, I've: (a) started a Facebook account in order to reconnect with people I haven't given a damn about in twenty years, (b) organized all our Christmas decorations, rewrapping the delicate ornaments I'd tossed carelessly back in the box seven months ago and testing each string of lights, (c) made significant headway in teaching the dogs to bark on command until Fletch reminded me they don't need any more encouragement in the barking department, and (d) read the first two *Twilight* series books. Twice.[33]

"Yeah? How'd that happen? And what kind of recipes?"

"I was writing and I had the Food Network on in the background. Then I noticed some woman getting a massive check for some lousy chicken recipe. Seriously, my chicken is so much better than what won,

----

[32]*Good Enough to Eat*, available September 2010. Buy it!

[33]Team Jacob!

and she got something like a hundred grand. For a shitty chicken paprikash! I clicked my Word document closed and began to Google cooking contests. I found a ton of them, and I've been entering them ever since. Right now, I'm all about Plugra, the European butter people." Stacey describes the various butter compounds she's created, and by the time she's finished, my mouth is watering.

"The one with bacon and maple sounds amazing!" I gush.

"Would that not be ridiculous on pancakes?" she raves.

"How are you making all this stuff and not gaining, like, a million pounds?"

Stacey wrinkles her nose. "Oh, please, I'm not making anything; I'm just coming up with ideas. I've already submitted forty different compound recipes."

I'm dumbfounded at this news and it takes me a moment to digest what she's saying. "Wait, you're not entering *recipe contests*; you're entering *writing* contests."

"That's about the size of it." She nods thoughtfully.

"Ha! On the one hand, I applaud your ability to avoid your deadline, but on the other, you're totally gaming the system. You're obligated to cook; otherwise, you're a butter cheater."

"Listen," she says, sending away another duo of frogs with a wave. "I've probably made each of these compounds a dozen times. I'm just writing down the work I already did. Obviously I'm hoping to win the grand prize, but they're also giving away a bunch of ceramic butter bells to the runners-up. I'll win some of those, because come on, I've already entered forty times and these recipes are gold. I'll make sure to give you one."

At that moment, lightning flashes across the sky and thunder cracks and we dunk ourselves one more time to remove any stray frogs before scurrying out of the water.

I don't say anything, but I'm pretty sure this storm is God's way of punishing Stacey for her butter—cheating.

After dinner, I convince Stacey our evening would be best spent watching *So You Think You Can Dance*.

During a particularly stirring piece, I turn to her and say, "Before I started watching this show, it never occurred to me that you could actually tell a story through dance. Like, who knew dance could make you *feel* something?"

Stacey gives me the kind of endearing, indulgent smile reserved for kittens and children taking their first steps. Since she possesses a master's degree in an arts-related field and was the educational director at the Goodman Theatre for seven years, I guess Stacey might already be familiar with the power of art. "Listen," she says, "if you like dance that tells a story, I can get us tickets for Marta Carrasco."

"What's that?"

"Marta's a who, not a what, and she's the leader of a very cool Spanish dance troupe that does really artistic pieces. I've seen her a few times at the Goodman and she's amazing."

"Neat! I'm totally in."

We finish watching the show, and at my insistence, view some quality Flavor Flav–based programming on VH1.[34] I finally retire to the guest room for the evening, where I watch an iPod Touch episode of *Living Lohan* before falling asleep and dreaming that Bret Michaels and I win *Dancing with the Stars*.

....

[34]She pays me back in the morning by making me watch Olbermann.

Stacey and I go out for pancakes in the morning. When I note that my breakfast probably would be better topped with a bacon-maple butter compound, she smirks in response.

I totally love when they do Latin dances on *So You Think You Can Dance*, and I'm all excited to see what I imagine are a bunch of flamenco dancers with all the flounce-y shirts and castanets and eyeliner. Stacey used to work here and still knows everyone, and since we have time before the curtain rises, she takes me around to meet important people.

All of the Important People gush about how wonderful Marta Carrasco is, which piques my interest. And, frankly, my curiosity, because each of them mentions we might not want to sit in the first few rows. As soon as the production designer we're talking to steps out of earshot to eat a quick dinner[35] before the show, I ask Stacey, "Why do they keep saying stuff about splash zones? Is this going to turn into a Gallagher show complete with sledgehammers and watermelons?"

Part of Stacey's old job was to teach local gang members to appreciate the Bard, so her patience level is infinite, and this isn't the dumbest question she's ever been asked.[36] "No, I'm sure it has more to do with sight lines. My guess is we don't want to be too close so we can take in all

---

[35]A McDonald's caramel sundae—I love those! And they're only a buck!
[36]Probably.

the action on the stage." I'm glad for the warning because I'll surely be uncomfortable if I can see the dancers' underpants.

We find some seats toward the back, and as my eyes adjust to the light, I take in the detail on the elaborate set. The backdrop is kind of fascinating—on the far wall, there are dozens of antique white garments hung from ropes at various angles, including a straitjacket. Staircases lead to a platform midstage with lots of little doors built into it.

Four old, crooked bookcases are spotlit at the front of the stage, and they're filled with a variety of items, like inflated latex hands and sparkly shoes and Kewpie doll heads. They take on a sinister quality grouped together like that. Honestly? The set kind of reminds me of my grandmother's attic. She lived in a creepy old house, and because she lived through the Depression, she tended to keep everything she got her hands on, and I mean *everything*. As soon as I took my first psych class in college, I diagnosed her with a hoarding disorder, but my mother said I was being ridiculous. Yes, because it's perfectly normal to keep three broken fridges in the kitchen for thirty years. My bad.

The accumulated junk in my grandparents' house wasn't what made the attic so eerie, though—it was the perfectly preserved, neatly wallpapered bedroom up there in the middle of all the chaos of forgotten possessions. I once asked my noni if she ever kept hostages up there, but she told me I was being fresh.[37]

Anyway, I feel like these are odd surroundings in which to showcase flamenco dancing, but what do I know? The lights in the theater go down, the audience politely applauds, and then the show starts. The bookcases slowly part and a pretty woman slides onto the stage on a rolly

---

[37]Her generation's version of "ridiculous."

chair with a rolly desk, and we watch her smoke an entire cigarette.[38] She doesn't dance; she just smokes.

Then other people in vintage outfits crawl onto the stage, except for one lady who's toting an IV pole. When IV Lady squeezes her bag of saline, it laughs.

No one dances.

The sound track is some French song that gets louder and faster and includes the sound of puppies yelping. I lean into Stacey and whisper, "Boy, if Loki were here, he'd be having a fit!"

As the music gets louder, the smoking lady begins to twirl in her rolly chair and her rolly desk. Someone gets slapped, but no one dances.

A man enters stage right in a tutu, which is promising for dancing, and a scrunched-up baby mask, which is not. Someone slaps him, and then there's a whole bunch of shouting in Spanish. Everyone in the audience laughs, except for those of us who thought it would be *très amusante* to take French in high school.

A woman then comes out with her head in a grandfather clock and sways back and forth.

The swaying is the closest we've come so far to dancing.

I'm beginning to suspect I'm not going to see any flamenco tonight.

More puppies yelp while two shirtless guys fly onstage with some woman in a ball gown. She gets thrown back and forth between them. Then a different girl in a *Mad Men*–looking dress enters stage left. She begins to shout in Spanish, and I lean into Stacey, saying, "Seriously, if I wanted to hear people yell in Spanish, I could have just stayed in my living room and opened the windows."

....
[38]I stifle the urge to shout that smoking is now considered a hate crime in the city of Chicago.

After she finishes shouting, the whole audience laughs except for me. Apparently she said something hilarious, but I have no idea what. Stacey's Spanish is a bit less rudimentary than mine, and she says she thinks the woman was reading a recipe.

Yes. Because that makes perfect sense.

A different woman comes out in a ball gown and a gas mask and drops rubber babies out of her dress as she slowly walks by. The tutu baby man then picks up the babies and slaps them.

There's still no dancing.

A giant Velcro mattress is wheeled out and placed in a vertical position in the center of the stage. A lady in Velcro pajamas throws herself at it for a while. Every time she hits it, her hair fans out, and it looks like she's been electrocuted. This is my favorite part so far.

Tutu Baby Man revisits the stage and shouts more[39] while a couple of guys in pajama bottoms at the front of the stage yank another woman's shirt down and begin to slap all her naked bits.

Have I mentioned the no-dancing part yet?

And why was I not warned there would be nudity?

In my peripheral vision, I see Stacey stifling her laugher because she knows I'm so prudish that I actually spell out words that are even vaguely sexual. She catches my eye and mouths, "I'm so sorry. I had no idea!"

Then Marta, the lead dancer, comes out wearing a circus-tent-sized shirtdress. She strips from the waist up and begins to make out with a statue for a while.

Like, a long while.

Then the whole stage is covered with an enormous sheet of dry-cleaning film, and Marta and her naked self writhe against it for a very

....
[39] Possibly giving hints on preparing a perfect paella?

long, naked while. She almost dances but is likely too busy being naked and trying not to suffocate when she breathes in the film.

I guess this is why they put all those warnings on the plastic.

Then the entire ensemble assembles onstage with giant plates of watermelon,[40] and they spit chunks of it into the air and at the audience. They pour water all over themselves and swim around on the wet, watermelon-y floor.

And then it is over.

With no goddamned dancing whatsoever.

The audience goes batshit crazy with applause and gives the "dancers" an extra-long standing ovation while I try to make sense of what the hell I just saw.

As soon as everyone finally finishes applauding, I turn to Stacey and say, "You realize this is exactly why my side keeps cutting funding to the arts. And by the way, I totally called the watermelon."

Later we find out that Marta Carrasco and company were retiring certain pieces and that what we saw was essentially a medley of her previous work. Stacey tells me, "By cutting them up and mixing them around, the continuity was lost, as was most of the dancing. In the original context, you'd have seen that the smoking and desk spinning in the beginning was her interpretation of losing a job and having nothing but time on her hands."

I nod. "Now *that* I'd understand. When I got laid off, I remember I'd sit in my desk chair and spin and spin when I was trying to think."

....

[40]Watermelon!!

"Exactly. And I give you props for not leaving the moment the first n-i-p-p-l-e made its Goodman Theatre debut," she adds.

"You know what's funny? Even though I had no frigging clue what any of the performance meant, I like having had the privilege of getting a glimpse into an artist's mind. I mean, what I saw was disturbing and dark—"

"And watermelon-y."

"And watermelon-y," I agree, "but the experience wasn't without value, you know? Like, my world is a tiny bit bigger for having seen that."

Stacey seems pleased. "That's what I always used to try to get my students to see. The value in a performance like that isn't understanding every nuance the artist implies. It's the interpretation and feelings *you* get from it."

"Well, mostly I ended up thinking I wasn't in on the joke. But there's a part of me that feels like I learned something from the performance, even if it's how to fight my way out of a giant dry-cleaning bag."

Seriously, something about this performance yanked off the big white dustcover that's been protecting the critical thinking part of my brain. There were no producers here to explain every little nuance of the action via a single-camera confessional, and it was up to me to interpret what I saw. I had to *engage*.

Intellectually, I sort of feel like I did the first time I ran on the tread-mill. Most of my body was screaming no . . . but a tiny part of me shouted yes.

Dear Neighbor,

Remember this weekend when you idled right outside my bedroom window? And you played shitty house music as loud as your fifteen-year-old Buick's radio would allow? With your bass turned up so high my fillings rattled? For, like, twenty minutes? At 3:00 a.m.? And when I went outside to glower at you, all you did was move two spaces up? Remember that?

No?

Too bad.

Because that'd go a long way in explaining why I was organizing my purse right beneath your open bedroom window late last night, playing Natasha Bedingfield as loud as my Harman Kardon speakers would allow.

By the way, I don't have a day job.

But from the looks of your pajamas, you do.

Check and mate, bitch.

Best,

Jen Cognito, Association President

P.S. Next time, I'm breaking out my Wham CD. Consider this a warning.

---

[41]Who says I can't write fiction?

C·H·A·P·T·E·R F·O·U·R

Do You Have Love for New York?

I've reached a new height in procrastination.

Thirty-four thousand feet, to be exact.

With a book deadline looming, I decide the most effective use of my time is to join my friends in New York for a girls' weekend instead of sitting down at my computer and finally putting a dent in my book.

My friends planned this trip last year but I knew I'd be on deadline, so I begged off months ago. All that changed last week when I got an e-mail from an associate producer working for the Travel Channel. She was in charge of finding residents to appear on a Chicago edition of Samantha Brown's *Great Weekends* show and would I be interested?

Would I be *interested*?

In seeing my enormous head *on national cable television*?

On what's technically *a reality show*?

Which in turn might be seen by the producers of *Survivor*, who will immediately appreciate how snarky I am and fall all over themselves to cast me because even though I trend a little acerbic,[42] I'm way more likable than that mean girl Courtney from the China season. Sure, she came up with the greatest zinger in reality show history, describing the be-mulleted lunch lady as someone who "sucked at life," but still . . . I'm pretty sure I'd be better. Plus, I have some *strongs* left inside me from all the working out I did for *Such a Pretty Fat*, so I would kick ass in the challenges, especially those I had to throw my weight into.

Also? I rock the house at Scrabulous and can totally solve puzzles.[43] And the plotting and the scheming and the cultivation of minions that goes along with *Survivor* game play? I mean, I was the rush chairman of my sorority—believe me, I can bully people into doing unpleasant shit. You think those kids *wanted* to cut literally thousands of stars out of aluminum foil?

The only problem could be that with my big, fat mouth, I may eventually get on other survivors' nerves, especially when I keep crying about how bad my hair looks—unless we were in the desert, in which case I would be fabulous—so there's a possibility I wouldn't make it to the tribal merge, but who cares?

Yeah, I wrote back to the associate producer, *I think I might be interested.*

(Sidebar? Much as I'd like to be on television, I'd never want a reality show where cameras followed me in my everyday life because I like being married to Fletch. Seriously, look at the Hogans, Carmen and Dave, Nick and Jessica, the tattoo-necked guy and Miss USA,

....

[42]Some might say bitter.

[43]Unless they involve addition, subtraction, or God help me, fractions.

Britney and Kevin, Danny Bonaduce and his stupid wife, and the Os-bournes. Everyone divorced![44] Okay, fine, Ozzy and Sharon made it, but their kids went to rehab![45] Try to give me my own TV show and I say no, no, no.)

The AP told me everything sounded good after a preliminary chat, but she said a New York–based executive producer needed to meet me before any decisions could be made. Then the EP and I went through all the machinations of getting together, but unfortunately his scouting trip to Chicago was too hectic, and at the last minute, we couldn't coordinate.

My desire to see my enormous head on national cable television transcends most rational thought, so after our missed connection, I told him, "Hey, I'm going to be in New York next weekend with my girl-friends—why don't we meet up while I'm there?" Seriously, I'm as crafty as Yau-man when he made that fake hidden-immunity idol on *Survivor: Fiji* or when Eval Dick spent the week terrorizing the *Big Brother* house and STILL got Eric to vote to keep him.

The producer agreed, which meant that I found myself scrambling for a ticket with a week's notice and suddenly felt a tad less brilliant. As I clicked around Orbitz, I winced at the last-minute prices and was almost ready to give up when Fletch suggested I check our banking re-wards points. I logged on and found we had enough saved up for a nonstop round-trip ticket. Victory!

"Aw, wait," I said, remembering. "I can't use these points."

"Why not?" Fletch asked, reading over my shoulder. "I don't see any

---

[44]You can add Jon and Kate's spectacular crash and burn to this list at the time of writing. Won't someone please think of the children?

[45]And yes, they grew up into fine adults, but it was rocky there for a while.

restrictions or blackout dates." Since apparently Fletch standing next to me constitutes a party, Maisy hopped off her couch and wedged her way under my desk. She perched her head on my knee and gazed up soulfully at me. I began to stroke her silky ears.

"Yeah, but if I waste these for a flight, then I won't have enough to get the reward I really wanted. Check this out." I pulled up the page and showed Fletch an image of a group of fit, attractive people in matching pink life vests careening through a deep canyon on a churning river. "See how much fun that blond family's having on those rapids?"

He scanned the page. "You want to redeem award points for a trip to the Grand Canyon? Wow. Never thought I'd see you opt for an active vacation." Whenever we've gone to Vegas, I've parked myself at the pool from ten a.m. until six p.m., taking every meal in my lawn chair and only getting up to swim and use the bathroom.[46]

"Oh, please, I don't want the trip; I want the boat!"

Fletch squinted at the screen and then back at me. "What *the hell* are you going to do with a twelve-foot raft?"

"*Pfft*, white-water rafting, dude!"

Fletch drew in a really big breath and slowly released it through pursed lips, causing a little plume of dust to fly up off my desk and onto Maisy's sweet head. I brushed it away, prompting her to give my knees a thorough licking. "You have any idea how to operate a white-water raft?"

"I'm sure it comes with an instruction booklet. And how hard could it be? You sit, it goes. Kind of like a riding lawn mower. Easy-peasy."

"You have any idea how to operate a riding lawn mower?"

....
[46]Which, coincidentally, tend to occur in the same place.

"No, but that's beside the point. Forrest Gump could drive a riding mower. Think about it—he was s-l-o-w."[47]

"Your logic is irrefutable." He rocked back on his heels, placing a hand on my shoulder. I detected a hint of smug about the eyes but chose to ignore it.

I pointed at a line of text on the screen. "Says here this is a twelve-foot rigid inflatable. I'm not sure what the means, but it sounds awesome!"

"Awesome," he agreed. "And you plan to white-water raft . . . where? The wild rapids of the Chicago River? Gonna perfect your sweep stroke while you cruise past the steel recycling plant on Elston? Or navigate the strainer at Navy Pier?"

"There's got to be somewhere in Illinois to go, right? Oh, but we'd have to get a couple of those silly little helmets first.[48] We might have enough points for those, too." I tabbed through the other pages of rewards.

"Sure, sure, that all sounds like a fine plan. But, um . . . where will you store your twelve-foot rigid inflatable?"

"In the rafters up in the garage. Naturally, I'd have to deflate it first. Also, I'd have to get rid of the baby pool currently up there, but I'd be willing to make that sacrifice." Maisy lay down on my feet in a show of solidarity. "See?" I asked, pointing to the dog. "She supports my decision fully. Remind me to get her a doggie life jacket so she can come with us."

....

[47] I try to be extrasensitive now after a reader got mad at me for making fun of a kid who had to wear a helmet in the apartment beneath me in one of my first books. Shit, I didn't know that meant autism! I didn't even know what autism was back then. I just thought helmets were funny. I mean, come on. Picture a helmet on anything else, like a cat or a pumpkin. It's hilarious! But still, I'm totally sorry.

[48] And if I wore one, you'd be allowed to laugh. See? It's only fair.

"I'm certainly glad you've secured the dog's vote. But tell me, you plan to reinflate the raft . . . how?"

"Bicycle pump, *duh*."

"Of course, bicycle pump. You could blow up your raft while you watch television."

I nodded. "That's the plan."

"Our living room's only eleven feet long."

"I'll angle it."

"We used a twelve-foot rigid inflatable in the Army. Took seven men on either side to paddle it. Wasn't easy paddling, either; each stroke of the oar was like lifting a shovel full of wet sand. So, if fourteen fit men had trouble moving the raft from point A to point B, how do you plan on making it go?"

"I have plenty of *strongs*, and the rapids will do most of the work for me. Plus, Maisy can sit in back and provide ballast." At the sound of her name, her tail began to thump.

"Well," Fletch said, clapping his hands together, "I can see that you've thought long and hard about this. Tell you what. I *insist* you give up your opportunity to see yourself on television and have a great weekend with your friends in New York to get this raft. Here, let's get it right now." He scooted me out of the way and went for the keyboard.

I stiffened in my seat. "Whoa, wait. . . . Hold up. I should maybe reconsider the raft for a second. I mean, summer's mostly over, so I won't get in a lot of sailing—"

"Rafting. You're only sailing when there's a sail."

"I mean, *rafting*—what are you, Captain Stubing now?—and I really do want to see everyone. And what if I can't find a matching life vest for Maisy? Maybe it's a better idea to go to New York? Plus those little helmets would mess up my hair."

He mulled over the idea for a moment. "If you don't get a raft, you won't have to throw your baby pool away."

"We do like sitting in the pool when it's really hot out," I admitted. Although I always have to monitor Maisy when we're wallowing because she won't get out to pee, either. This dog truly is my soul mate. "Maybe I should just get the plane ticket."

"Only if you feel like that's a better idea," he called over his shoulder as he walked back to the living room.

I chose New York, so I'm here in my first-class seat,[49] trying to figure out how many free Bloody Marys it will take to assuage the guilt I feel about being a thousand miles away from my unfinished manuscript.

I blot at a tomato juice spot on my black Lacoste, then lean back and sigh contentedly.

Looks like three is the magic number.

The girls pick me up from the airport and we drive straight to the beach. When we landed, the pilot said it was ninety degrees out, so it's the perfect day for a nice wallow in the Atlantic.

Most of us live in different parts of the country and rarely get together, so the car's alive with excited chatter as we make our way up the Long Island Expressway. If being together weren't enough, today's extra-exciting because we're taking our friend Angie to see the ocean for the first time.

"I just don't understand how someone can be our age and have never seen the ocean," I say. I mean, I know it's possible—the kids on *Amish in*

----

[49]Scored an upgrade, woo!

the City—my second-favorite reality show ever[50]—had never seen the ocean before, but they'd also never ridden on escalators or tasted coffee or had zippers on their pants. Plus, Angie's not Amish.

"I grew up on a Great Lake. Ask anyone in Michigan, and they'll tell you it's the same thing," Angie replies. She doesn't need to demonstrate on her hand where she spent her childhood because we already know she's from the Thumb. Plus, she's shown us a dozen times before. What is it with people from Michigan? They throw up their hands as often as a newly minted fiancée flashes her diamond. Is it because Michigan's the only state shaped like something familiar? I wonder if Italian folks are always rolling up their pants to show you where they're from on their boots?[51]

My WASP-y pal Poppy, who spent every second of every summer for twenty years on Atlantic beaches before moving to the Midwest, interjects, "It's *so* not the same."

"Do you feel like you've been missing something?" Wendy asks.

"How can I miss it if I've never had it?" Angie replies.

I can't wrap my mind around this. "You haven't even been to the Caribbean? Or, like, Florida? I bet you've been and you just don't remember. You've seen it. You must have seen it."

Angie frowns at me. "I've repressed my memory of the ocean?"

"Yeah." I bob my head enthusiastically, agreeing with my own conspiracy theory.

"No."

I persist. "But you just flew into New York yesterday. Did you not notice that big band of blue surrounding LaGuardia?"

....

[50]First is the original *Paradise Hotel*.

[51]If they do, I bet the Europeans roll their eyes, too.

Blackbird glances back from the driver's seat. "Jen, that's the Long Island Sound."

"No," I insist. "I'm talking about the other water around the airport."

Blackbird raises one elegant eyebrow in the rearview mirror. "The East River? Flushing Bay?"

I deliberately switch tracks. "Angie, did you or did you not see the Statue of Liberty on your flight in?"

"I did! How cool was that? I can't wait to tell the boys!"

"Aha! Then you saw the ocean that surrounds her!"

Poppy chimes in, "That would be the New York Bay."

Wendy leans around Angie, who's sitting between us in the backseat. "Jen, I thought you lived here. Shouldn't you know this?"

Okay, so maybe I suck at math AND geography.

But not at life. I'm *awesome* at life.

"*Pfft*, that was thirty years ago. I'm allowed to forget. Anyway, Ange, you never felt like just packing up the family and taking everyone to the beach for a few days?" I ask.

Blackbird jumps to Angie's defense. "Do you understand the amount of coordination that would take? That'd be tougher than a military strike. With all those boys, she probably counts herself lucky if they're all wearing pants when they leave the house."

"Yet you admit it's kind of weird to be an ocean virgin at almost forty," I counter.

"Oh, yeah, totally fucked up. But *understandably* fucked up," Blackbird clarifies.

"How do you think you'll react when you see it?" Wendy asks.

"Maybe she'll cry," I suggest. I remember when Mose from *Amish in the City* saw the Pacific for the first time. He waded in wearing jeans and got all emotional because the endlessness of the water made him even more appreciative of God's majesty. I didn't just cry when I watched that episode; I *sobbed.*

Angie shoots me a puzzled glance. "Why would I cry?"

"Because it's kind of an emotional thing. You'll feel way insignificant and you'll question your place in the universe because you'll have never seen anything so vast before."

Angie's having none of this. "Give me a break; I've never seen anything as vast as the laundry all the men in my house produce. One of the little guys is on two baseball teams this summer. Two teams! That's two full uniforms a day in addition to whatever else he wears. If that doesn't make me cry, I assure you, nothing will."

"I can't wait to see how you react when you smell the salt air for the first time. Bird, open the windows before we get there!" Poppy demands.

When we arrive at the beach, Blackbird throws the car into park, and we each hump a huge load of supplies over the dunes past the beach roses and saw grass to the boardwalk. We've got chairs and coolers and blankets and towels. We haul sandwiches and beverages and umbrellas. Beach toys and first-aid supplies balance out our loads. Our fruit is bountiful and fresh and water stock plentiful. Given our massive stash, you might think we're planning to colonize the beach. It's like we're on *Survivor: Mommyblogger.*

Seriously, the upside of traveling with a bunch of moms is that they're prepared for every eventuality. You'll never find yourself wanting for a Kleenex or a hard candy or hand sanitizer (or a corkscrew) with this group. The downside is today isn't helping me gear up for *Survivor,* because the contestants only get to bring one small pack. I remember on the first season[52] contestants were allowed to bring one small personal item like tweezers, but eventually they stopped that, knowing someone like me would probably bring my Kindle. The worst of the seasons was China, when they let contestants take only the clothes on their backs. About halfway through, production had to give everyone swimsuits because their underpants appeared to be rotting.

Wait, why do I want to be on this show again?

Anyway, none of us is paying attention to where we're going; we're all just watching Angie's face. The boardwalk is interminably long and our loads ridiculously heavy, but we know the effort will have been worth it when Angie sees the water for the first time. I want my *Amish in the City* moment!

Poppy and Blackbird lead the assault, so the second they spy a strip of salt water, they begin to walk backward. Moments later, when Angie finally sees the ocean, her expression is . . . fairly neutral. She merely gives the vista a quick once-over and tells us, "That's exactly what I thought it would look like."

Seriously, she must have more laundry than we can imagine if the entire Atlantic fails to bowl her over.

We choose a prime spot close to the water to set up camp. Most of us want to get a little color before we get wet, so the four of us settle into our chairs while Angie strips off her cover-up and heads down to the shoreline.

"She's going! She's going!" Wendy cries.

"*Shh*, quiet! We don't want to spook her!" Blackbird commands.

....

[52]Which I didn't watch at the time but eventually caught up on with the DVD series, coincidentally after I finished my last book.

Maybe we didn't get our big, dramatic reveal when she saw the water for the first time, but surely *swimming* in the ocean will be significant. The four of us lean forward in our chairs as Angie sizes up the situation with one hand on her hip and one shading her eyes.

"How's she going to approach this? I mean, she's never seen a wave before, and they're breaking big and hard today," I say.

Blackbird adds, "I saw riptide flags posted farther down the beach. Powerful surf out there."

Wendy agrees, "This water has to be superintimidating. And freezing. Mostly freezing."

We hold our breath as Angie ventures in up to her ankles and clutch one another as the water reaches her knees. Will she be shocked at how cold the Atlantic can be, even in late July? Will she wade in, only to do a *Baywatch*-worthy run out the second rippling water hits her thighs?

Angie glances to either side for a moment and then the greatest thing in the world happens—she just shrugs at the majesty of the whole new world before her and dives in headfirst.

We lose our minds.

Blackbird begins shouting first. "What? WHAT? Did you . . . Have you ever . . . I mean . . . HOLY SHIT!"

Wendy's up on her feet, mouth agape and eyes wild. "Did you see that? Did you see *that*? Did! You! See! That?"

I can't believe she just dove in. I'm stunned. That's the absolute opposite of what I'd do if this were my first time. I'd test the water about fifteen times. I'd consult the lifeguards. I'd query everyone on the beach before maybe hitting the snack bar, having a cheeseburger, and then waiting the requisite half hour before even thinking about approaching the water again. I'd construct an elaborate list of pros and cons and then I'd run the whole thing past Fletch not only to get his opinion but also to encourage him to come up with the kind of bribe or challenge I almost always require before I'll try something new.

But just diving in?

That's the last thing on earth I'd have done. "Nobody just dives in the Atlantic the first time they see it! No one!" Then I clarify, "I mean, dogs maybe, but not people!" My heart hasn't felt this buoyant since Zora and Evan Marriott got to split the unexpected seven-figure check on *Joe Millionaire*!

Poppy's Boston accent comes out when she's tired or drinking or under duress. She's much more succinct in her reaction. "Oh, my mathafuckin' Gaaawd!"

"She dove! I can't believe she dove. That's the bravest thing I've ever seen. I . . . I . . . I need to smoke now." Blackbird scrambles in her bag for cigarettes and a lighter. Speechless, Poppy holds her hand out for one, too.

Angie emerges from the surf, brushing sand and stray bits of seaweed off herself. She heads back in our direction, and Blackbird and Poppy rise and give her a long, slow clap while Wendy tosses her a striped towel.

As Angie dries herself, she says simply, "So *that's* the ocean. . . . I like it. And, hey, why do I have so much sand in my crotch?"

Okay, seriously?

This is so much better than a twelve-foot rigid inflatable raft.

To: gina_at_home

From: jen_at_home

Subject: suddenly my life has meaning again (okay, it had it before, but still)

I just found this while procrastinating in the TV/Film/Radio Jobs section on Craigslist. Tell me this isn't the best trashy TV news you've heard in a while. (P.S. My thoughts are in italics.)

VH1 and BRET MICHAELS will hit the road literally . . . to find true love on the . . . "ROCK OF LOVE BUS with BRET MICHAELS"

VH1 is loading up a tour bus filled with beautiful babes and taking them on tour across the country. *The Rock of Love Bus with Bret Michaels* takes contestants out of the mansion and on the road in true rock star style. This season will feature all new ladies vying for Bret's affection while traveling across America following Bret on a monthlong tour. The contestants will face new challenges to see if they can handle the rock star life on the road! If you are a sexy single lady looking for love who can party like a rock star, then this is the show for you! Ladies must be ages 21 and up. *(No STDs? No problem! We can provide them for you!)*

TO BE CONSIDERED, E-MAIL THE FOLLOWING INFO TO YOUR CLOSEST AUDITION CITY:

1. Your Name *(Bonus points awarded if it ends in an I or Y)*
2. Age *(Don't bother if you're over 25. This bus does not stop in Cougar Town.)*

3. What city you would like to audition in *(Meaning "In which city is your strip club located?")*

4. Best phone #

5. Little about yourself and why you would be good for Bret *(Meaning, "Send shots of yourself naked. Lots and lots of naked.")*

6. And be sure to ATTACH A FEW RECENT PICS of yourself AND Web page/MySpace url *(See above.)*

Aug. 1–10 CHICAGO (IL): ChicagoRock @xxxxCasting.net
Aug. 11–18 CINCINNATI (OH): OhioRock @xxxxCasting.net

Location: Chicago only

Compensation: $100/day

($100? I guess that's the going rate for dignity these days. And, no, I can't wait!)

C·H·A·P·T·E·R F·I·V·E

Outwit, Outlast, Outclassed

$\mathcal{I}$ got my ass kicked at the beach yesterday.

After Angie's first dip, I joined her in the water. The other girls declared the water too cold—or the company too compelling—and stayed in their chairs. When I was a kid, I went to the beach all the time and kind of figured swimming in the Atlantic is like riding a bike—you never forget. Maybe I'd have to reperfect my wave-diving and body-surfing skills, but that would only take a minute. Plus, I needed to hone my water proficiency for *Survivor*, anyway.

Here's the thing—if I were to make it onto *Survivor*, my main goal would be avoiding the Shame Rattle sound effect. Ever notice that any-time a contestant says or does something particularly stupid, the produc-ers overlay this little *chucka-chucka-chuck* noise? Happens on *The Bachelor* and *The RR/RW Challenges* and *The Amazing Race* and *Hell's*

Kitchen all the time, plus tons of other shows. Producers use the Shame Rattle as a way to highlight a contestant's lack of self-awareness, but they also love to lay it over failed feats of athleticism. Personally, I love the Shame Rattle, but since my plan is to sit out on the running events, I've got to be extra-fierce in the water-based ones, lest it rattle for me.

I've always been a strong swimmer, so imagine my surprise when what looked like a gentle tide grabbed me by the shins, pulled me under, gave me a ten-billion-gallon swirlie, and then threw me onto a bed of jagged rocks and broken shells so forcefully that I skidded almost all the way back to our beach camp.

Huh, I thought. *Perhaps the three Bloody Marys I slugged down on the plane made me a bit wobbly. Jeff Probst would mock me mercilessly if I only tried this the once, plus the Shame Rattle would sound, so I should go in again.*

I'd waded in up to my ankles when another teeny wave suddenly turned white and not only knocked me ass over teakettle but also wedged buckets of sand in my every orifice.[53] Next to me, Angie was receiving a similar beating.

Oh, ocean, I mused, *I'll best you yet. I'm just out of practice.*

This time I dashed into the water full force, mouth wide-open à la *Braveheart,* which is exactly how I ended up swallowing a hogshead full of briny water, seaweed, and possibly one dead jellyfish.

Sixteen increasingly unsuccessful tries later, I hauled myself back to my group of girls, battered, bloody, and wearing what felt like a diaper full of sand, whispering only, *"Ocean—monumental fail,"* before collapsing into my beach chair.

If we were on *Survivor,* I'd have to hike to the freshwater spring to

---

[53] And I mean EVERY.

get the nonsalt variety, bring it back through the jungle, boil it, and then wait for it to cool. But here, all I have to do is ask for one of the million bottles of Dasani the girls packed. Sometimes real life is even better than reality television.

Moments after my surrender, the lifeguard put up two huge red flags on either side of where I'd been attempting to swim. He must have been sitting in his tall chair the whole time, thinking, "The big, tan, sturdy one keeps getting knocked over. Hey . . . I wonder if there aren't some riptides right about here."

Point?

I'd rather be getting ten thousand violent sand enemas right now than standing on a New York City sidewalk that's so hot it's melting the rubber on the bottom of my sandals in the minute it takes Poppy to get her bags out of the car.

We all stayed at the beach last night, but today we're in the city proper. I have my Travel Channel meeting this afternoon, and the other girls have their own agendas. Poppy mentioned something about her devoting her day to "spending quality time at the mother ship,"[54] but that still counts as a plan.

We were all going to sleep at Wendy's brother-in-law's loft in Chelsea, but when we got there, we discovered it was smaller than we'd expected. Sensing we might be cramped, Poppy invited me to stay with her at the Colony Club.

"Um . . . okay. How much does it cost?" I asked. Given her taste in three-hundred-dollar scarves, I was a tad cautious about the lodgings she might choose.

"Nothing because it's on me," she replied.

....

[54]Hermès.

"Then I'm totally in." Given her taste in three-hundred-dollar scarves, I was a tad delighted about the lodgings she might choose.

I was ten years old the last time I was in New York in the summer. I recall skipping down streets, the sun at my back, delighting in how abandoned the city was, the majority of the residents having left the island in pursuit of sand and surf. I remember how calm everything was—there was none of the festive chaos we'd encountered the previous fall when my dad took us to the Museum of Natural History or the following December when my Girl Scout troop saw the Rockettes and watched the enormous tree being lit.

What I don't remember is the stifling heat.

It's not that I'm unfamiliar with hot. Sometimes I seek it out. Hot only becomes part of my Unholy Trinity of Unhappy when it's involuntary. Seriously, I dig the desert, and I purposely vacation in Vegas on the Fourth of July. I ride with the windows open as often as I can in the summer because I love how a warm breeze feels on my skin. On tour last month, I even parked myself poolside for a few hours midday in 115-degree Scottsdale, Arizona.[55] Yet none of these experiences has prepared me for how sweltering this city can be. Who knew that the second it hit eighty degrees, all the bricks and concrete would conspire to turn the city into the world's largest pizza oven? I'll take 115 degrees in Scottsdale over ninety-two degrees on the Upper East Side any day of the week.

There's so much sweat pooling in my ears that I don't even hear Poppy approach with her things. "Shall we?" she asks.

Since we're at what I assume is a hotel, I expect someone in a scratchy suit and silly hat to swing open the doors and welcome us. Seems like the fancier they are, the more ridiculously the doormen are dressed. At one

---

[55]Yes, frozen blueberry mojitos were involved. Is that a problem?

place in Vegas, all the guys were dressed like the Crocodile Hunter. Crikey! Judging by the number of Rolls-Royces lined up on the sidewalk here, whoever comes out to get our bags should be done up like an organ grinder's monkey. Okay, fine, there are only two Rollses idling at the curb, but since I'm not sure I've even seen one before, two seems like a surfeit.

Turns out there's no doorman at all. Instead of a delightfully costumed staffer rushing out and whisking away our things, Poppy has to ring a discreet little bell at the side of the door in the middle of a hulking brick building. From my spot on the sidewalk, I can hear her going through the same kind of ritual Dorothy performed before being granted access to the Wizard. Poppy answers a litany of questions while I try not to liquefy in the sun.

We're finally ushered in moments before the heat kills me dead, splat. We bypass any sort of license-showing, credit-card-verifying sort of check-in procedure. The guy in the drab gray suit who opens the door knows exactly who we are and where we're from. This'd be creepy if we hadn't already played twenty questions.

This building's enormous, and all of it seems to belong to the Colony Club. I always feel boxed in when I come to New York because everywhere I go is tiny and crowded, and everyone's fighting for their square foot of space. But not here—the ceilings are high and the rooms we cross are vast and airy and empty, save for some really elegant groupings of fussy-footed fine furniture. What did the Colony Clubbers do, exactly, to merit so much prime Park Avenue real estate?

On the way to our rooms, we pass fastidiously appointed receiving rooms and tasteful touches like enormous porcelain bowls full of crushed lavender. Couple the meticulous decor with our prime Upper East Side location, and I begin to wonder exactly what I've gotten myself into. I mean, I don't even know what a receiving room *is*, but this building is lousy with them. What's everyone receiving? Other than checks, I mean.

This place feels less like a hotel and more like I'm staying at a great-aunt's house. Correction, the house of a very, very wealthy great-aunt who smells vaguely of gin and isn't terribly fond of, well, anyone. I'll be honest, I'm not entirely comfortable here. Every inch of this reeks of old-world exclusivity, and I'm getting an intense "you don't belong here" vibe from the furniture alone.

Stupid, intimidating armoires.

The premises are completely deserted and, save for the two idling cars with their blackened windows, I haven't seen another guest or staffer since we walked in.

"Poppy," I whisper, "is this really a hotel?"

"Yes and no. Basically, Colony Club was founded at the turn of the century because society women couldn't come to the city and just stay at a hotel by themselves; that would've violated the social norm. So a few ladies got together and created the club. I guess you could say it's a hotel for women."

"Oh, I get it. Like on *Bosom Buddies*."

That's when the disappointingly dressed doorman turns to me, curls his lip, and hisses, "Not like on *Bosom Buddies*. Not at all. This is a *private club*, not the YWCA."

Seriously? Nice attitude, jackass. Okay, not to be all classist or anything, but *you're* the one carrying *my* suitcase, and I'd appreciate a little less condescension. I'm already uncomfortable enough as it is. I'm ready to tear into the guy when Poppy gives me a circumspect head shake.

Oh. Okay. No fistfights in her fancy club. Got it. Shame Rattle averted.

I glower at the back of the doorman's neck and pursue a different line of questioning. "How'd you become a member of a New York club?"

"My club at home has reciprocal privileges." Poppy lives in the tony North Shore suburbs, fifteen miles and one entire world away from me.

Fletch and I belonged to a private club once, but all it had was a dining room with mediocre food and a stunning view. There were no fancy sister outfits in other cities. As I mull things over, pieces of Poppy's puzzle begin to fall into place. Over the few years we've known each other, she's had more than her fair share of black-tie benefits and box seats at the opera and . . . it finally dawns on me. "Wait a minute. . . . You're . . . you're . . . a socialite, aren't you?"

Poppy says nothing, but instead offers me a slight, embarrassed grin.

I guess the first rule about WASP Fight Club is you don't talk about WASP Fight Club.[56]

How did I not figure this out earlier? I mean, the husband and the houses and the Hermès scarves were all clues, but then she spends most of her time doing charity work, which threw me off. I guess I've watched too many shows starring bimbos from Orange County and members of the Hilton family to realize sometimes socialites use their resources for good.

My head's still reeling when we drop Poppy off at her room. My friend's a socialite. That's like suddenly finding out I've been hanging out with Batman. If *I* were a socialite, it'd be the first thing out of my mouth whenever I met someone new . . . probably one of the myriad reasons why I'll never *be* a socialite.

Then the doorman takes me to my room. Surliness radiates off this guy as we go down the hall and around the corner. I'm not sure if he's hostile because he knows I have no business here or if the heat's gotten to him, too. Grudgingly he unlocks my door and begins to beat a hasty retreat as soon as I'm in.

....

[56]The second rule of WASP Fight Club is the martinis must be as dry as Cheever's wit. Why? What did you think it was?

"Hey, wait!" I say, chasing after him with a crumpled ten-dollar bill. "Here you go." I've been clutching it in my sweaty palm ever since we got out of the car, so the bill is a bit limp. One might even call it flaccid. But still, ten bucks AND you insulted me for referencing an old Tom Hanks sitcom? YOU'RE WELCOME.

The sneer I'm given in return takes me by surprise. "We don't accept gratuities."

"I'm sorry?"

"No tipping."

"Oh, come on," I say conspiratorially. "It's freaking hot out there. You carried my bag, you're working hard, and it's not like there's anyone who'll see. Go on." I gesture toward him with the bill. "Please. Get an iced coffee or something. I want to say thank you."

The doorman clenches his jaw. "We *do not* accept gratuities, and I *do not* want to have to repeat myself."

Wait, what? "But . . ."

He rolls his eyes heavenward and, with more than a little contempt, says, "If you're so anxious to reward my service, then you're welcome to contribute to the employee Christmas fund." Then he spins on his heel and stalks away.

Which is why I can't be held responsible for then muttering, "Oh, yeah? Well, I'm not going to *be* here at Christmas, motherfucker!"

There goes that damn Shame Rattle again.

"How'd it go?"

We're having dinner at Park Avenue Summer, which is so trendy and swank that I'm sure we only got in because every resident had the good sense to get the hell out of this city this weekend.[57] We're drinking lovely pink cocktails and catching one another up on the day's adventures. Angie's asking me about my meeting with the Travel Channel.

"I came superclose to blowing it," I admit.

"I'm sure you didn't," Poppy reassures me.

"Bup, bup, bup—hear me out. We went to a restaurant a couple of blocks west of here, and they had their big front window open so people could eat inside or on the sidewalk. We opted for in, what with the sweat pouring into the crack of my ass and all."

Angie shudders. "Matthew Broderick said it best. This place is Africa hot. Tarzan couldn't take this kind of hot."

"Anyway, this totally chichi place is filled with what looks like a bunch of extras from *Gossip Girl* and it's nine thousand degrees in there and none of them is sweating. No one. The producer kept asking me questions, but instead of really listening and giving him the kind of insightful answers that will get me on *Survivor*—"

"Wait, I thought this was for *Great Weekends*?" Angie asks.

"In my mind it would lead to *Survivor*.[58] Anyway, I couldn't stop bitching about how hot it was and begging the server to crank the air. And why wasn't anyone else hot? Some of the guys were in blazers and long pants! Eating big, creamy plates of pasta! In billion-degree heat! Not a bead on them! What's up with that, Upper East Siders? Are you some superior breed born without sweat glands?"

Poppy snickers and says, "Privilege doesn't perspire."

"Too freaking true. I finally just scooped some ice out of my glass,

....

[57]We're probably the only people in here who aren't from, like, Kansas or something.

[58]In my mind, everything kind of leads to *Survivor*.

stuffed it in my napkin, and began to hold it against the back of my neck to keep my brain stem from melting.[59] Good thing I did, because an entire conversation about my ass crack was about to tumble forth, and I managed to head it off at the pass, which I'm sure is the only reason they agreed to let me be on the Chicago episode."

"Well done!" Poppy cheers.

"Yes!" Angie exclaims, and we all clink glasses. "So, what's the hotel like?"

Poppy and I reply at the same time. "As expected." *"Bizarre."*

"You go first," Poppy says.

"Well, I tried to go downstairs and pay for my room because I didn't realize how swanky it was when Poppy invited me and I didn't want to take advantage."

"No! You're my guest," Poppy argues.

"Well, it's a nonissue. The snotty door guy was all, '*We don't accept cash, check, or credit card. You can't pay for a room unless you're a member.*' And then while I'm trying to figure out what to do next, this Rolls-Royce deposits some lady out front, and the guy has to go and let her in. Then he's got to take her up to her room because she's carrying a great big hatbox."

"When was the last time anyone bought anything in a frigging hatbox?" Angie asks.

"Exactly! So I was all, '*Fine, screw it. I'll just go with it.*' I kept thinking back to you yesterday, Angie. You just dove right in, and I thought maybe it's time for me to tear a page out of your book."

I hold up my pink cocktail and silently salute her while I continue. "I decided I'd try to get into the spirit of the place since I'm probably

---

[59]Shame Rattle, Shame Rattle, Shame Rattle.

never going to have this kind of opportunity again. I went back up to my room and stood out on the balcony. The wind was blowing a little *finally* and the sun was starting to set and all I could see were manicured roof gardens and maids walking little yip-yip dogs. Seriously, there was opulence everywhere I looked. And, I don't know, I guess I was overcome by how glamorous and otherworldly it was, and I suddenly felt like *I* was on *Gossip Girl*. I found myself stepping up a little bit on the cement balcony barrier with my arms spread out in the wind shouting, '*I am Blair Waldorf!*' I dove in, you know, and it was incredibly liberating."

Getting a glimpse of New York that so few other people have seen, I felt younger and thinner and wealthier, and I suddenly had the urge to buy a whole bunch of headbands.

I continue. "But then someone on a roof nearby must have heard me because they shouted back, '*No, you're not*,' and that freaked me out. Sometimes when you dive in, you hit the bottom and break your neck, you know? So I went back to hide and watch VH1 reruns until dinner. By the way, did you know that Poppy's a socialite?"

Angie takes a quick sip of her cosmo. "She has three houses and box seats at the opera. How did you *not* know that?"

Today I'm filming my segment for the Travel Channel. It's been a fascinating experience as I'm learning that even the most documentary-like shows require some tweaking. When my friends and I meet Samantha on camera, we'll have not only already been introduced, but we'll have chatted at some length. I always wondered if people had a little forewarning when they film reality stuff, and this seems to confirm that they do. I mean, it's still real, but when you take the time to sign a release and get miked up first, a little bit of the spontaneity disappears.

The one idea I managed to pull out of my ass (crack) in New York was to talk about why Chicago was the better city, so that's what I'm supposed to bring up on camera today.

And I do . . . but instead of being playful and charming about it, I become combative. I end up turning my benign chitchat with Samantha Brown—possibly the nicest, most genuine and gracious person on the planet, by the way—into a single-sided duel. I hear myself badgering her, and I can sense that my aggression is not exactly appreciated, but I can't stop myself because I have no idea what else I can discuss.

What am I going to talk about? The new exhibit at the Art Institute?[60]

The delicious tandoori chicken at the Indian place on Devon?[61]

Any one of the amazing dramas at Chicago's world-class theaters?[62]

My friend Gina, who's unbelievably social and able to talk with anyone about anything, keeps diving in to try to rescue me, but the damage has been done.

I'm upset with myself because not only is my awkwardly aggressive camera time not what *Survivor* producers would want, but this isn't how I want to be. This is a problem.

Correction, this is a problem in need of a resolution.

But how do I fix a problem when I'm not even sure what it is?

I spend a lot of time soul-searching over the next few days, and I don't like the conclusions I reach.

....

[60]Never been there.

[61]Never tried it.

[62]Never seen them.

The issue here is that I'm a dangerous combination of stupid and mouthy.

Wait, that was way harsh, Tai.

Let me rephrase that—it seems that the root of the problem is that I've stopped challenging myself, and I've become intellectually lazy. I mean, for Christ's sake, I just expressed my existential angst by quoting *Clueless*.

That's just messed up.

I was laid off seven years ago, but I realized only recently that it had nothing to do with incompetence. My hubris led me to believe I was perfect in my job because of my outstanding sales record, so I never cultivated the softer social skills I needed outside of a meeting. Back in the office, shouting was my canvas and insults my paint. Sure, I could sell, but I was incapable of dealing with anyone in my organization with-out a healthy dose of condescension. Gritting my teeth and simply being nice wasn't nearly as easy[63] as hurling smart-assed retorts, so that's the path I chose.

Maybe I'd have never been laid off in the first place if I could just have an innocuous conversation about boring stuff like theater or dining or art or something.

Okay, now I'm *seriously* having an epiphany.

Maybe when my old company was forced to make cuts, they didn't keep me, despite my numbers. Instead, they kept the people they *liked*.

Maybe not being an asshole was more important than being good.

I don't want to let that happen again. I don't want to lose the chance to continue to live my current dream because I'm too lazy to Google

------

[63]Or funny.

Baudelaire and too lippy to avoid mocking everyone. In this case, being a successful author has something to do with writing but even more to do with being savvy enough to conduct myself professionally. Up to this point I've done well by spying on my neighbors and calling people "asshats" but that can only take me so far.

I'm worried that as my career grows and I'm presented with more opportunities, I'll keep screwing them up if I don't learn how to be smarter and more gracious in professional situations.

My fans tell me they love my books because they're guilty pleasures. But I wonder if I'm able to overcome my crippling intellectual lethargy, my books might simply be pleasures, sans the guilt.

Maybe the problem is that I'm currently reaping everything I've been putting out into the universe. You know, garbage in, garbage out. If I spend my days watching Flavor Flav take baths with skanks, what possible good can I expect to come of this?

I bet if I spend less time with the television and more time pursuing activities that enhance my life and expand my knowledge, I won't freeze up in business or social situations.

When I took on the project that resulted in *Such a Pretty Fat*, I was able to better my own world by putting forth physical effort. A lot of what I did was hard and kind of sucked, but the sweat was worth it. I failed at a whole bunch of stuff along the way, but I never let myself quit.

Maybe it's time to do the same thing for my brain.

Maybe it's time to leave my cerebral comfort zone.

To try new things.

To challenge myself.

To do what I'd always written off as boring or hard or scary.

To put myself in positions I've never been in.

To not allow myself to run away the second it doesn't work out exactly like I want it to.

To fill the universe with something other than my constant commentary on this season's new batch of *The Apprentice* contestants and scathing retorts.

My Shame Rattle has sounded for the last time.

I guess I could say the tribe has spoken.

Now I've just got to figure out what to say back.

To: fletch_at_work

From: jen_at_home

Subject: I'm like Batman, only fatter

Hey,

So I was sitting at my desk in back watching a nonhomeless-looking person walking down our alley. He appeared to be checking things out, and that bothered me. Think about it—there's no reason to be in our alley because it's not a shortcut to anywhere.

I watched as he strolled past our house, and when he noticed our back door was open, he stopped in his tracks and immediately made a beeline through the vacant backyard next door and headed right toward our house.

What he didn't expect was for me to step out of the shadows with a pit bull and a huge shepherd-wolf mix, shouting, "NO FUCKING WAY."

He left a vapor trail in his wake.

I kick ass.

XO,

Jen

P.S. This is why I need a gun.

To: jen_at_home

From: fletch_at_work

Subject: re: I'm like Batman, only fatter

This is exactly why you can't have a gun.

Extreme Makeover: Dumb-Ass Edition

*B*y Jove, I think I've got it!

I totally figured out how I'm going to ease my conversational impediment.

I'm going to go Eliza Doolittle all over my ass!

Here's the thing—I'm not concerned with passing myself off as a lady of high society; I just don't want to give strangers the impression that I'm a dumb ass anymore. Plus, I don't want to make them feel all uncomfortable when I spout a bunch of thoughtless commentary because ultimately, if I say the wrong thing in the wrong place, I could offend the wrong person or even kill my career. Basically, I need to stop using my mouth as a weapon.

To do so, I'm going to have to get me some learnin'.

What I need is a cultural renaissance.

Scratch that. I need a cultural *Jen*aissance.

My handicap isn't that I'm incapable of learning but that I'm rarely motivated to do it, so I'm going to battle my natural propensity for sloth by forcing myself to get off the couch and acquire a base of cultural knowledge. I need to broaden what I'm familiar with by reading and dining and patronizing the arts[64] so when I'm in the middle of an important conversation, I won't just panic and start blurting nonsense. For example, this past winter, if I'd maybe read a book on petroleum politics, I wouldn't have immediately launched into a diatribe about how Clooney killed *The Facts of Life*.[65]

The thing is, I'm easily influenced and gorging myself on a steady diet of shitty reality television has clearly had an effect. Reality television's a terrible influence on me because the participants are put in absurdly unnatural situations, and they have a team of producers behind the scenes encouraging them to, figuratively, go for blood.

Ipso facto, if I surround myself with positive influences, I'll be more erudite.

I already have plenty of cultivated (yet fascinating) people in my life—I mean, I know a master sommelier, so why don't we ever get together to drink great wine? One of my friends works in a big museum— why haven't I ever taken her up on her offer of a backstage tour? Apparently I know socialites, so why do I struggle with even the most basic of social graces? Plus, through Stacey I've met chefs and lots of theater people—shouldn't I be able to learn from all of them? I mean, if I actually put forth the effort and don't shake and rock and go all hot-

---

[64]I mean attending, not talking down to them, even if they are trying to pass off Vaseline barbells as art.

[65]But admit it, he did.

water-burns-baby every time they try to talk about what I previously found mind-numbing?

I mean, maybe I'll learn I've actually been very happy avoiding opera my whole life. Maybe I'll discover that my initial impression of the Vaseline barbell was on the money. Maybe I'll discover stinky cheese tastes exactly as bad as it smells and my love for Kraft American singles is forever.

And maybe I won't. And that's okay.

The real value will be in having had the experiences in the first place.

I'm willing to wager that being able to draw from a greater depth of knowledge and experience will make me a better writer because I'll finally be able to describe someone as evil without having to reference Blair Waldorf or Mr. Burns.

Because, *dude*, it's time.

Perhaps my first official foray outside of my comfort zone should have involved wearing a bra.

To backtrack, once in a great while, I'll come across a book that totally alters my perspective. Years ago, when I read Ayn Rand's magnum opus *Atlas Shrugged*, it forever changed the way I looked at the relationship between industry and government.[66] And a college course featuring *Catcher in the Rye* brought out the foulmouthed cynic I never knew lived inside me.

....

[66]Some of you may argue it turned me into a conservative, compassionless douchebag. Some of you might not be wrong, but that topic is not currently up for debate.

That may or may not have been a good thing.

What inspired me in *Eat, Pray, Love* was that Elizabeth Gilbert put herself into situations that were initially uncomfortable, but that ended up helping her meet her goal—finding fulfillment in body, mind, and spirit. She tried all kinds of crazy stuff, some of which she liked, and some she didn't, but each try brought her a step closer to her goal.

That's why I'm here, top off, facedown on this terry-cloth-covered table. I decided the best way to push myself out of my comfort zone was to revisit something I'd previously written off, so I'm getting a massage. I know, I know. . . . Everyone loves a massage! Except me. First of all, massages hurt. A lot. I'm generally so tense that even a little manipulation *kills.* Second, the least relaxing thing I can think to do is to take my pants off in front of a stranger, no matter how professional he or she may be. Third, I actually thrive on stimulus bordering on chaos, so lying in a dark, quiet room, hearing the sound of nothing but whale music and the occasional rippling of back fat is NOT my recipe for a good time.

I figure if I can get past my discomfort—you know, just dive in—I might find some value in it. Plus, it's easier than going to a museum.

I'm lying here, trying to clear my mind. But the thing is, the second the masseuse turns off the light, my thoughts begin to race:

I wish the masseuse had eucalyptus oil. I hate lavender and my only other choice was lemongrass, which smells nice, but it totally makes me want another one of those lemongrass mojitos we had when Stacey invited me to the opening of that new hotel. I guess now that I think about it, it was kind of disrespectful for me to mock the PR girls for going on and on about the giant tuna they were going to carve into fresh sushi. But the second we walked in, everyone was all, "Did you see the fish? Did you see the fish? You have to see the fish!" like it was the second coming of Christ or something. So, I ask you, how was I not supposed to bend over by its still-

intact head and take a MySpace-style self-portrait with it? Hilarious! And maybe I shouldn't have loudly announced, "Let's go eat our sandwiches over by those models so we'll feel extra-good about ourselves!" but come on, it was pretty funny. Stacey thought so and OW, that fucking HURT and HOLY OW, that hurt even more.

You wouldn't think this tiny little masseuse would have such strong hands, but she does. Bet she would kick so much ass at a thumb-wrestling match. Okay, she's touching my shoulders, and OW, I don't like that AT ALL and now she's massaging my head and HEY, LADY, YOUR HANDS HAVE OIL ON THEM AND I JUST WASHED MY HAIR. Oh, great, I'm going to be a big, greasy lemon head for the rest of the day because I am not showering again because I just showered an hour ago and I have better things to do than lather, rinse, repeat all the damn day and I kind of still have a book due and JESUS CHRIST, you are going to pop my head clean off!

I'm paying a buck a minute for this?

Okay, okay, I'm not being terribly Eat, Pray, or Love right now. I feel more Eat, Aim, Shoot. I need to clear my thoughts and relax and be in the moment but it's really hard to do when this little person is SNAPPING MY SPINAL CORD. OW!! And how am I supposed to relax when I'm only wearing underpants and a sheet? I know this person is professional and sees people undressed for a living, yet THIS IS STILL REALLY UNCOM-FORTABLE FOR ME IN EVERY SENSE.

You know what helps me relax? A shirt. Some pants. Maybe FULL UNDERWIRE SUPPORT. And what's the deal with this music? It's just one long pan flute solo? Is it more than one guy playing? When does he take a break? And why does it have to be all New Age-y? Why can't they play opera? From what Poppy says, opera is very nice and it tells a story that maybe I could concentrate on while this little tiny person is MURDERING ME ONE HANDFUL OF BACK FAT AT A TIME.

I wonder if she'd rather work on a person who's heavier than a really skinny person? I bet massaging them would be like gripping a Baggie full of chicken bones, while I probably feel like a Stretch Armstrong doll. Do they still make those? And what'd they fill them with, anyway? I remember how mad my grade school friend Donna was when I bit a tiny hole in her Stretch doll to see what he was made of, and if I recall, it was some kind of green goo and MOTHER OF CHRIST, I THINK MY ARM'S DISLOCATED NOW. You know what I like? I like when I'm lying on the bed on my stomach reading and my six-pound cat Maggie walks on my back. Sometimes she makes little biscuits and it's soft and sweet and DOESN'T FEEL LIKE TORTURE. FOR GOD'S SAKE WHY NOT JUST WATERBOARD ME WHILE YOU'RE AT IT?

Um . . . yeah.

Apparently I still don't like massages.

But I do have something new to talk about. So there's that.

Last year, Fletch and I agreed to make the big move out to the suburbs. However, we've yet to decide which one is the real us. We hemmed and hawed so much we had to renew our lease to buy more time. But this is it—when this lease is over, we're leaving the (773) for good.

Last weekend we were up in Winnetka looking at a stately stucco home within walking distance of the lake. The house was at the top end of our budget, and we're not quite ready to make an offer, but we took a peek anyway.

"I don't know about this place, Fletch," I said.

"Why not? It's practically perfect," he replied, having already mentally set up his media room in the finished basement. "Too expensive?"

"Nah, that's not it. First of all, where are the rats? I don't see evidence of a single rodent. If Loki doesn't have a backyard stocked with vermin, how's he going to keep up his excellent killin' skills?"[67]

"You make a fine point," he agreed, getting into the spirit. "I've noticed there's no garbage on the sidewalk—what are the rats supposed to eat once we import them?"

"Listen." I paused for a second to take in all the quiet. "The windows are open and cars keep driving by, but none of them is blasting salsa music. Where's my relentless mariachi serenade?"

"No thumping bass line yet, either. How are we supposed to enjoy other people's music if they don't share it with us?" he wondered.

"Worst of all, what if one of us suddenly develops an interest in illegal drugs? Place like this, you can't just walk out front and buy crack. Serious inconvenience."

Then we drove back to the city, laughing all the way until we got to our depressing neighborhood and still-squalid home. Then everything was a lot less funny.

I feel like once we figure out where to settle in for good, and after I complete this manuscript, only then can I get down to the business of fixing what's wrong with me.

Finally.

"What was that thump?"

"Was that a thump? Sounded more like a crash to me."

---

[67] Although I've yet to understand why that damn dog happily kills outdoor rats, but couldn't lift a paw in opposition to indoor rats.

Fletch and I are in the living room, drinking coffee and watching FOX News. We're heckling every story we see Stadler- and Waldorf-style, which makes this a pretty typical Saturday. We planned to look at houses today, but we're in the middle of a vicious September rainstorm and neither of us wants to brave the expressway in a monsoon. Plus, I'm already two weeks overdue on my manuscript and I've got to get it done,[68] so I'm in for the day.

"You really want to debate the semantics of the noise we just heard instead of getting up to inspect it? *Oh, hello, Mr. Breaking-and-Entering criminal! We're in here! Come and murder us!*" I singsong toward the back of the house. This might be funny if there hadn't been a spate of B&Es in the neighborhood in the past few weeks.

"'S fine," Fletch assures me, eyes still on the screen.

"Really?" I huff. "You're not even going to get up? FINE YOUR-SELF." I hurl myself out of my seat and stomp into the kitchen.

"Can I have more coffee while you're up?"

"Can't. Busy being stabbed," I yell back. But there's no evidence of breaking and entering. Or entering, anyway. Something definitely broke.

"What the hell's going on here?" I mutter to myself. I bend over to inspect the problem. One of our hardwired under-cabinet lights has just fallen out of the wall and into a puddle on the counter. "Swear to God, if that little bastard took a leak on here again, we're having him for dinner." Our surly cat Bones has taken to peeing up here lately. I assume this is how he expresses his unhappiness with the litter-box situation. I admit I haven't provided the level of sanitation he normally requires, but ever

---

[68]The first person who asks, "Why didn't you start writing it in January when it sold?" gets a solid kick in the teeth.

since I got hit with a flying rat this winter, I seem to have lost my passion for keeping his toilet perfectly spotless.

"What's the problem in there?"

"Light fell out of the wall."

Apparently this is too interesting—or his cup is too empty—not to see firsthand, and Fletch approaches from behind me while I furiously dry and decontaminate the counter. "Here, I'll fix it." He tries to place the fixture back up, lining the screws up with the holes in the wall, but it immediately falls out again. He tentatively touches the drywall underneath the cabinet . . . and his finger goes right through it.

"This is soaked," he reports.

"How'd that little shit manage to wet the wall?" I wonder. "Did he back up to it? Does he need to go to the vet?"

"If Bones peed hard enough to saturate the wall, he needs a priest, not a doctor. This isn't urine."

"Well, hurrah for us being slightly less squalid than anticipated! But if this isn't pee, what's been flooding the counter? Is this from the bathroom?" I ask.

"Can't be—we're fifteen feet away from those pipes, and this is an exterior wall. This is coming from the roof over the back porch."

"Do we have a problem?" I fret.

Fletch gives it a dismissive shrug. "I'm sure it's nothing to worry about. Now let's get some more coffee."

I head back to the living room, glancing at the wall over my shoulder. "Okay . . . if you're sure."

"Trust me."

Does the statement "trust me" ever NOT become famous last words?

Over the next few weeks we find out that not only is our roof leaking, but our foundation has cracked. Water has saturated the electrical panel and the back wall's become structurally unsound, which is causing the porch—you know, the place where I'm supposed to finish writing my book—to sink.

As in my house is sinking.

Myhouseissinking.[69]

This is bad.

I'm in my office giving my manuscript one final read. I finish scanning the last page, click SAVE, and then SEND.

That's it.

I'm finished![70]

I turn my attention to the two men in full hazmat suits who're about to tear out the drywall ten feet away from me.

"I bet you find a little bit of mold," I tell them. "I've been really wheezy in here, and my eyes have totally been burning. The thing is? I kind of think it's some kind of beneficial supermold because I've been able to concentrate in here like never before. Seriously, I'm talking crystal clear focus. I'm pretty sure it's a penicillin-y strain of mold that's like

....

[69]Kind of puts that whole ratinmyhouse thing into perspective, doesn't it?
[70]WHEW!

brain medicine. Which, really? Perfect timing because I'm about to take on a project that'll require me to use my mind, like, all the time."

The two men look at me strangely, and then they each strap on respirators. "You might want to wait in the other room," the older one says.

"Okeydokey," I reply, practically skipping off toward my television. But before I can even get past the opening credits of *I Love Money*, the younger mold-remediation guy comes in—pale and shaking—to say, "We opened the wall because we were going to start the cleanup in your office and OH, GOD THE MOLD, THERE WAS SO MUCH MOLD. OH, GOD, OH GOD, WE HAVE TO SEAL IT UP AND LEAVE RIGHT NOW."

Oh.

God.

I guess we're moving.

We have no choice.

Now I need to find a new house.

And probably pack, too.

My cultural Jenaissance will have to go on hold indefinitely.

Well, THAT was one enormous, six-week-long pain in the ass. I never want to see another cardboard box again.

We have to stop at the old place one more time tonight to drop off the garage door opener. The old homestead looks so different now. They began major construction the day we moved out, and now the entire kitchen has been gutted because of the water leak. All forty-seven of my former pretty white cabinets can be found scattered throughout the wee first floor. My old landlords are such nice people and I feel awful for them.

As I walk around the kitchen, I can see the wall where the cabinets had barely been hanging on to a rotten stud, surrounded by giant blooms of black mold. I know from looking around, there's no way we could have stayed here. There's too much damage.

And then in a bittersweet moment, I'm vindicated for a year's worth of argument.

"Fletch, check it out!" I demand.

"What am I looking at?"

"In there, in that space between where the wall and floor meet. Do you see?"

He peers into the open area and then recoils.

"So you see it," I confirm.

He blanches. "Whoa."

What I'm pointing out are droppings. Not mouse droppings like he'd assured me, but rat droppings. Turds. Poop. Doody. Big, fat, filthy, disease-ridden rat scat. Gah. I'm so grossed out that if I had a gun right now, I might just put myself out of my own misery.

"I guess you were right," he grudgingly admits. "There really was a ratinourhouse."

I nod, but I don't savor the win.

To: jen_at_home

From: stacey_at_home

Subject: Monday

You up to hit *Desire Under the Elms* with me Monday? My date had to cancel at the last minute.

To: stacey_at_home

From: jen_at_home

Subject: RE: Monday

Totally! What kind of food do they serve?

Property Ladder

"**A**re you finally settled in?"

"Yeah . . ." I trail off.

"Do you love the new place?"

"Yeah . . ." I respond unconvincingly.

"Okay, what's the problem? That house seems pretty nice, judging from the photos you posted." I'm on the phone with Angie, and I can hear her huffing away in the background. I suspect she's getting in a quick elliptical workout while we chat, as she doesn't know how to avoid multitasking. One time we were talking and I could hear sawing. At first I thought a kid was snoring in the background, but it turns out she was on her hands-free phone, preparing for Halloween by building a six-foot-tall witch out of plywood from a pattern she'd seen in Martha Stewart's magazine.

We lucked into renting brand-new construction, so the chances of this house sinking are considerably reduced. The rooms are sunny and quiet, and there's enough yard space for the dogs to run laps. They're so thrilled that Maisy only pees indoors now to make a point.

There's space enough for me to have my own office in a room with big windows. The kitchen's quite functional, with dark granite and cherry cabinets, both of which are perfect for masking dirt and the paw prints from cats who refuse to stay off the counters. And if we really love it here, we have the option to buy once our lease is up, thus settling the whole where-do-we-want-to-live dilemma. The best part is this house has all the benefits of a suburban homestead, but I still live only five minutes away from Stacey, and yet . . .

"I'm not playing around with you, Lancaster. Cough it up." Yeah, she's definitely exercising. The endorphins make her aggressive.

I hesitate. "Well, the new house is . . . boring, okay? It's boring. I mean, technically we moved to what isn't as good a neighborhood as the one we were in—"

Angie barks but tries to cover it with a cough. "*That* was a good neighborhood?" Apparently the large retaining wall covered with gang graffiti across the street led her to believe otherwise.

(Sidebar: I always wanted to go out there and, you know, *disrespect* the local Latin Kings by covering their crowns and tridents with arrows and my old sorority letters, but Fletch thought that was my worst idea yet. He was all, "*What if they catch you? What would be your line of defense? Not inviting them to your mixer? Gossiping about their baggy pants and plain white T-shirts at the Phi Delt house?*"[71]

It didn't matter in the end because you—meaning *I*—can't buy spray

---

[71]Again, wouldn't be an issue if he'd just let me have a gun.

paint in city limits. I grilled the unhelpful associate in the paint department at the home-improvement store about this stupid local ordinance. I tapped my loafered foot, adjusted my pearls, and repopped the collar on my Lacoste while we spoke. "I'm sorry. Do you think I'm going to stuff your spray paint in my Coach purse, drive home in my German car, and then start tagging walls?" The associate just stood there in his smock, looking scared, not saying anything.[72]

I sigh and gaze out at my tidy little backyard. "Yeah, smarty-pants, we lived in *Bucktown*, which is superdesirable, even though we were in the weird little pocket of it that bordered Logan Square. Now we're in the Square proper, which isn't considered nearly as nice. That's why we were able to rent something bigger and newer for about the same price. The thing is, we're in the very best part of the Square and . . . and . . . our neighbors *suck*."

"Aren't you used to that?" I can't tell if she's snorting or just breathing hard.

"No, I mean they suck in an entirely new way. We've got construction on one side, so no one even lives there. On the other side, we've got a house identical to ours. A lovely young couple lives there. They wave when we see them, and they're always out raking leaves and stuff."

Angie begins to huff louder. The jury's out as to whether she's reaching a critical point in her workout or if she's just getting annoyed. "Weren't you going to put out a hit on the weird old neighbors who never cut their lawn? Didn't you squeal to the City about them all the time? You stole their tree![73] Now proper landscaping is a prob-

....

[72]Fine, that's exactly what I was about to do, so perhaps it's for the best.

[73]Okay, that was fan-freaking-tastic. Here's the thing—you can get your rotten old tree trimmed so its falling limbs don't crush my garage, or I will convince the City that it's a nuisance and needs to be removed. Your choice.

lem? I'm sorry. I guess I'm having trouble keeping all your proclivities straight."

Unfazed, I continue. "Appropriate yard upkeep isn't getting to me. The problem here is they don't annoy me! They don't do anything wrong!"

In her most patronizingly soothing voice, she says, "Wow, that's just *awful*. Perhaps you can convince the ex-con to move in behind you again."

Since I'm on the cordless phone, I'm free to pace between the kitchen and dining room, my socks slipping on the hardwood. Maisy gets off her doggie bed in the corner of the room and joins me, her entire backside wagging in happiness at our being together. "Hear me out—I've made a career out of writing about the foibles of my neighborhood, and now I live in the city's version of suburbia and I'm coming up empty! My next subtitle's going to have to be '*Who Are All These Lovely People and Aren't I Lucky to Have Them Live Next Door to Me?*' That blows goats! Don't get me wrong. I love how quiet and civilized it is here, but what the hell am I supposed to write about? I need struggle! I need to be angry! Annoyed! I don't have any of that right now because it's all peace and fucking quiet."

"Tragic," she snarks.

"The worst part is I've already gotten notes from the neighborhood association about banding together against crime. There's an actual Web site! My new alderman's even involved. Getting this stuff organized—or, rather, bitching about how this stuff isn't organized—is MY job. What am I supposed to do now?" I flop down on the living room couch, and Maisy flops beside me, resting her head on my shoulder and looking at me as if to say, "*I feel you, my sister. Now let's have a cookie.*"

"You could be thankful."

"Bite me. What else you got?"

"Jen, it's simple. Try something new."

"I hate new." I do. I hate it. I like old, established, just like it always was.

"You enjoy living indoors?"

"Very much so."

"Then my advice stands—try something new. Why don't you work on that thing you were telling me about a couple of months ago? You know, the one where you go to plays and listen to jazz and try to not be such an asshole?"

Okay? This? Is exactly why I like her. Here I had this huge epiphany, and the second I started to pack, I completely forgot about it. "Maybe it is time to revisit that, although . . . it seems kind of hard, and things are really starting to get exciting on this season's *Biggest Loser* and *Amazing Race* and *America's Next Top Model* and *Lost*—"

Angie interrupts me. "Hey, remember when you had to work all those temp jobs and people made you get them coffee?"

I shudder. "Yeah." Although I finally got into the swing of temping by the end, the first time I walked into an office to be someone's secretary after having been an executive was among the worst moments of my life. What if I lose my current momentum? What would it be like to have to fetch lattes again? I really never want to know.

"Then that's your alternative." I hear a beep, which I assume means she's finished with her workout. Although with Angie, she could be baking a pie or building a fallout shelter.

I get off the couch to glance out the window again, and Maisy follows. I'm hoping desperately that an episode of *Jerry Springer* will have broken out on the neighbor's lawn so that I can report on it. Instead I see their tasteful Fall Harvest decor spilling down their spotless front stoop. There's nothing but gourds and cornucopias and shit out there. Damn. Then I look in the mirror and see my pajama-clad self—even though it's lunchtime—with my best friend in the world at my side, and I again appreciate the life I've created for myself.

The way I see it, I have no choice.

I'm going to try something new.

Even if it kills me.

Cultural Jenaissance, it is.

FYI? Things *Desire Under the Elms* Is Not:

A trendy new Gold Coast bistro

A trendy new River North bistro

A trendy new Fulton Market bistro

A trendy new bistro of ANY sort

A high-end furniture store

A day spa located on a particularly woodsy part of Elm Street

A florist specializing in decorative bouquets filled with cut branches

(This would be a great name for ANY of these businesses and you're welcome to help yourself to my ideas—provided I'm given proper credit—if you're feeling entrepreneurial.)

Apparently *Desire Under the Elms* is a classic Eugene O'Neill play.

Having studied O'Neill in college,[74] I probably should have already known this. Then again, I flunked out a semester after I took it, so it's possible the strictest attention was not paid.[75]

Stacey's long-standing association with the Goodman Theatre means she's comped seats for all kinds of events, and the offer extends to almost every theater in the city, too.

"What's the deal with this thing specifically?" I ask. I'm at her house for our usual Wednesday night whatever's-on-Bravo get-together.

Stacey pauses the program we're watching. "Um, *specifically*, it's O'Neill's version of a Greek tragedy, so it's got all the classic elements, like anger and betrayal and lust. Eben—the son—suffers because he's got an abusive father. Ephraim—the father—suffers because he's so wrapped up in his own hubris that he can't admit the world's mocking him for what's happening under his own nose. The father's hot new young wife, Abbie, suffers because she's sleeping with the son and lying about her baby's parentage. Basically everyone's miserable, and it's completely awesome."

"Is it modern? And does it take place in the South?" I ask. I have a penchant for stories about dysfunctional Southern families, likely stemming from my love of the *North and South* miniseries when I was in junior high school.

"Nope, it takes place in New England during the gold rush era. None of that matters so much because it's a timeless story. Could take place in ancient Athens; could take place now in Atlanta. I can guarantee the acting will be superb."

....

[74] Correction, having BRAGGED about studying O'Neill in college.

[75] Also, you might want to check with the O'Neill estate before you swipe that name, too.

"How can you be so sure?"

"For starters, it stars Brian Dennehy."

"Big Tom Callahan? *Really?* I guess I can't see him onstage. I mean, come on, he only lasted twenty minutes in that movie."

"Jen, he's won Tony awards and studied drama at Yale. Just because you've only seen him in *Tommy Boy* doesn't mean that's all he's done or is capable of doing."

"Excellent point. I'm surprised, but now I remember how sad poor Chris Farley was when he died in *Tommy Boy*. I guess his acting must have been convincing because I totally teared up. I could see how Chris Farley's wanting to honor him prompted him to travel cross-country with David Spade to sell auto parts to save the company. Yeah, I guess he could be okay."

Drily, Stacey replies, "He'll be relieved to hear it."

"Hey, do you think David Spade will be there?" I mean, maybe they became friends during filming, right?

"My guess is no. But Carla Gugino stars as Abbie, and Pablo Schreiber is Eben. The Goodman always casts the most amazing actors."

"Wait, Carla Gugino? From *Son in Law*? That's so badass!"

Stacey looks suddenly exhausted as she winces and holds up her hand. "Before you ask, Pauly Shore probably won't be there. If for some bizarre reason he is, you'll get to meet him and all the other actors at the cast party."

"NO WAY!" I may or may not shout this so loud that I shake the frames hanging on the wall behind us. Shoot, I'd have said yes to theater tickets years ago if I realized it would make me her plus-one at the after party.

I've seen Stacey's scrapbooks from various productions and heard the stories about all the famous people she's worked with. I've always been impressed, but Stacey says it's no big deal because they're just folks doing their jobs. She says most actors are regular people who come to work and then go home to enjoy their lives and spouses and friends. They aren't out getting shitfaced at Hyde or Club Les Deux or throwing cell phones at their assistants or "accidentally" flashing their girly bits to the paparazzi.

I'm deeply disappointed to hear this.

The more Stacey fills me in on the details of this particular production, the more excited I get. I'm superpsyched about what I can learn from seeing a show in such an august theater by such a renowned playwright. This is exactly the sort of thing that's going to make me better-rounded intellectually, and I'm eager for the personal growth opportunity it will afford.

Okay, that's total bullshit.

I'm mostly jazzed to meet famous people.

"Are you worried I'm going to embarrass you with my nervous-talking thing?" I ask. Stacey was a firsthand witness to the slurring, sweating, and shouting spurred by my meeting a *Top Chef* winner recently, and she was just on a cable network.[76] The second I come into contact with anyone who's been on mah tee-vee, I turn into a complete moron. Whatever internal filter I possess[77] switches off, and I end up spewing every bit of nonsensical blather that pops into my brain. As their level of fame increases, so does my incoherence. I'm afraid of what might happen when I meet an *actual* movie star.

"If I were worried, I wouldn't have invited you," she assures me. "I *want* you to come with me, and we're going to have a fantastic time."

....

[76]Because she was on *Top Chef*, I grudgingly tried her fois gras dish. And you know what? Two thumbs up—it's like meat butter!

[77]Paltry as it may be.

"Cool." I ease back into the couch, and we resume our program.

A few minutes later, I realize there's something still bothering me. "Hey, no one's going to be naked in this, right?"

Stacey does the verbal equivalent of patting me on the head. "Of course not, peanut. Of course not."

Before I begin to primp for my big night out, I run down to the basement to TiVo *24* and *The Bachelor*. Just because I'm trying to smarten up doesn't mean I'm not *me* anymore, right?

Since I'm going to the cast party, I take special care with my appearance. I mean, really, is Carla Gugino going to want to be BFF with some chick who can't be bothered to curl her hair and don three shades of eye shadow? I don't *think* so.

(Sidebar: If I ever have a CAT scan, I'm betting it will show a slightly shriveled part of my cerebellum that causes me to say everything I think when in the vicinity of fame. Next to it, there will be a dented piece that houses my absolute belief that every famous person will want to be my friend, given the opportunity.)

Since I plan to go to a lot of shows this winter, I've bought a proper theater outfit since my daily cold-weather accoutrement of track pants and pullover fleece jackets won't cut it. For someone whose book covers feature dresses and purses and footwear, you might think nothing makes me happier than shopping.

Not true.[78]

....

[78] At least, anymore.

The truth is, my laziness manifests itself in my wardrobe, too. I don't own thirty Lacostes because I love them more than any other shirt ever made[79]; I own them because they're cute, they're colorful, and they fit well. This explains why I have six pairs of the same khaki shorts. I have twelve different sundresses that I wear on tour, and they're all cut identically. I mix and match each of them with a solid cardigan, of which I own seven. I'm fortunate that the preppy look's timeless because if I'd become attached to parachute pants and *Flashdance* sweatshirts, I'd be screwed right about now.

I bought a long blackwatch plaid, pleated wool skirt and a navy V-neck sweater, which I've paired with a pointy-collared, crisp white blouse. "Flattering" is the best description of the cut, and the fabrics should keep me warm in even the draftiest of theaters. I feel cute wearing this, despite the whole "world's oldest Catholic school student" vibe.

Before I slip on my skirt and pull on my sweater, I'm predressed in a stretchy black camisole, a tan girdle, black boots, and black leggings. My hair is up in hot rollers.

I have to laugh as I glance at myself in the mirror: *Worst. Superhero. Ever.*

When we arrive at the Goodman, I stop by the snack bar first, even though we've just come from dinner. I'm pleased that they have the white wine I like and delighted by the big cookies. But if the ushers are to be believed, I'm not supposed to take either of them into the theater.

---

[79] Although I'd be hard-pressed to find something I prefer.

"I can't bring snacks?" I ask Stacey.

"No, you have to finish them in the lobby," she says, gesturing toward the garbage cans.

"Snacks and entertainment go together like chalk and cheese."

"I'm pretty sure you're using that expression wrong."

Huh. I guess that's why it never made sense. "Okay, fine. Well, at the movies you can eat popcorn. In fact, *they* encourage it."

"This isn't the movies."

"THAT'S why plays will never win! Ha! Movies–1, plays–0."

Stacey gives me a good-natured eye roll. "This also isn't a competition."

I gulp down my wine and deposit my glass in the trash. Just as we're about to enter, I spot a girl carrying the most awesome tote bag I've ever seen. I nudge Stacey. "Check that out."

Stacey lapses into LOLcat, uncharacteristic for her, but an unfortunate side effect of being around me too much. "Ooh, want. Do want!"

The spectacular tote in question features a line drawing of Shakespeare and a caption that reads, "Shakespeare got to get paid, son."[80] Word.

We arrange ourselves in our seats in the first balcony. Our view, not only of the stage, but of the whole opening-night crowd, is excellent. Nice seats; they must like Stacey a lot around here.

"Sure are a lot of fur coats in here," I observe. "If I were with PETA, I'd totally stand in the lobby with buckets of red paint."

She casts a sidelong glance in my direction. "I imagine the ushers would take issue with that."

"*Pfft*, they're each about a thousand years old, and they're unpaid.

---

[80]Ten bucks says the Bard allowed popcorn in his shows.

No senior citizen is going to voluntarily take a bucket of paint in the teeth to save your chinchilla. Foolproof is what this idea is."

Sometimes when Stacey and I are together, I leave her at a loss for words. This is one of those times. After a very long silence, she says, "I can honestly tell you that in all my theatergoing years, I've never had that thought."

"Maybe I'm expanding your horizons, too."

"My question is *why would* that even occur to you? Judging by some of your Facebook wall posts, you hate PETA."

"I do, but I feel like it's my purpose in life to coach people who are doing their jobs wrong.[81] I mean, PETA could be so much more efficient. As it is now, all their paint-tossing activists have got to wait for Fashion Week. Here, they could do it every night from November to April. And twice on Saturdays!"

"Noted."

I continue to scan the crowd, which I wouldn't do were I otherwise distracted by, say, popcorn. "There are a lot of kids in here, too. That's going to be trouble. I bet you're glad you're no longer responsible for all the little monsters being forced to see the show."

Stacey's eyes light up at the mere mention of her old job. *"Not at all,"* she says emphatically. "I loved teaching those kids. And I *kept* them from being monsters."

Since the theater Nazis won't let me have a beverage, I drink in the scenery. The set's so elaborate. On the right side of the stage, there's an enormous pile of rocks, leading up two full stories and exiting stage left.[82]

---

[81] Or perhaps it's just my hobby.

[82] My familiarity with fancy theater-speak comes from years of watching Bugs Bunny cartoons.

On the left, there's a perfect rendition of an old farmhouse, but it's hanging about twelve feet above the stage from ropes, which I find a tad disconcerting. What if it falls and crushes poor Brian Dennehy? Then what?

Scattered above the whole set are more enormous boulders hanging from what look like nooses. Nowhere onstage is anything that looks like an elm tree. I bet this is where my lack of theater education shows the most. I'm probably being way too literal here. Perhaps having an elm tree in a show with "elm" in the title is all weird and awkward and obvious, like when someone wears a band's shirt to that band's concert or when my mom says, "Don't go there, girlfriend."

The play begins and I'm instantly enthralled. I haven't been to a show since Fletch and I saw *Cabaret* in the late nineties with a couple of college friends. Bless his heart, Fletch tried to like it, but big musical productions are never going to be in his wheelhouse. Even though I was mesmerized by the performances and haunted by some of the songs, I never went to anything else. I could have forced Fletch to accompany me, but he was so miserable that I couldn't bring myself to torture him.

Still, I'm full of regret for letting all that time pass. If I'd taken the initiative, I'm sure I could have talked someone else into coming with me. Or I could have gone alone.

I forgot what a thrill live theater can be. I mean, *this* is the ultimate reality program. Anything can happen, and there's no tape delay for the West Coast broadcast or team of editors to fix what went wrong in postproduction. Stacey's recounted various hilarious snafus that happened during her tenure—props breaking, actors breaking wind, forgotten lines, cues missed, and once a director's French bulldog wandered into the middle of the scene and refused to be coaxed off the stage.

I used to love seeing plays and even thought I'd be a stage actress myself at one point. My plan was to be a big triple threat on Broadway—

despite being utterly tone deaf and uncoordinated—and then to break into television, having established my credibility as a Serious Actress. Despite only being able to play characters who were exactly like me, I really thought I had a shot. I dreamed of greasepaint and standing ovations.

So, I signed up for theater class as a college freshman. But after a brief, mandatory internship in the costume shop, my dream died. Since I couldn't design or tailor or even sew a straight line, I got stuck spending hours with an industrial iron, smoothing out enormous sheets of muslin, which were the costumes for the casts of *Medea* and *Oedipus*. I remember telling the director, *"Jocasta accidentally did it with her son. You really think she gives a shit about wrinkles?"*

Oh, wait, maybe I was *asked* not to be a part of the theater department.

Regardless, I'm absolutely sucked into everything happening on-stage until I hear a weird sound. What is that? Is something supposed to be going on in the background? The acoustics in here are perfect—I can hear even the softest of Eben's sighs and the rustle of Abbie's skirts. So what is that noise? Is it stomping or marching? No, that can't be it. Why would anyone march? There's no war in this play. The sound is too close and familiar but I can't identify it. It's almost like a . . . grinding?

Or crunching?

I crane around in my seat, spot the source of the noise, and hiss in Stacey's ear, *"That kid is eating Cheetos!"*

She leans in close to me. "Distracting, right?"

"It's making me stabby!"

She shrugs. "That's why they don't allow popcorn."

"Point taken," I whisper.[83]

....
[83]Movies–1, plays–1.

I shouldn't be surprised by the crunching because there are a few very rude people in here, all of whom are drawing my attention away from the stage. Phones have been ringing, hard candies unwrapping, and two assholes a couple of rows back are having an outside-voice conversation about where they're going for drinks afterward.

How can this be? I'm essentially a theater virgin and even I know this stuff is verboten. And this is opening night. You can't just be some guy off the street and get tickets to opening night; they aren't for sale. Opening night is by invitation only. You have to have a friend in the production or be a member of the media or be an actor yourself. Ergo, every single person in here *should know better*. They're all theater veterans. None of these people should even dream of talking or chewing or texting because their family, friend, colleague, or client is part of the production. We should all be watching this play with our undivided attention. Yet here we are. This lack of common courtesy is astounding and disrespectful and marginalizes everything these poor actors are trying to accomplish.[84]

Hey! I think I just had an epiphany about the importance of social graces!

And yet before I can ponder it further, one of the actors *strips naked onstage*. I cast a sidelong glance at Stacey, who's all squinty and shaking silently. I guarantee she won't look at me for fear of laughing out loud.

After the final curtain call, I turn to her. "Apparently I have the ability to make shit happen just by mentioning it before the curtain goes up. Tonight? Naked. At the Marta Carrasco show? The watermelon. I'm a frigging psychic. Next time I'm totally going to worry in advance about people throwing five-dollar bills at me."

....

[84]Perhaps they'd learn their lesson if I were to throw PETA paint on them.

"I was dying for you," she admits. "When he stripped down, your eyes were saucers. You've got to admit though, since it was Pablo, it was *good* naked."

"I'll be honest, after Pablo turned into Senor SansHisPants and Carla went topless, I got real worried about seeing Dennehy in the buff. And, fine, I can't argue that all the nudity didn't make sense in the context of the story. The story was supposed to be raw, and what's more raw than being completely nude onstage? I get it. I'm okay with it. Plus, we didn't have any nonsensical dry-cleaning film moments."

As we make our way to the cast party at Petterino's next door, Stacey listens to me go on and on about how much I enjoyed the show. The set was spectacular and the acting was top-notch. I loved how the tension built and built and I appreciated the few comic moments in the beginning with Eben's brothers. As I gush, Stacey nods encouragingly, but she doesn't heap her own praises on the production.

Granted, some of what happened onstage puzzled me. I don't quite get why the other sons shouted so much in the first scene (even though it was funny) or why the house was suspended by ropes,[85] but I figure there are excellent, artistic reasons for these decisions, even if I'm not privy to them.

The party's in a huge room filled with giant round tables, which means people are going to sit with us and likely expect to have conversations of the nonbanal variety. This makes the back of my neck start to sweat.

Oy, what am I going to say to sophisticated theater people?

Am I going to accidentally grill them on tonight's *Bachelor* evictions?

....
[85]Or how come we never saw a damn elm tree.

Or talk about all the bad weaves on this season's *Rock of Love Bus*?[86] Or am I going to bitch about how rude a handful of people were? And that doesn't even begin to take into account where my mouth may go when I meet the actors. Will I bring up *Tommy Boy*? Or, worse, Pauly Shore? I feel like I've already painted myself into a corner, and we just got here.

While we're getting refreshments, I tell Stacey, "I don't trust myself not to sound like an asshole. I mean, I didn't even realize I couldn't eat popcorn during the show. What am I going to say to people?"

Stacey takes her drink and tips the bartender before turning to face me. "First of all, you're being too hard on yourself. So what if you don't know that much about live theater? Who cares? No one starts out an expert. So many people dismiss activities like this out of pocket, without ever having tried, but you're here trying. People will appreciate you wanting to learn, I promise. Talk about why you're here and explain your project. You may even meet someone who can help in your education."

And she's right, of course.

I have great conversations with all kinds of theater people—a costume designer, a director, scene builders, and a couple of choreographers. Each one encourages me to continue my pursuits. The consensus is they respect what I'm attempting, and one of the choreographers thinks I'd enjoy some of his productions.

What's ironic is the costume designer is leaving the party shortly because she's addicted to *Rock of Love* and hasn't yet watched this week's episode.

As our table clears, I tell Stacey, "I feel like my takeaway from tonight is that it's okay to love shitty television, provided you make an effort to appreciate other kinds of entertainment."

....
[86]Team Beverly rules!

"Ultimately, it's all about striking a balance," she agrees. "Now you want to go upstairs and meet the cast?"

On our way out of the downstairs festivities, we stop and chat a dozen times to say hello to all of Stacey's former cronies. No one could be nicer, but I'm not quite fully engaged because I'm on the lookout for the rude people. I don't bump into any of them, which is probably for the best.

By the time we get up there, I'm feeling much surer of myself. Stacey introduces me to Brian Dennehy, and we have a brief but lovely conversation about the show and his performance. He's so gracious that I don't even start with the nervous talking. And when we shake hands, I have the wherewithal not to compliment him on his commitment to moisturizing, despite the fact that his hands are as smooth as a little girl's. Progress, I say!

The thing is, I suspect my burgeoning confidence stems not from a growing sense of self or a shadow of familiarity with the world of professional theater but rather from a number of free glasses of sauvignon blanc.

When I meet Carla, I'm so moved by her having given the performance of a lifetime on one of the most prestigious stages in the world that it doesn't even occur to me to bring up Pauly Shore or *Spy Kids*.

And yet I cannot add this interaction to the win column.

"Hi, I'm Jen. It's so nice to meet you." I'm rewarded with a friendly greeting and a sincere handshake. I'm also possibly blinded by my first real-life, thousand-watt, million-dollar, movie-star smile, and it triggers that weird little part of my brain to switch on. Uh-oh.

Now that I have her attention, do I tell her I'm a fan? Do I bring up that whole "artistic professional" thing and say that I'm an author? Do I mention my project?

No.

The only words I can find are about the wig she wore onstage.

"Hey!" I exclaim. "That wasn't your real hair. It really looked like your real hair. Your hair is dark. I almost missed saying hi to you because you look different with your real hair."

Hey, self, now might be a good time to shut up about her hair if you plan on being BFFs.

"That is your real hair, right? It's way darker than I thought. I went dark now, too. Not as dark as you, though. Yours is superdark. Like, black. Inky black. Superblack. Tar black. But good, you know? I like it. Black is the new black, ha ha!"

If I shut up now, she might still want to have lunch every once in a while, even if we're not besties. And yet something inside me presses me on.

"The dark is nice, but the wig was also nice. Didn't your hair used to be the color of your wig? Yes! It totally did. You've had, like, ten different hair colors in stuff I've seen you in. You want me to name each of them?"

With that, I've officially exited the Potential Friend Zone and I'm careening quickly toward Stalker City. And that's when the pseudointelligence kicks in.

"You know, you could kind of look at the play from your wig's perspective. I mean, your do told a story. First it was all tight and rolled, and then it got sort of loose, and then it got all messy and then—"

Please, someone get me away from her before she calls the authorities. Seriously, I am fixed to this spot. I can't move and I can't shut up. Someone please throw PETA paint on me so I shut up! Help!

Fortunately, Stacey notices Carla's making fraidy-cat-get-this-weirdo-away-from-me eyes, which neatly coincide with my what-the-fuck-am-I-doing-and-why-can't-I-stop expression, so she interrupts to tell me it's time to go. For good measure, Stacey yanks me away by my coat pocket, which is fortuitous because my paw, completely of its own volition, was starting to snake up in the direction of Carla's hair.

So I end the night with a little bit more culture and a little bit more perspective and a little bit more knowledge.[87]

Best of all is that out of a whole theater full of people at this posh event, only one of them might believe I'm a dummy.

I'd definitely say that's progress.

....

[87]And a lot of a buzz.

To: stacey_at_home

From: jen_at_home

Subject: S-a-t-u-r-d-a-y Night!

I've dined out on my theatergoing frequent-flier status all week.

"Oh, sorry, I'm busy that night with a premiere."

"You wanted me to drop it off when? Nope, can't. Theater tickets. You know how it is."

"Listen, I'd love to, but I've got another opening night and cast party. I hope you understand."

Okay, pretty much I've just said this stuff to Fletch, but still, it sounded cool. (The polite thing would have been for him to at least pretend to be impressed.)

See you at 6:00?

C·H·A·P·T·E·R E·I·G·H·T

The Biggest Winner

J'm all decked out in my theatergoing outfit and I'm on my way to tonight's artistic endeavor. Stacey and I are in her car, headed to a play in the northern suburbs. I feel like quite the sophisticate, even though our glamorous après-theater plans include heading to the Four Moon Tavern for grilled cheese sandwiches.

"This is twice in one week I've stolen you away from your husband for an evening. Is he going to miss you?" Stacey asks. She steers her car expertly through the steadily falling snow. I'm helping her by occasionally punching the imaginary brakes on my side of the car and second-guessing her navigation.

Given tonight's inclement weather, I'd have preferred to stay home, wrapped in blankets, quaffing hot chocolate, and parked in front of *Survivor*. Instead, we're plowing through a wealthy suburb. With the abundance of snowcapped trees and adorable storefronts and antique streetlamps, this would resemble a Currier and Ives scene if it weren't for all the Starbucks.

"Are you kidding? He's got the big TV all to himself for the whole night. No one's going to make him watch anything in which roses are accepted or torches are extinguished or top models are sent packing for only showing Miss Tyra one look.[88] I'm pretty sure his plans include his special-occasion small-batch bourbon and a German death metal concert video. He's thrilled."

Despite the weather, I'm glad for another opportunity to work toward my Jenaissance. I couldn't have started this whole process of self-improvement at a more fortuitous time because I've got to get my fat mouth in check soon. It's not just that people think I'm a jerk; that's nothing new. But lately my thoughtless chatter has cost me serious cash. Case in point? The new television. We didn't get it because we both wanted it or planned for it or, for that matter, even agreed on it. Nope, I kind of had to buy it for Fletch because I said something dumb.

My favorite indie book store, the Book Cellar,[89] arranged a rock-and-roll book event, and my friend Jolene was in town to participate. She wrote a memoir about being a Goth girl in the eighties and how music helped her through a desperately dark time in her life. A few other authors were included—one woman who wrote a YA novel about how punk rock led her back to her mother and another guy with the best title ever—*Hairstyles of the Damned*. The last author at the event was Chris Connelly.

According to Fletch, if you *don't* have the musical sensibilities of a

....

[88]Even though that sounds kind of awesome right now.

[89]They serve wine!

strip club DJ, you'll recognize his name. Should your memory need re-freshing, Chris played with Ministry, RevCo,[90] and Pigface, all of whom are famous for their groundbreaking work on the industrial music scene. Chris wrote a genuine life-of-an-alternative-rock-star memoir, which he read from at the event.

Jolene had to point Chris out to me at first because I was expecting a mohawked/dreadlocked/guy-linered thrash rocker all done up in leather and skinny jeans and anarchy patches. What I didn't expect was an affa-ble fellow with a haircut that could pass muster at any investment bank. He was clad in a green wool sweater and regular old loose-fit jeans and looked exactly like someone you'd ping for advice about whether organic heirloom tomatoes were in season if he was shopping beside you at Whole Foods. Seeing him messed with my preconceptions—I didn't know you could *be* punk rock without *looking* punk rock.

I decided to ask Chris to sign a book for Fletch because he was in some of his all-time-favorite bands and Fletch has such respect for him. In fact, he credits Chris's music for his own Renaissance.[91] Last summer, Fletch was drowning in job stress and drinking more than he should to compensate, and he wasn't happy with his overall physical and mental state. Although he enjoyed working out, he'd yet to make it a habit. One morning, he woke up early and decided that instead of rolling over and going back to sleep, he'd get up and go to the gym. He'd put on his iPod and crank RevCo, and that would inspire him to push harder every time he hit the gym.

Now he gets up at four a.m. almost every day to lift weights before

....

[90]I am not writing out their whole name, as the "Co" does not stand for "com-pany."

[91]Fletchaissance? No, that's pushing it.

work. His dedication to his new lifestyle is an inspiration. He's energized, he's happy, and he's lost a good twenty pounds. He looks and feels better now than he did in college. Cocktails are for special occasions because otherwise they mess up his workout schedule. I'm superproud of him and I only resent him a tiny bit for not starting the summer before when I was working on *Such a Pretty Fat*.[92]

Anyway, when it was my turn to get the book signed, I recognized the gravity of the situation and my nervous-talking thing took hold and my mouth hip-checked my decorum into the wall.

"Ohmigod, hi, Chris, hi!" I exclaimed, thrusting a copy of his book at him. "Can you make this out to Fletch? That's my husband and I want this for him because he spends every morning at the gym with you! You've, like, totally turned his life around and he's all healthy now because of your music, which frankly is a bit shouty for me, but that's neither here nor there. Point is that every day at the ass crack of dawn he's up and he's got you on his iPod and he's working away and . . ." And I kind of went on like this for another few minutes. I'd relay the entire conversation, but my shame at what happened next is making me blank out on the details.

Apparently while I was busy babbling—possibly[93] spitting—at some point in my superspeedy diatribe I gave Chris the idea that Fletch was not listening to his music while huffing away all punk rock by lifting heavy iron bars but instead that his music was spurring Fletch on *in spin class*.

Chris signed Fletch's book wishing him the best of luck and to

....

[92]He says I can resent him for not starting soon enough or simply be happy that he's extended his life. My choice.

[93]Definitely.

"Keep spinning." And Chris is a rock star, so I didn't want to correct him and tell him, "No, no, you got it wrong," so now Fletch's idol thinks he takes *spin class* and most likely walked away from our encounter wondering how the *hell* one spins to Pigface.

And then—then!—I asked to get a picture together and he sweetly obliged each of the fifteen times I demanded because the shots wouldn't save because I'd filled up my BlackBerry's memory by taking too damn many photos of my new dining room table, which I then inadvertently admitted out loud and Jolene had to take the photo with her camera because I was really starting to make him nervous.

To recap, Fletch's icon believes: (a) he *spins* and (b) he's married to an idiot with a predilection for fast-talking and table porn.

This would be the equivalent of Fletch telling Candace Bushnell I bought all my handbags at Kmart.

After that, I pretty much had no choice but to buy Fletch the new flat-screen TV he wanted for the media room. Granted, all of our money is pooled, but somehow he found victory in me writing the check.[94] Fortunately, I had the wherewithal not to tell Chris that Fletch couldn't come to the signing because he'd had a run-in with Thanksgiving leftovers that had turned; otherwise I'd have been on the hook for a surround-sound system, too.

For a while we drive in contented silence. Stacey's paying strict attention to the slick roads while I'm lulled by the gentle back-and-forth motion of the windshield wipers. Stacey breaks the stillness by asking me, "How are you feeling about tonight? Are you still worried about talking to people at the cast party?"

----

[94]This is where I'd like to be all snarky and describe how Miss Tyra should never be seen that big/in such high definition, but she's flawless up close. Argh.

"Actually, I'm kind of okay. I figured out what my problem is. It's confidence." I wag my finger at her before she can protest. "Bup, bup, before you disagree, I realize I'm always going on about my own self-confidence. I mean, we've established that we're both girls who like ourselves and how we look and what we're about. That's not the issue. What's going on here is *situational* confidence. I discovered I can only be confident in a situation if I've been in it before. I have trouble with firsts."

"Since you've already been to a cast party, it's old hat? No big deal?"

"Exactly. I can be my usual calm, cool, collected self now. It's totally the Eliza Doolittle syndrome."

Stacey clicks on her turn signal and we ease onto a side street. The tires crunch in the snow. "How do you figure?"

"The first time she had to talk like a lady in public, she was sharting herself. She was under pressure not just internally, but from Higgins and, at least tangentially, Pickering, too. But as soon as she got that initial conversation under her belt, it was easy-peasy. She'd done it before and knew what to expect, so she handled herself beautifully."

"Except for the *'move your bloomin' arse!'* bit."

I stare straight ahead. "Rome was not built in a day, Stacey."

"So you're good."

"I am unflappable," I agree.

"And what happens when you meet Vince Vaughn?"

"HOLY SHIT, IS VINCE GOING TO BE THERE?"

"No, just testing." She flashes me a playful grin.

"Oh. Don't do that to me. I just had, like, fourteen heart attacks. Otherwise, I'll be the frigging Miles Davis of cool; just you wait. What are we seeing tonight anyway?"

"It's called *Old Glory*. I honestly don't know anything about it, except that it will be done well because we're going to Writers' Theatre," she tells me. She pulls up to an intersection and yields to oncoming traffic.

"How do you know?" I ask.

Stacey takes her eyes off the road to glance at me. "Because we're going to Writers' Theatre."

I reply, "So, *post hoc ergo propter hoc*?"

Stacey's forehead scrunches. "What?"

"I don't know; it just flew out." I've been reading some smart stuff lately and I thought I used that right. I guess not.

She ignores my ham-fisted attempt at Latin. "All the plays performed at Writers' Theatre are thought-provoking. These productions put a huge amount of value on words. There's no theater in Chicago that's as much about the writing. You'll notice that the set's simple and the cast's small. They do it that way because it creates intimacy. Whatever the story is, it's going to feel huge, and yet you're going to feel like you're a part of it."

"How will it be different from *Desire Under the Elms*?" In my head, I've already painted all iterations of "theater" with the same brush. It never occurred to me that there may be nuances.

"*Desire*'s set probably cost three hundred thousand dollars. Tonight's set may be a couple of old couches. Or, better example, picture your friend Carla Gugino's wig. You were blown away by it, right?"

"I was mesmerized. Her wig was more real than her real hair."

"And it probably set them back fifteen hundred dollars. Different theaters have different budgets and standards of production. I've been to shows in small theaters where the wigs came from someone's grandma's attic. Sometimes they're so bad it's hard not to laugh."

"Which are better? Big shows or little ones?"

"Depends. Tell you what. We'll take in a variety of productions at different venues so you can decide for yourself. There are almost two hundred theaters in and around Chicago."

"Whoa. *That* sounds like a lot of work. Why don't you just give me your educated opinion?" I suggest.

She smirks. "Or you could just put in the effort and decide for yourself."

"You're not going to let me be lazy, are you?"

She simply raises her brows in response.

We pull into a spot right in front of the theater, which is in an old North Shore mansion. "We're here!" she says. "Do you want to walk up to the door, princess, or shall I carry you up on my back?"

"Okay, okay, I get it," I mutter as I trudge through the snow and into the building. As we enter, I notice a number of posters hanging in the lobby describing our country's failings in the war on terror. "Aw, shit, Stacey, did you bring me to a show that's going to tell me how everything I believe is wrong?"

Stacey and I are on vastly different teams politically. We both respect each other enough that when we see a point differently, we discuss it rationally. We've never changed each other's minds, but we can appreciate the perspective the other one brings. Also, we make a point not to rub anything in—I never insist she eat any of the cake I bake every year for Ronald Reagan's birthday, and she only made me watch Maddow that one time because there was a segment she thought I'd like.[95] With us, we have so much other stuff in common that there's little reason to discuss our differences.

What's ironic is politics is the one topic outside of reality television

....
[95]Stacey was right. He's hilarious. (Oh, settle down. I kid. I kid.)

on which I'm well informed. Every week I listen to hours of talk radio and I read a ton of conservative magazines and blogs. Yet besides Fletch, almost none of my friends share my ideology, and I try not to include any political opinion on my own blog, so it's rare that I ever get into the kind of discussion that proves I actually have a basis for my opinions.

"No! I swear! Even though it would be funny, I'd never do that!" She grabs a program and begins to scan the description. "See? It says right here: *'No politics, just people.'* I promise if the show does somehow sneak in politics—"

"Or nudity," I interject.

"If they sneak in politics or nudity, grilled cheeses are on me."

"Deal." We shake on it.

I'm immediately struck by how different this theater is from the Goodman. The space is tiny, with maybe a hundred seats. When I walked into the Goodman, I felt small and insignificant. I was one tiny cog in the giant wheel of audience. You could conduct an entire circus on that stage. The Goodman is cavernous and impossibly tall, whereas this place feels like an afterthought, or the end result of some kind of *Our Gang* hey-kids-let's-put-on-a-show. I'm a tad surprised there's no curtain made of stitched-together bandannas and old overalls.

Our seats are hopelessly close together. We wedge into our slots and I tell Stacey, "This makes me long for a middle seat on an airplane. In coach."

"Yeah, it's tight," she agrees. "But the shows here are always worth the squeeze."

"Just so you know, I'm putting my arm around you unless you want to fight me for the armrest for the next ninety minutes."

The seating area is divided into three sections of risers, forming a U around the stage. We're in the section on the far right, but that doesn't matter—there's not a bad seat in the joint. And even the back row is within twenty feet of the stage. Although there isn't a stage, per se. There's just a clearing filled with various pieces of a set. One portion looks like an Army barracks, another is a bar, and the third contains a couple of fancy armchairs. The whole performance area is barely bigger than my old living room.

Between the cramped seats and simplicity of the stage, I've already decided that I prefer elaborate productions and I mentally cross Writers' Theatre off my list of places to return. This is too small. I can hear the dude next to me breathing and I can smell vanilla. I suspect someone here had cupcakes right before they arrived.[96]

This is too intimate. I don't want to be this close to the audience or the actors. What if I sneeze over someone's line? What if my stomach growls in anticipation of my pending grilled cheese? The old guy to my right has a whistling nostril—what if this eventually causes one of the actors to snap?[97] I don't want to hear the cadence of someone else's breath or feel their pulse through a shared armrest. It's creepy.

And this set? Ugh. It's so plain. Look at all the unused space above the stage. You could totally suspend big rocks or maybe part of a farm-house over this thing. And why do all three settings have to be onstage at the same time? They can't carry the wing chairs in and out between breaks? I can't fathom what Stacey meant when she said this show will be "huge." This whole setting is too small to be "big."

I shift uncomfortably in my tiny chair and wait for the damned thing to begin.

....

[96]Share, why don't you?

[97]I mean, if I don't first.

"What'd you think?" Stacey asks me as we walk up the mansion's stairs to the cast party.

I need a minute to formulate my response. I'm not even sure how to begin. But I get what Stacey meant by "big" now. The story involved an accidental shooting on an Army base in Fallujah. Friendly fire. I've heard a million stories about what it's like to be deployed—the pride of service tempered with boredom and laced with loneliness and punctuated with brief flashes of terror. Without once foisting an agenda on me, the playwright nailed all this. When I watched things go terribly wrong, I kept thinking, "That could have been my husband. That could have been my friend. That could have happened."

I finally reply, "This play is going to stick with me for a long, long time."

The unexpected end result of being in such close quarters is that the drama is amplified ten thousand times. When the woman in front of me sucked in her breath at a plot twist, I heard it. When my neighbor's pulse quickened in response to a tense moment, I felt it. And being ten feet away from the actors made me feel less like I was an audience member and more like an accidental participant. It was awkward and off-putting and . . . exhilarating. "Who knew a story could be so powerful with such a modest set and so little space?"

Stacey nods a tad smugly. "That's Writers' Theatre."

"When I compare this in my mind to what we saw at the Goodman, well, there is no comparison. This play blew the other away on what, maybe five percent of the budget?"

Once we hit the party, I get a glass of wine and Stacey has a ginger ale. We grab a table close to the bar but I'm having trouble saying anything. The drama's left me tense and raw.

The soldier named Rat reminded me so much of what Fletch might have been like in the Army—introspective and motivated. Quietly intelligent and sick to death of dealing with the bullshit stemming from hillbillies and assholes. Rat tried to make sense of his world by reading philosophy while his bunkmate delved into comic books. Rat's frustration with the state of affairs during wartime was nothing I hadn't heard from my own husband a dozen times when he recounts Army stories.

The climax came when one soldier accidentally shot another. All I could think was, given the events that led up to the situation, my poor husband could have been on either end of that gun. And despite there being no pricey pyrotechnics, the moment was so real.

Silly though it may sound, I immediately e-mail Fletch when it's over to see if he's okay. He writes back saying: *I'm watching a Rammstein DVD.* When I prompt him to find out if he's *really* okay, he replies: *I'm having a splendid time skidding on the hardwood floors in boxer shorts and Ray-Bans, drinking Chivas Regal, and licking a frozen dinner.* I e-mail back: *Really?* He responds: *Don't worry, I'll keep your crystal egg safe. Have a good night.*

(Sidebar: This? Right here? Is why I could never truly be a cougar, despite my deep and abiding ardor for Robert Pattinson and Chuck Bass on *Gossip Girl.*[98] I don't care how sculpted your abs are or how firm your jawline is; if you can't quote a twenty-five-year-old Tom Cruise movie, well, then it looks like University of Illinois for you, Joel.)

I'm off-kilter for a while and only begin to calm down when I see the

---

[98] I know he's a character played by Ed Westwick, but I don't love Ed Westwick—I love the character. The opposite applies to Pattinson as I find Edward Cullen creepy. Do you see the difference?

actor who played the protagonist enter the party. I eavesdrop and hear him say he can't stay because he's moving in the morning and he has to go home and pack. For some reason, this fills me with an enormous sense of relief. Yet I notice I'm not the only person in the room who's visibly relieved that he's actually alive and well. I'm even happier when I see the woman who played the heartbroken mother arrive at the party not in her frumpy scuffs and dowdy elastic waist pants, but in sparkly lip gloss and a darling floral dress. My mood further lifts when I hear some people in the party do the Jon Lovitz Master Thespian bit from old *Saturday Night Live*. "Acting!" "*Genius!*" This cast truly suspended my disbelief, almost a little too much.

Some of the folks I met at the *Desire* cast party gather around our table. They bring their heads in close to ours and I discover something very interesting about theater people: They never criticize whoever's providing the free wine afterward. That is, not at *that* party. If they don't like the show, they find *something* nice to say about it. Like if the acting is a hot mess, they'll praise the blocking, or if the set's ridiculous, they'll rave about the lighting design.

"Can you believe that steaming pile of crap we saw last week?" Stacey's friend Richard asks. "I mean, sweet Lord, O'Neill is turning over in his grave. You can't cut that much text and not destroy the integrity of the story!" Richard clamps his eyes shut, turns his head, and splays his fingers over his heart, as though the memory is just too painful to bear.

"Wait, someone edited the dialogue? You can't do that, right? I mean, you can't possibly think that your interpretation would be better than the original." I'm dumbfounded. So what if I just heard of this play a week ago? The arrogance of second-guessing Eugene O'Neill astounds me.

Stacey's other friend Billy jumps in. "Can . . . did . . . snap! The lies that flew outta my mouth when I raved about it? Child, I am going straight to Hell-o! And that house on ropes? When Eben and Abbie get together in his momma's parlor and they start to have sex, I turned to Richard and said, *'If this house is—rockin', don't come a-knockin'.'* I could barely keep from screaming with laughter. And the overacting? Girl, do not START me on the overacting, okay? Because screaming is not equal to 'dramatic.'"

A third friend joins us. Her name escapes me, but I remember that she has something to do with design. She whispers conspiratorially, "Are you talking about *Desire*?" We nod, glancing over our shoulders. "Jesus Christ, the boulders? Can we be a little more symbolic about the burdens everyone has to bear and the weight of it all dragging them down, please?"

"Wait," I say. "I liked the rocks. What was wrong with the set? How would you have done it?"

"Um, so, everything you saw? I'd have done the opposite," she replies.

"Would you have put an elm onstage?" I ask.

"I'd probably have represented it in some form, yeah," she replies.[99]

We chat a while longer and I take advantage of the open bar. I'm still a little raw and welcome the idea of anesthetizing myself. Eventually Stacey's friends drift off to mock *Desire* with other people.

"Does that always happen?" I ask Stacey.

She nods. "Tough crowd."

"That was seriously bitchy," I note. "I like it. But you know what's funny? I didn't even know I didn't enjoy *Desire Under the Elms*. Here I thought it was great until everyone told me why it wasn't."

"Theater's subjective. That's why I didn't agree or disagree with

---

[99]Hey! Two points for Jen!

what you thought of it—I wanted you to draw your own conclusions based on your own experience."

"My conclusion's entirely different after talking to all these experts."

"Are you happy with how your conversation went?"

"I kept up, I said things that contributed to the overall dialogue, and I felt comfortable. You know why?" I ask. "Because I had confidence."

Stacey gives me a high five. "Nicely done."

We're only alone for a minute before another of Stacey's buddies joins us. I'm introduced to Todd and learn that he's a Tony Award–winning scenic designer. Neat! I try to get some dirt out of him on his opinion of *Desire*, but he's all closemouthed. I guess you don't win big awards by denigrating potential employers.

Instead, I grill him about what it's like to win a Tony.

"Did you watch the show?" he asks.

"*Pfft.* I hate award shows. I'm not winning anything, why should I watch?" I reply.

"Interesting point," he concedes. "With the Tonys, for me it was a rush and it knocked the breath out of me to hear my name."

"Maybe you were just better than all of them and that's why you won," I say helpfully.

Todd tells us, "I don't look at it that way at all. It's surreal just to be standing there and recognized in front of the people I admire."

"And," Stacey adds, "that's not the whole story. Todd's being modest. He's also up for an Olivier Award in London next month."

"Are you going to win?" I ask.

Todd shrugs. "That doesn't matter. I'm honored just to be nominated in a group of—"

"No!" I blurt and bang my hand on the table. "Cut it out! That's loser talk! Enough with this humility crap; I want to hear some confidence. You already won one award, so you totally know what to do next. You need to tell those other scenic guys they're goin' down! Taunt them! Talk smack! Tout yourself! Send them snapshots of your mantel with the Tony on it and point out where the Olivier's gonna go. Be in their faces! *That's* what's going to win you an award." I nod wisely.

"Hey, it's about time I get that grilled cheese in you," Stacey suggests. We extricate ourselves from the table and begin to say our good-byes. She hustles me out the exit while I call back to Todd, "Remember! Confidence! Talk like a winner! Be the ball, Danny! Be the ball!"

Okay, I see where I went off track here.

I ended the night with my own *"Move your bloomin' arse"* moment. And I'd been doing so well.

And yet, later in the spring, when Todd wins the Olivier Award, I can't help but feel a tiny bit responsible. Maybe for once my big mouth actually helped.

Also, I skip the next opening-night party Stacey invites me to.

I loved *Old Glory*, so I want to avoid hearing any experts at the next event telling me why I shouldn't.

To: stacey_at_home

From: jen_at_home

Subject: Welcome home!

Hey! Hope you had fun in New York! Since you've been gone, I've joined Twitter—here are all my very important updates you've missed:

going all CSI *to determine the stink in the family room. Cats are at the top of my suspect list.*

has located source of carpet stink. Culprit not identified, but dogs pretty much cleared; not capable of this kind of evil. Cats on notice.

initiating vacuuming and deodorizing sequence.

has informed cats of their rights and advised them not to leave town.

is queasy from Arm & Hammer fumes and currently being mocked by both cats and carpeting. On to the soap-and-water-scrub portion of our show.

is AAARRRGGHH! CARPET STINK IS JUST LIKE GREMLINS! NEVER ADD WATER! RUN! SAVE YOUR-SELVES!

has gone to DEFCON ONE—carting my lazy ass down all those stairs to get the Spotbot.

overheard cats by water dish whispering, "Steam cleaner, pfft. She's going to need NASA to get that stink out."

gives up. Cats–1. Jen–0.

can't believe that even with the aroma of pies baking and briskets . . . brisketing that The Stink Abides. Maybe something did die in the wall?

I still haven't determined the source of the stink. But aren't you really anxious to come over now?

C·H·A·P·T·E·R N·I·N·E

The Flavor of FAIL

"*g*ross."
　　　"Double gross."
"Yikes."
"Sausage factory."
"Boob-tacular."

I'm in the master bedroom in front of my full-length mirror with a pile of clothes heaped up on the bed behind me. I'm headed out on book tour again next month and I'm having yet another wardrobe dilemma. I got all these well-fitted dresses to wear on tour last year and now . . . they don't fit so well.

The truth is I kind of slacked off on my intensive exercise regime. I haven't lapsed back into my old habits—at least not completely—but I've definitely back-burnered my previous level of effort. For example, I haven't trained with Barbie since we moved. I'm only about three miles west of where I'd been living when I was so devoted, but now the trip to the gym takes an extra twenty minutes because of traffic, both ways. I mean, I meant to go see her, and we certainly chatted via e-mail, but I had a deadline and then I had to move and it took almost two months to completely settle into the new place and then it was the holidays and then the January editions of all my favorite shows came back on and . . . you know. Life got in the way.[100]

Yes, I've since realized the value of consistency. I did a solid run on the treadmill earlier today, but thirty minutes of a moderate jog isn't enough to make up for six months of lethargy, no matter how well intentioned it may have been. According to the scale, I haven't gained more than a few pounds, but I'm pretty sure that's because I've lost muscle mass. Plus, I don't feel my *strongs* like I used to.

I'm pissed off that I didn't police myself better, although I can still get back on track. I could be all "Oh, no! I'm fat again!" but I already wrote that book and through it I figured out how to set myself right. I learned from the effort, which is actually why I have the tiniest of problems with folks like Bret Michaels and Miss New York and Flavor Flav. When I see them doing the same damn show over and over again—as much as I love 'em, can't miss 'em, and plan my week around 'em—I have to wonder if any of them has even a shred of self-awareness. Do they not see their own patterns of relationship-destroying behavior?

Or are the checks just so big they don't care?

Or is everything so far removed from reality that it's nothing but show business?

....

[100]Although, seriously, if I recited this litany of excuses to Jillian on the *Biggest Loser* right now, I'm pretty sure she'd ram her foot up my ass. I guess it's best that I never made it onto the show.

As for me, I took the first step today—thirty minutes of them, in fact. And I'm definitely more energized for having run. I forgot how much I liked the feeling of my heart pounding (for a reason other than social anxiety) and the V of my T-shirt dampening (not in terror sweat). Plus, I finally have a great bathtub—seems like I'd want to go out and make my muscles ache so I'd get to really enjoy a soothing, effervescent soak.

The problem is I have less than a month before I leave, and given my schedule, there's no way I'll be able to work off what I've put on between now and then. So until I have the time to fully embrace fitness and clean living, I need to employ a little subterfuge. Maybe if I distract everyone by looking fantastic from the neck up, they won't notice my embig-gened[101] ass. I appraise myself long and hard in the mirror to assess the damage.

I don't need a trainer right now; I need an esthetician.

And a dermatologist.

I peer at myself more closely.

And a cosmetic dentist.

And a hairdresser.

I glance over at the pile of discarded dresses behind me.

And possibly a seamstress.

As soon as I put all my clothes away, I sat down with my address book and began making calls and booking appointments. I figured that any-thing I got done would need time to settle in, so I planned a solid week of beauty rivaling anything you'd see on the now-defunct *Extreme Make-*

----

[101]It's a real word. Just ask *The Simpsons*.

over.[102] Granted, my "journey" didn't include a team of therapists standing behind me spouting positive affirmations because really? I already know I'm worth it. Also? No knives. I'm far too young[103] for anything requiring stitches or general anesthesia.

My rigorous week of beauty boot camp is over and now I have six throbbing red bulges in my forehead from Botox. My lip's not only inflated as big as the twelve-foot rigid raft I'd so admired, but also severely bruised from Restylane injections.

When I woke up this morning, Fletch actually screamed when he saw me. And then Maisy jumped out of bed and hid when she heard him because she hates conflict, so I had to give her all kinds of love and encouragement to coax her out of the closet. And then I saw myself and screamed and Maisy hid all over again.

The bruise starts out all purple and blue at the upper inner tube presently taking the place of my lip and has blossomed to the exact size of a fist across the right side of my face. The contusion begins to yellow about halfway up because I got injections in the nasal-labial folds around my mouth, too.

In the unbruised parts, my face is like corduroy, with alternating red and white stripes running up and down from microdermabrasion. Normally my skin isn't so sensitive, but my face was terribly tender from having my mouth pried open for so many hours earlier in the week, first for the tooth bleaching and then with the new veneers. By the way, I can only drink room-temperature liquids at the moment, and I have to breathe through my nose because my gums are the consistency of a flank steak.

Did I mention the hair? My tour is eighties-themed, so I had hair

----

[102]The non–Ty Pennington version.

[103]And chicken.

extensions put in to better embody that time period. What I didn't realize is that for the first week, all five hundred individual extensions feel like grains of wild rice digging into my scalp and that it will hurt so much, sleep's pretty much impossible. So, even though I haven't actually been given two black eyes, the deep, exhausted shadows replicate them nicely. Couple that with the eyeball redness and lid irritation stemming from the prescription lash-growing medicine I've been applying, and there's officially not one part of me from the chin up that's better than when I started.

Suddenly having strangers wondering if I'd put on a few pounds doesn't seem so bad.

You know what? This is exactly why producers made all *The Swan* ugly ducks live in apartments without mirrors during their treatments. I'm seriously hideous right now. What's funny is I wanted the enhancements to make me all pretty and polished and *Real Housewives,* and instead I'm much more scabby and bruised and *Flavor of Love.* Argh.

"Maybe we shouldn't go to the dealership today," Fletch says, wincing every time his eyes light upon me. "We could wait until you're less"—he waves his hand across his face—"whatever you call this." He doesn't say "terrifying"; he doesn't have to.

"Are you kidding me?" I say. "We *must* go. Next weekend will be too late." Today we plan to trade in the ten-year-old, dented, Maisy-scented[104] SUV that I'm stuck driving, and I couldn't be more excited. I'm getting my first car. I mean, yeah, I've had a license for twenty-four years and I've owned plenty of other automobiles, but I've never once been the one to decide what I've gotten. The locus of control went straight from my dad to my husband.

....

[104] I call her an armpit bull for a reason.

Okay, technically I never actually *wanted* to pick out my own car, but still . . . Also, I kind of made Fletch do all the research and the cost comparisons, so I'm going to choose from the four models he hand-selected. But if I want it in silver, damn it, I'm getting silver. Also, since this'll be my car, I can eat in it whenever I want. HA!

"Why are you insisting we go today? I mean right now you're . . . wow. I think the kids call it 'tore up.' You really want to be outside like this?"

"Of course!" I'm completely emphatic.

"But *why?*" he beseeches. "You don't get the mail before you put on your makeup. You look like you've gone three rounds with Mike Tyson, so what's up?" Maisy's been particularly concerned about me this week and I have to keep dodging her tongue. I guess she's noticed that I'm all banged up and would like to heal me.

"Simple," I declare. "It's all part of my car-buying strategy. When the salesman sees my face, I'll say, *'Oh, please, sir, give me a good deal or my husband will beat me again!'*"

"Excellent call," Fletch dubiously agrees. "That can't *not* work."

"Exactly."

While he heads off to take a shower, I try to decide what kind of sandwich I'm going to eat in my new car first.

I think maybe turkey.

You know what?

I should never be allowed to talk, ever. I should get surgical tape to slap over my mouth every time I leave the house. The second I opened my bruised cake hole at the dealership, I'm pretty sure I added ten per-cent to the price.[105]

According to my husband, Donald Trump, it's poor negotiating strategy to squeal, *"I love it so much that I'll do anything in my power to possess it!"* when out for a test drive.

But come on—there's a refrigerated compartment in the console. I could keep cold sandwiches in there *all the time.*

How do I *not* get excited about that?

"You have fun at the museum?"

I'm sitting on the edge of the bed while Fletch changes out of his work clothes. "Sort of. I had trouble with the car."

"What happened?"

What happened is I picked a vehicle because it had a refrigerated compartment, which I haven't even used because what sane person drives around with a bunch of sandwiches in her glove compartment? Also, the new car's way bigger than the old one, and I keep getting it stuck in places because I continue to underestimate its size. Today I got wedged in the wrong way in the parking garage and had to make a sixteen-point turn to get out. Then, once I finally made it onto the street, a bus stalled in front of me, and I got trapped in the middle of the crosswalk at the commuter train station. At rush hour. For five full lights. I can't even begin to count how many people shouted at me. The crowds' consensus was "moron," although "asshole" made a strong showing as well.

....
[105]Undercoating? Yes, please!

"The usual," I sigh. He nods; he's ridden with me.

"As for the Art Institute . . . I was surprised at what I did and didn't enjoy." As part of my project, I've been hitting all the local museums. I've been to most of them before—the Field Museum, Museum of Science and Industry, Adler Planetarium, Museum of Contemporary Art, et cetera. However, I've never set foot past the gift shop in the Art Institute of Chicago until today. "I thought I'd be completely gaga for the Impressionist stuff, but I'll be damned if Cher Horowitz wasn't right. Up close, they're a big old mess."

Granted, there's something a little amazing about being able to put my face *thisclose* to the actual pieces of canvas that van Gogh and Monet and Gauguin touched. But in the end, the pictures weren't what caught my attention. Instead, I marveled at seeing the texture of the paints and the imprints left from the brushes they used. That's a moment frozen in time forever. Had the decrepit old security guy not gotten all shout-y with me, I could have stared at the up-close detail all day. Given time, would I have spotted stray fibers or specks of dust or maybe even one of the artist's hairs affixed for eternity?

I read each of the little placards under the paintings, so I've pieced together a vague understanding of why the Impressionist movement set the art world on its ear, but I'll be honest, I still prefer the older stuff. I love the French and Italian church paintings from the Middle Ages. But I'm also interested to learn more about who was the first to make the leap from religious art to secular. That couldn't have been a small feat. Who was brave enough to say, *"You know what? Enough of Jesus. I'mma paint me this here bowl of fruit and then I'mma paint my girlfriend . . . naked!"*

Did artists revolting against church tradition bring on the Renaissance? Or did the Renaissance happen and that inspired all the new art? Seems like something I should find out for myself. You know what? Suddenly art history doesn't seem like such a bullshit major, and I feel like there are a whole lot of former college classmates to whom I owe an apology.

Still, I could look at the older works all day long. I'm fascinated by how vibrant the colors still are. What kind of paint did they use that they're still so bright five to seven hundred years after the fact? Is there some kind of preservative brushed on them? I want to know the mechanics behind the art. And I wonder how these artists would feel if they knew their work would continue to live on so many centuries later.

Seeing these paintings makes me want to discover more about how they came to be. I want to read the backstories about the artists and their inspirations and their lives.

I guess today's lesson is that although pictures are interesting, I'm always going to be more captivated by words.

"Do you feel extra-cultured now?" Fletch removes his work shoes and promptly fills them with cedar shoe trees.

"Yes and no. On the one hand, I was excited to take it all in, but on the other . . . I couldn't stop being me while I was there." Maisy and Loki then enter the room, both with big yay-my-people-are-all-home grins on their doggie faces. Loki curls up at the foot of the bed and Maisy wedges herself in next to me. I hug her, inadvertently taking a whiff. Good thing she's charming because that dog has a stink no bath can conquer.

"Meaning?" He then neatly folds his pants before depositing them into the dry-cleaning bag.

"Meaning I couldn't turn off the hyperparanoid, danger-danger-danger part of my brain. I kept thinking about that short-lived show *Traveler*, where the bad guy blew up the museum and I was all *'Today will really suck if I get exploded.'* I kept looking for hipsters with video cameras and backpacks and roller skates. Then I really started to assess the security situation, and it turns out the whole place is staffed with guards who are either old enough to have modeled for the artists featured in the Impressionist wing or as fat as me. Plus, they carry walkie-talkies, not weapons. Maybe they have a nightstick or something, but that's only going to work if they can keep pace with whomever they're trying to clobber."

I stretch and reposition myself on the bed before continuing. "So then I started examining each doorway to see if they had those metal bars that would clamp down when the alarm goes off like in *The Thomas Crown Affair*, and they had nothing! All I saw were unobscured doorways! I'm telling you that place is wide-open for any wannabe art thief to come in and steal a priceless Degas because neither the Oldies nor Fatties are going to have the wherewithal to chase 'em down. You don't need to be Thomas Crown to steal fine art; you just need a razor blade and some sneakers."

Fletch pokes his head out of his closet. "Tell me that I'm not going to get a call at work that you tried to run off with a Renoir."

"Oh, please, that's not a problem. I'm not fast enough."

Yet.

"How's your face?"

"Better, thanks! Everything's shrunk back to an appropriate size and kind of smoothed out, and I can't see my top lip when I look down anymore. Plus, all the bruises are gone and I can eat hot food again. Just in time, too, because I've got to fly out to my meeting tomorrow."

I'm sitting on the kitchen counter talking to Angie. Normally I don't like to put my butt where my food goes, but the cord on this phone's really short, and there's only the one working phone jack on this floor. One of the few downsides about this house is that although there are plenty of jacks, most of them haven't been wired. And yet I really need the exercise I get every time I have to run for the ring, so I haven't yet gotten them fixed.[106]

"Wait, what's tomorrow? I thought you didn't leave for your tour until next week," Angie says.

"I don't. I've got a dinner with a retailer tomorrow who carries my books."

"Are you nervous about talking to them?" There's clicking in the background, and I can't tell if Angie's checking her e-mail or initiating a launch sequence.

"I get the feeling I'll be okay. I mean, I've been putting in a lot of effort on the whole Jenaissance thing, so I've got some great topics of conversation. For example, you know my friend Gina? Well, her dad's this famous blues musician, so I set up a time to talk with him about why I hate jazz."

"Yeah? How was that? You still hate jazz?"

"Actually, yes. But now I know *why* I hate it. Gina's dad explained how jazz doesn't really follow the standard format of orchestral music, which is four movements which go from theme, to theme development, to buildup, to the fourth movement, which wraps it all up. Symphonies totally make sense to me now, whereas modern jazz is harder to follow

---

[106]This is why I answer every call breathless and panting and sounding like a reverse obscene caller.

because it doesn't stick to typical linear progression and I'm all about a good story, you know? I need a beginning, a middle, and an end. I have a better appreciation for how technical jazz is, even if I don't like it."

"Cool! Can you eat waffles again?"

"Had 'em for breakfast, baby! Anyway, you know what's funny? I'm totally fascinated by the blues now. I used to hate them, too, because I always thought they were totally depressing."

Angie laughs. "Hence the name."

"Hence the name. But Gina gave me this huge box series of DVDs by Martin Scorsese about the birth of the blues, and I've been so drawn in by them. I can't stop watching. Plus, Mr. Barge explained to me that they started off as slave chants and progressed into what they are now. Men would sing about how much their woman mistreated them while they were sweating in the fields, but really the lyrics were just code about how awful the foreman was. Workers used the blues to express themselves in situations where speaking the truth was too dangerous."

"That actually does sound interesting!" I can still hear her tapping away on her keyboard. Her ability to pay attention to so many things at once astounds me, particularly if she's, like, repositioning satellites and not just checking comments on her blog.

"That's what I'm saying! So I was sitting there in Gina's kitchen with my notepad, all *Jen Lancaster, Girl Reporter,* but the minute Mr. Barge started telling stories, I put my pen down and just listened. Fletch was with me and we were both . . . I guess enchanted, for lack of a better word. Enraptured? I mean, we started off talking about music, but as he told us about his past, I began to pick up on stuff that blew my mind. Back when he was touring in the sixties, he wasn't allowed to stay in the hotels he'd play in. He had to check into guesthouses on the edge of town, which led to a discussion of the civil rights movement. He mentioned how his friend Doc did this and how Doc did that, and I was all, 'Hold the phone. Do you mean you knew *Dr. Martin Luther King?*' And he did."

"Holy shit!"

"And then—then! Mr. Barge tells Gina to show us some of her scrapbooks, and very matter-of-factly, Gina pulls out photos of when she was a kid hanging out in the recording studio with the Jacksons—"

"As in Michael?"[107] Angie's always had a soft spot for Michael. She's tried to turn her kids onto him, but they somehow can't grasp that the creepy sunglass guy with the blanket-covered kids used to be the most beloved man on the planet.

(Sidebar: My theory is if you grew up in the eighties, there're a couple of icons you just can't help but love, no matter what stupid shit they pull. George Michael comes to mind. Have as many public bathroom trysts as you want, buddy! We're still pulling for you. And I'll always have a special place in my heart for Madonna because no one could ever be cooler than the girl writhing around in a slutty wedding dress singing *Like a Virgin* at the VMAs.)

"And Tito and Jermaine and Marlon and the other brother whose name I always forget. Is it Gary?"

"No, that's where they're from. Randy, maybe?"

"Yeah, that sounds right. But that's not even the best part. Gina gets to a page that's kind of a misty gray stage shot of some stadium filled with thousands of concertgoers. And she's all 'Oh, yeah, that's the summer when Dad toured with the Rolling Stones.'"

"What?!" Her shriek practically pierces my eardrum.

"I guess their regular sax player couldn't do the European leg of the tour, so they asked Mr. Barge. That's when my head exploded all over

....

[107]People, enough with the dying while I'm writing this damn thing already.

her kitchen. I was all, *'How is it that I never knew this stuff?'* And Gina just shrugged, like it was no big deal."

"How long have you known each other?"

"About three years."

"And you knew *none* of this."

"Nada."

Angie contemplates for a couple of seconds before she laughs. "Hey, you ever consider that maybe your takeaway from this project isn't going to be that you need to learn what to say? Maybe what you need to figure out is how to *listen.*"

I'm spending the night away from home tomorrow for my big out-of-town dinner, and that entails luggage.

Used to be when I'd travel, I'd lose all ability to make wise packing choices because I'd get so freaked out about flying. I'd find myself standing in my closet in my nightgown at midnight, crying because I had to get up in four hours, and all I'd managed to stuff in my bag was a dated copy of *US Weekly* and my two rattiest pair of underpants.

But ever since last year's tour and the twenty consecutive daily flights I had to take, it somehow got less scary. I still don't love flying, but it no longer paralyzes me.[108]

I also took Stacey's advice and contacted her friend the costume designer, and he whipped me up all kinds of adorable madras pants and shorts and skirts. The colors are all complementary, so I can grab any bottom to pair with any of my Lacoste shirts and V-neck sweaters and

---

[108]Now I'm much more likely to be annoyed—a far more natural state for me.

have a complete outfit. Essentially, my dream of adult Garanimals has come true, so packing was a breeze.

I manage to be so organized that I have my bags filled and ready by the front door at eight p.m., all without scrambling . . . or sweating . . . or crying.

I'm not sure if the fates are conspiring, or if maybe this is simply the result of having finally purchased a grown-up carry-on bag. Regardless, I'm able to relax and enjoy my evening stress-free.

But it's really not stress-free.

Where's that feeling of doom stemming from having packed nothing but three bags of Skittles and a girdle? What will it be like to go to the airport on no more than forty-five minutes of REM sleep?

Despite being completely ready, I feel out of sorts. I take a bath, but that doesn't make a difference. I hug Maisy really hard. It helps a little. I take an Ambien. And that helps a little more. So I have a single glass of wine on top of it. And that helps a lot. Having achieved a state of perfect relaxation, I get into bed.

Okay, that's a lie.

Instead, I log on to Twitter, where I am @AltgeldShrugged[109] and, well . . . I'll just let the following speak for itself:

AltgeldShrugged—is so organized that I have time to drink a glass of wine, swallow an Ambien, and trot off to the Internet where I'll dispense advice.

AltgeldShrugged—Not that anyone has asked, but I'm here at the ready, or at least until the pharmaceuticals toss my ass in bed.

....

[109] Altgeld is my old street, and I love Ayn Rand. Get it?

AltgeldShrugged—which, letsh be honests, is rapidly approchaing.

AltgeldShrugged—I understand all the words in this tweet, but not their meaning. Am I in Cnn? Which this book? Am I the book cococachoo?

AltgeldShrugged—I bet Ashton Kutcher NEVER chases Ambien with wine and then runs to the computer because he's all "professional" and shit. (He has people 4 that.)

AltgeldShrugged—Ashton's curing malaria? With what? Eric Foreman's dad's Datsun? Dude and Sweet tattoos? A big bag of weed? So confused.

AltgeldShrugged—Ambien might have mentally just tossed my salad. WITH CROUTONS.

AltgeldShrugged—Purple monkey dishwasher.

AltgeldShrugged—I'd chose me, but only if I were Kelly Taylor and didn't want to date old men.

AltgeldShrugged—Yous are lazy? Mine are always "blah blah blah business plans, blah, sustainable growth, and solid P&L." My monkeys suck.

AltgeldShrugged—I would kill each and every one of you (well, not you jessedup) for a very small cheeseburger with a pickle and mustard on an itty-bitty bun.

AltgeldShrugged—I keeed! I keeed! I would only rob you for your wee, wee (but not pee-related) itty-bitty burgers.

AltgeldShrugged—I can stagger like a muthafuckin ninja. (Typed that wroed ninja weong but had the wherewithall the fix it.)

AltgeldShrugged—You say it like findifng my shoes (or my feet) is an option right now.

AltgeldShrugged—am getting al;l cookied up in honor o0f casey's biethdyay. She likes it when I gets slurry.

AltgeldShrugged—FYI? THis? Right here? Is why I was so poipular in collage.

AltgeldShrugged—Having a relazed sense of moreal turpitude didn't hurt either.

AltgeldShrugged—Mrs. Kutcher, you're washing cars? Wowie, I guess the economy is hitting everyone harder than expected.

AltgeldShrugged—Yegatory.

AltgeldShrugged—Just lost a bunch of followers. But if they don't like Sauvignon-Ambien Jen, why the fuck where they even hanging around?

AltgeldShrugged—I find college rewarding, too. All those little pictures sitcking on top of each toher.

AltgeldShrugged—No but last week I orderd $4k of bedroom furniture. They showe d up and I was all SURPRISE! Oh, wait.

AltgeldShrugged—Neither, you'll end uip with three pole dancers name Tiffany shoing up at yoru place in twenrty minutes.

AltgeldShrugged—Pfft, not a rant. This is what I DO. Must remember to save this to end a chapter in some lateR book.[110]

AltgeldShrugged—And it's floral. What's supresad is i've had one wee ambien andone wee glass of wine. Fatasslightweight.

AltgeldShrugged—Glass emptyee pill digested, peanute btutter bpretzels, tastey, bednowyeskthxbai.

AltgeldShrugged—HEY YOU PEPIOLE ARE MOCKING ME . . .Not undesrrtverd, but still Mocking. I'll go to bed & be unpleasantly surprised whenb I log on in the AM.

AltgeldShrugged—Internet = 1, Jen's dumb ass = 0

AltgeldShrugged—Godspeed, ninja. Am strealing that. Good night. Off to PotteryBarn.com . . .

The good news is there's no evidence I did any online shopping last night.

The bad news is at some point after this dialogue, I had a run-in with a can of spray tan.

This is probably why I should never pack early.

---

[110]And here we are.

To: angie_at_home, stacey_at_home, wendy_at_home, poppy_at_
home

From: jen_at_home

Subject: yet another Jen-point quiz

You are out of town at a business dinner with a bunch of book buyers from an important retailer. After you do an excellent job of regaling your companions with recitations on Chicago theater, Impressionist art, and the blues, you find yourself out of highbrow conversational material.

What do you do next?

(a) You thank everyone for a truly lovely evening, refuse the last glass of wine, and return to your hotel, savoring the victory of not having made an ass out of yourself.

(b) You quietly smile and nod while other topics are being discussed, causing all diners to believe you're wise and knowing and that you're the kind of still water that runs deep.

(c) You not only slug down the last glass of wine, but you insist the table order another bottle because you're just warming up to launch into a fifteen-minute diatribe about how that screaming nancy-boy Adam Lambert massacred "Ring of Fire" last month on *American Idol* and how you hope that Johnny Cash returns from the grave to stomp all over his poseur ass.

(d) You encourage, nay, *insist* the entire group drink the restaurant out of a particular vintage but then accidentally ruin the party atmosphere when casually recounting a conversation where someone told you Don Knotts was gay, which then makes everyone increasingly more shout-y as the table splits into two opposing teams hotly contesting the influence of a neckerchief on one's sexuality.

(e) Answers C and D.

I'm pretty sure I don't have to explain the scoring key on this one.

C·H·A·P·T·E·R   T·E·N

Survivor: Chinatown

My enormous out-of-town dinner FAIL tells me that I've got to step up my effort in getting more cultured. The one thing I've got going for me is I'll be at events every night during prime time for the next month and thus will be removed from the constant barrage/terrible influence of reality shows.[111]

I'm going to be in a whole bunch of big cities, and each of them is filled with important museums and world-class dining and landmarks rich in historical significance. My time's pretty limited but, damn it, I'm going to capitalize on the opportunities in each city.

I am. I swear. Just you wait.

....

[111]Although I may or may not have three DVRs, and they may or may not all be preprogrammed.

Detroit: Um . . . it's the first stop and I'm staying in the hotel at the airport. But if I weren't all the way out here, I'd totally hit the Detroit Institute of Arts. I would. Really.

Boston: I lived here for a summer in college, so I've actually been to a lot of the museums, which is why I don't feel bad about deciding to spend what free time I have in my hotel instead. Someone in the travel department had a contact at the Four Seasons and they got a superdiscounted rate, so I'm staying here tonight!

I get the feeling there's very little I'd see in this city that could compare to my pretty room with the unencumbered view of the Boston Common. Not only was my ice bucket already filled when I got here, but then my doorbell rang—*my room has a doorbell!*—and a staff member delivered a copy of my book *made out of chocolate.*

This? Is so much better than Disneyland.

I figure I can see art any day of the week, but when am I ever going to be in a Four Seasons again? In a room with a *doorbell?* I can't *not* take advantage of this situation, so I park myself on the couch, order a room service cheeseburger, and tune in to *Deadliest Catch* reruns.

Sadly, I'm leaving shortly to do a televised interview, so I put on all my eighties gear—madras plaid Bermuda shorts, layered pastel Lacoste shirts, and a cable-knit sweater over my shoulders. Right now, especially given my setting, I could pass for the quintessential John Hughes villain. Whoever's wearing this outfit on-screen will absolutely be the one who makes Molly Ringwald cry. I stuff my enormous mane of fake hair into an impressive ponytail and tie it with a coordinating madras ribbon, topping the whole do with a pair of polarized Ray-Bans.

As I admire myself, my eyes trail back up to my hair. I feel a moderate level of existential angst over these hair extensions. While they were being applied,[112] the stylist explained that what I'd gotten was Indian temple hair. Because of its sturdy texture and ability to hold a curl, this is the best kind of hair to use. I was intrigued, so I went home to have a consultation with Dr. Google.

Apparently devoted Hindi women spend their whole lives growing out their hair in order to eventually give it to Vishnu in offering. Once ready, they go on a pilgrimage to the Tiripati temple, which can take days of travel for some of them, often in squalid conditions. Upon arrival, they submit to the temple barber, who shaves their heads, which hopefully prompts the gods to heap good fortune upon their shiny bald noggins.

So, the idea of a religious pilgrim spending her whole life preparing this gift and then traveling hard for hundreds of miles only to have me tease her sacrifice with a can of Aqua Net so I can look like an asshole on a book tour isn't sitting so well with me.

Guilt aside, I'm pleased with my level of authenticity and am particularly proud of the electric powder blue eye shadow I managed to find, which I've now blended artfully with the sparkly powder pink stuff. I am currently coming across more eighties than I even was in the eighties.

I grab my bag and head down to the lobby. The elevator's crowded, but I notice no one's meeting my gaze. And then I remember my twenty-year-out-of-date look. I'm more than a little embarrassed when I start

---

[112]By someone who found it appropriate to snap her gum for six straight hours, and my God, do you know how hard it was not to smack the Dentyne right out of her?

walking through the lobby. I don't know why I didn't feel like an ass yesterday, but maybe it's because I was in a hurry and didn't have as much time to devote to detail.

I head outside to wait for my ride. As I take in the surroundings, I notice a familiar man to my right. Hey, that's Lenny Clarke, the stand-up comedian! Cool! First official celeb sighting! I go to introduce myself because he's friends with my cousin who performs in Boston comedy clubs. Before I get over to him, I realize he's in the throes of an animated conversation with another guy I recognize. Even if I hadn't seen the second man's face, I'd know that smoky, gravelly voice anywhere.

Denis Leary.

I'm standing right next to Denis Leary.

First a doorbell and now Denis Leary? There's nothing this hotel can't provide!

I want to interrupt him and be all confident and outrageous by telling him that my new book's going to be the one to knock his down a notch on the *NYT* hardcover nonfiction bestseller list but (a) this may be an utter and complete fabrication as there's zero evidence this'll happen, and (b) there is no b. Wait, here we go—(b) I look like an asshole all done up like this, and not the good kind Leary's always singing about. Damn it.

Before I can come up with a clever way to spin my appearance, my ride arrives and I have to go. We pull out of the Four Seasons driveway, while I gaze longingly back at my missed opportunity.

I guess there's no cure for confidence, either.

New York: I take in no culture, but I do have a hot dog from a street vendor that's *practically* a work of art.

Washington, D.C.: I take in no culture, unless watching *Four Chrismases* on pay-per-view counts as a cultural experience. (It shouldn't.)

Dallas: Nothing.

Houston: Nada.

Charlotte: My timing gets all screwed up in North Carolina, and I end up running behind on most of my itinerary stops. Let's just say this does not positively impact my disposition or level of patience. So, not only do I take in no culture, but I later learn that all those Southerners who remark, "You must be a Yankee," whenever I lapse into bitch-panic mode aren't just making an observation that I'm from the North.[113]

Nashville: Zip.

Atlanta: In a twenty-four-hour day, I'm on the go for twenty-one of them, so at no point do I get to visit the Martin Luther King Jr. National Historic Site. But I do manage to slip into the big Macy's with the fantastic plus-size department at Lenox Square Mall for a few minutes.

Sometimes I really earn the Shame Rattle.

Portland: I knew that I'd have the whole day to myself after my morning television appearance. Before I even got on the plane, I researched what cultural attraction I'd most like to see, and I decided upon the Portland Museum of Art. They've got an extensive collection of silver pieces and lots of European art. Since I'm still intrigued by this whole Renaissance thing, I figure there's knowledge to be found. Maybe I'll even pick up a history book in the gift shop.

Before my day-o'-learning, I first have to do my interview. I leave my

---

[113]Bless their hearts.

hotel, where the doorman—dressed up in full Beefeater gear, *thank you very much*—directs me to my ride. I get in the car and quickly discover that I'm leaving a whole hour before I actually need to.

"Do you want to go back inside for a while or would you rather go get some coffee or donuts and take a little tour of the city?" the driver asks me.

My desire for caffeine trumps the need for sleep, so I say, "Ooh, yes, where's the nearest Starbucks?"

The driver's expression immediately sours, and he winces as though he's been slapped. "I'm not taking you to Starbucks in this town."

Instead, at his behest, we go to an independent coffeehouse called Stumptown, which is full not only of delicious coffee but also of hipsters, but the hipsters here seem awfully sincere about it. Like, they might actually *be* artists instead of just dressing like them. I may have even seen paint splattered on a few of their iconic seventies T-shirts. A couple of them milling around the tables smile, and the one behind the counter says, "Thank you," really earnestly. I'm willing to wager she didn't spit in my latte.

(Sidebar: These are the first hipsters I've seen who don't make me want to beat them with my shovel. The kids here aren't at all the stupid poseur hipsters currently invading my neighborhood with their beastly facial hair and lensless plastic glasses. I swear, these idiots in their headbands and American Apparel have completely ruined my favorite lunch spot with all their yawping and pouting and ennui. Why the long face, kids? Your parents still pay your rent! How can you be so cynical about a world you've yet to experience?)

Coffee secured, we're off to our next stop—the donut place. Sure, I love donuts, but I'm not terribly likely to seek them out. If I venture out of the house for pastry, I'm more of a cupcake/birthday cake kind of girl. Buttercream frosting is my antidrug, you know? But Voodoo Donuts may have just flipped the script. This dark and depressing shop looks more like a terrible punk rock club yet holds treasures I never even imagined; these donuts are covered with items I've only seen in my dreams!

I'm pretty much mesmerized as I take in the circular case. I could get donuts topped with crumbled candy bars or crushed cookies or a generous dusting of sweetened cereal. I could have the Grape Ape, which boasts vanilla icing and grape powder, or the Arnold Palmer, made with lemon and tea powder. One of them has peanut butter and chocolate Rice Krispies on it, and one's all covered in pink marshmallow and coconut—basically, a SnoBall donut. Can you *do* this kind of stuff to a donut? Is this even *legal?*

And then I spot it, my prize . . . my precious . . . my pastry. The hipster behind the counter promises me this is their very best donut, so I place my order and then practically run out of the store to make sure no one steals what I've got in this paper bag. The item in question is a maple-bacon bar. When I take my first bite, I'm pretty sure all the secrets of the universe are revealed, if only for a second. This is like a cruller on crack— the cloying sweetness of the maple frosting mingles with the smoky saltiness of the two thick slabs of bacon to create the ultimate breakfast food. I eat it as slowly as I can, and after I'm finished, I spend a few minutes huffing the bag it came in. The driver doesn't even laugh at me—I suspect he's seen this all before.

I do my interview (checking first for crumbs) and when it's over, the driver takes me back to the hotel. "Are you doing anything good with your afternoon?" he asks me.

I'm delighted with myself for having made a plan for today. I haven't done anything cultural in weeks and I can feel myself dumbening[114] again. I mean, yesterday in the airport I spent ten minutes expounding on the

....

[114]See? I'm stealing made-up words from *The Simpsons* again.

virtues of Bethenny Frankel from the New York season of the *Real House-wives* until I realized the person next to me had been talking about a book by *Viktor* Frankl. My subsequent mortification seemed like a heavy clue about my stepping up my own search for meaning.

"Yes!" I exclaim from my spot in the backseat. "I'm spending the whole day at the Portland Museum."

He glances up at me in the rearview mirror. "But it's Monday—you know they're closed today, right?"

Shit.

I probably could have found something else enriching, but I opt for a pedicure instead because my feet hurt. Granted, salon treatments don't sound like what a person attempting an intellectual renaissance would choose, but this is no ordinary sore set of feet. Due to my penchant for shoes that are "jewel-encrusted and adorable" instead of "sensible with proper arch support," I've developed a screaming case of *plantar fasciitis*, Latin for "Holy cats, I'm being stabbed in the heel."

Every step I've taken in the past few weeks sends daggers of pain up my leg and into my lower back. I find myself staring longingly at the old men on the street clad in Rockports and little kids in their sturdy lace-up school oxfords. My dogs were barking so loudly last week that I almost rolled a maid in Manhattan for her orthopedic shoes. While I was hobbling through the airport a couple of days ago, I spotted Johnston & Murphy, the men's store where Fletch occasionally buys snappy dress shoes. And if I hadn't been rushing to make a flight, I'd have stopped in there, purchased a pair of well-constructed wingtips, and blissfully worn them with my khaki cargo shorts.

Now I'm in the nail shop perched in the big pedicure throne, crying to the tiny Vietnamese technician about how much my arches ache, begging her to do whatever it takes to make them feel less stabby.

Apparently "stabby" does not translate well to Vietnamese, and the technician has to call the owner over to translate. Hey, who knew? Apparently whining is *not* a universal language.

An older gentleman in a bowling shirt wanders over. "You feets hurt?" he asks.

"They're killing me," I moan.

He claps his hands together and declares, "You no worry! We give you extra-good massage and use ancient Vietnamese secret."[115] Then he quickly says something to the technician in his native tongue before heading out to lunch.

The pedicure begins like they all do—the big soak in bubbling blue water. I adjust the chair's massage settings and ease back into it. I keep my eyes closed during the polish removal and clipping and filing. This is the most relaxed I've been in weeks.

I'm just about to fall asleep—or possibly black out due to a sugar crash[116]—when the next part of my pedicure begins. My eyes fly open when the first punch connects with my lower leg. The next thirty to forty blows happen so rapid-fire that I'm paralyzed in my chair. What the hell?

Horrified, I glance down at the technician, who's smiling back proudly at me. "Ancient technique," she confirms. Then she stops assaulting me and instead uses her pointy little thumbs to create a wedge between my shinbone and tendon, much like I do when I'm stripping a

---

[115]Calgon?

[116]Yeah, I bought more than one donut.

roast chicken. This is followed by another rigorous bout of calf smacking. And because I can't figure out how to say, *"Hey, Evander Holyfield, slow your freaking roll!"* in Vietnamese, I sit biting back tears until the massage comes to its merciful conclusion.

The thing is, the owner's right—I really don't notice my sore feet afterward. This may have less to do with skillfully implemented Asian reflexology, and more to do with the fact that my legs are throbbing.

For the next three weeks, I'm stuck with huge, round black-and-blue spots all over my legs. The bruises are so bad I can wear shorts only if I first slather my legs in industrial-strength concealer.

Good thing about those bacon donuts, Portland, or I might not have forgiven you.

Seattle: Legs hurt too much to walk to any culture.

San Francisco: Due to the miracle of a canceled media appearance,[117] I find myself with a free afternoon! Woo-hoo!

When I was here on tour last year, my schedule wasn't quite as crazed, so I went into Tourist Mode, which encompassed shopping in Union Square, gobbling up Ghirardelli chocolate and corn dogs, bitching about all the steep inclines, and visiting the dock claimed by sea lions.

Last time I called Fletch from Fisherman's Wharf so he could hear

---

[117]Strangely, my publicist does not consider canceled interviews "miraculous."

the sea lions barking firsthand as I furiously forwarded photo after photo from my BlackBerry.[118] I spent an hour watching stout yet sleek creatures jockey for prime position on wobbly little docks, which were originally built for boaters and definitely not made to sustain the weight of multiple thousand-pound sea mammals. The fighting styles I witnessed consisted almost exclusively of chest bumping and baying in one another's faces—the sea creature's version of *The Road Rules/Real World Challenge*—and I couldn't tear myself away.

Once bested, the lesser beasts would tumble back into the water, emerging at a different dock, ready to rumble with new takers, again and again, all day, every day. I feel sorry for the boat owners who tried to remove the sea lions once they took up residence. It's impossible to move Maisy and she's only sixty pounds, so there's no way those poor sailors were ever reclaiming their slips after the sea lions decided to stay.

I whiled away much of my time last year with the sea lions, but I was still able to marvel at the architecture and ogle bridges and make awkward conversation with cabdrivers on how I'd sure hate to be driving a stick shift around here![119] And although I chose not to sport the fanny-pack-socks-sandals-T-shirt-of-where-we-currently-are-and-woven-straw-hats uniform made popular by so many of the city's other visitors, I'll admit to consuming more than my fair share of tourist chow, such as corn dogs, wine, corn dogs, chocolate, corn dogs, sourdough bread bowls, and corn dogs.

Having no obligations until six p.m. feels like a gift; I don't want to piss it away seeking out the perfect nitrate on a stick. I need to continue

---

[118]To get the full effect, he'd really need to smell them. You may think creatures who spend their lives in water wouldn't stink so much. You'd be wrong.

[119]Bet they've never heard that before.

my Jenaissance. Plus, if I want to experience a bunch of fat, surly, un-grateful creatures jockeying for position, I can watch my cats duke it out over the sunny spot on the ottoman.[120]

I'm ready to have an adventure, so I instruct the cabdriver to take me to Chinatown. Recently, I went to a book club and spoke with a woman who'd gone to a tea-tasting workshop, where she learned all sorts of obscure facts like leaf origins and how to brew the perfect cup. She explained that I should never, ever buy bagged tea because those are the pieces that aren't big enough/good enough to sell as loose tea.

What really sparked my interest was her story about learning the ritual of tea service. I paid special attention because I remembered in cycle three of *America's Next Top Model*, the models were in Japan and Tyra made them do a tea-service challenge. Which, by the way, was bullshit, because what does modeling have to do with serving tea?[121] Hopeful model Yaya—who I HATED—won that competition and got all smug about it, and for a minute I thought my girl Eva wasn't going to win. Thus I pledged to myself to take any opportunity to learn a traditional tea service because even though I may be fat and forty, in my mind these factors do not necessarily prevent me from being on *ANTM*. So, if Miss Tyra's basing top-model decisions on who best doles out the Darjeeling, I'm a shoo-in.[122] Ergo, Chinatown.

Coincidentally, this isn't the first instance of reality TV coaxing me into action. When I finally try out for *Survivor* I'm not going to be that asshole running around picking coconuts and fixing shelter roofs while

---

[120]Or spend time with my brother.

[121]Serving coffee, maybe. But not tea.

[122]Laugh if you want, but *ANTM* Cycle Eleven is all about petite models. Old and fat is coming, mark my words.

showing twenty million viewers my simian armpits, so I've started a series of laser hair removal treatments; when the time comes, I'll be smooth and camera-ready.

(Sidebar: If you have high-def TV, you'll thank me for having made the effort. Another selling point for casting me on *Survivor* is that I won't already look like I'm starving once I get there, so at no point will you take morbid fascination in counting every knob in my spine and each rib. And why, why, why, Burnett & Co., do you keep casting chicks who look anorexic when you know they're going to lose another thirty pounds? What were you all thinking when you chose Courtney for the China season? She *started off* at ninety-five pounds. Thirty-nine days of rice, grubs, and contaminated groundwater did her no favors. Although maybe since she was already possibly pro-ana, her hair growth was retarded? I recall being horrified that her femur was smaller than my forearm, but at no point did I find myself willing the crew to smuggle her in a Lady Bic. In which case, I reiterate that I'd be the perfect pick because I'll be stubble-free. Seriously, though, Mark Burnett, do you really want these little actress/model/waitresses to die on your islands? Because someone is going to kick off soon, I promise you.)

Ahem.

Anyway, Chinatown.

The cabdriver drops me off at the archway and warns me that taxis don't make rounds on these tiny little streets. He says I'll need to walk a few blocks down to an intersection, the street names of which I forget the second I close the door. But how hard can it be to find a way out of here? I started off downhill and now I'm partway uphill. All I need to do is descend and I'm golden.

I begin my ascent, planning to find a tea shop. But then I remember what happened last year when I went exploring on an empty stomach, and I decide to stop first to take in some sustenance. I smell something amazing and do a Toucan Sam, only my nose leads me to a bakery and not the Froot Loop jungle.[123]

I enter the front door, which is flanked by display windows almost completely obscured by posters covered in Chinese writing. They effectively block the light, so the store is considerably darker than the street. It takes me a minute to see what the store looks like and when I do . . . wow.

Okay, here's the thing—if feng shui is Chinese, then what happened here? This place looks like a train full of flour sacks collided with a truck transporting office supplies, leaving staplers and pencils and drifts of white powder scattered for miles. There are mountains of boxes stacked haphazardly, and the walls are covered in flyers and old calendars, and there is a bunch of ratty bamboo shoots surrounded by a million other pieces of detritus. I'm instantly claustrophobic and I kind of want to run.

Beneath a stratum of debris, the glass counter boasts many exotic offerings. I don't recognize anything, even though I'm a huge fan of Chinese food. Shouldn't something be moderately familiar? Like, where are the egg rolls? Or fortune cookies? Then it dawns on me this is real-deal authentic fare, and not the watered-down, Americanized, McAsian stuff I'm used to.[124] This food is scary and weird and I would like a corn dog now, please.

I'm about to leave when it occurs to me I may be overreacting. I scold myself for my vaguely xenophobic reaction to this place. Just because it's

[123]One of the other donuts I got was covered in Froot Loops. It was good, but it was no maple-bacon bar.

[124]I remember laughing at *ANTM*'s Norelle in Cycle Three when she said how she expected the food in Asia to be like what you'd find at Panda Express. It's not so funny now.

different from what I'm used to doesn't mean it's bad. I mean, the Chinese culture thrived for thousands of years without benefit of a Whole Foods Market. The point of this exercise is to push myself out of my pretty, perfect, plastic bubble, and if I scurry away every time something's different, I'm never going to grow.

Basically, I need to dive in.

I resolve to stay and order and not be the coward who, despite being in an amazing food city, opts for a room service cheeseburger. Again.

But what do I get? I gawp at all the choices for a full minute before I even realize there's a clerk waiting for my order.

"Hi," I say to the wizened old woman behind the counter. Her face has been deeply etched by the years, and her mouth has a permanent downward cast that bleeds all the way into her determined jawline. She's clad in layers and layers of mismatched shirts and a Paddington Bear–type jacket, and her outfit's topped with a dirty apron. She has sparse little tufts of downy white hair, which are a striking contrast with her shiny black button eyes. She reminds me of one those dried apple-head dolls. I want to whisk her away from this chaos and put her in my pocket because I don't want one of the massive walls of junk to topple over and crush her.

"How are you?" I inquire. I flash my best Midwestern grin. "Listen, I've never been to a Chinese bakery before, so I don't really know what to get. I'm not sure what I smell right now, but, really . . . ? It's kind of divine. Can you suggest something that might—"

"WHATCHU WANT?" she shouts.

Huh.

That's a really enormous voice for such an ancient little body.

"Oh! Gosh, I'm sorry. I guess I haven't decided. But I do need some protein. Real quick? Last year, when I was in town, I filled up on chocolate, and then I stopped in a winery's storefront and I accidentally got drunk on free samples and joined, like, four wine clubs, and now I have all these unopened cases in my basement. Can you maybe—"

"YOU NO WASTE TIME." She waves a crooked, clawed finger in my direction.

Wow, that outburst generated more than a little spittle, and it kind of rattles me. I inadvertently take a step back and begin to stammer. "But I . . . just want—"

"YOU ORDER NOW OR GET OUT."

The woman who's screaming is no less than a thousand years old and can't be more than four feet tall. Yet I think she may have just lunged at me.

I basically feel like I'm visiting another country, so I'm trying to respect her culture by not shouting back. Or maybe I'm keeping my fat mouth shut because I suddenly realize that even though she only weighs seventy-eight pounds, she scares the living crap out of me.

I ask her to just give me what everyone else is getting. She stuffs something into white paper and snatches the five-dollar bill out of my hand. Then she takes my change and eyes the tip jar. I make a "Please, you keep it" gesture and bustle out of the store with my bag. I have no idea what I got, but I suspect I'd better eat it and like it, lest the old gal has a go at my calves.

Once I'm a safe distance from the shop, I tentatively open the bag. There's a big golden something or other in there. I take a cautious whiff, and I'm delighted that it smells like whatever drew me to that bakery in the first place. The aroma's vaguely sweet and yeasty, and there's an undertone that's familiar but I can't quite place it. I grab a napkin and wrap it around the disk, examining it in the sunlight. This appears to be a . . . donut? Maybe? But it isn't fried, so maybe not?

The dough's puckered on one side, and it's really tender. There's filling inside, and I desperately hope it's not scorpion. Elyse from Cycle One of *ANTM* lives in Asia now, and she's always showing snapshots on her Web site of vendors selling bug-based roasted street meats. She's more adventurous than I am, though even she was squicked out by frog oviduct soup.

They wouldn't put oviducts in a donut, right? Not in *America*.

I sink my teeth in and tear off a small bite. The dough isn't that sweet, so it's not a true donut. What I taste next is rich and meaty and tangy and reminds me of Texas.

Is this . . . barbecue?

Like, barbecued pork?

Wrapped in an almost-donut?

Because that *would be genius.*

As I slowly savor whatever this thing is, someone in an Alcatraz Psych Ward shirt approaches me. "Excuse me, ma'am. Can you tell me where you bought that steamed pork bun?" My mouth is full, so I gesture to the claustrophobic storefront up the street. He and his socks-and-sandaled companion stroll farther up the hill, and I have my answer.

I finish my bun, quietly delighting in the fact that diving into a new foodstuff didn't go horribly, scorpion-tastically wrong. I make my way up the hill and spot a tea shop on the left-hand side of the street. I'm waiting at the light to cross when I see one of its employees walk through the open storefront and hawk the largest loogie I've ever seen onto the street.

Although I'm sure what he just did is ethnically appropriate, I'm going to skip that shop.

Another couple of blocks north, I find a clean, well-lit, loogie-free shop offering tea service. I decide this is the place I want to patronize.

Watch out, Miss Tyra and the rest of you top models—I'm about to get my culture on.

"I'm lost."

"Where are you?"

"I don't know. I'm lost! I'm somewhere in Chinatown!" I'm on the phone with Angie. As I've just finished my tea-tasting session, I'm both disoriented and hopped up on caffeine.

While looking for a nonspitty tea ceremony, I went off the beaten path and headed down some weird side street. As I wove my way past dark shops on slant-y streets boasting bizarre curios, I realized this was exactly where Billy Peltzer's dad bought him Gizmo in the movie *Gremlins* . . . and we all know how *that* ended up. I mean, yes, I understand the story was fiction, but the more authors I meet, the more I realize that fiction is never quite fictional. The writers I know all base their work on something real. Thus, it stands to reason that some shit went down here, so I immediately pledged to buy nothing for fear of accidentally unleashing an army of tiny, bloodthirsty monsters.[125]

When I left the shop, I guess I got more turned around than I even realized because now nothing looks familiar. I thought I could find my way out if I went back down the hill, but the problem is the hills keep going up and down. They're rolling! No one told me the hills would roll. I'm completely discombobulated, and the longer I'm here, the more likely I am to accidentally buy a monster.

Once, a couple of years ago, Fletch had some corporate training in

----

[125]FYI, this is also why I'm not having children.

Denver. On his last night, he went out in the city with a bunch of people from his class. On his way back to the company's suburban headquarters, his cabdriver got lost. So Fletch called home at two in the morning, asking me to pull up Google Maps to navigate them both back to campus. At the time I wanted to murder him, yet suddenly I'm a lot more compassionate.

"What are you doing in Chinatown? I thought you were going to look at the sea lions," she says.

"I wanted to learn a goddamned tradition, and now I'm lost! Also, I think I may have accidentally bought black tar heroin because I don't know how to say *no* in Chinese."

There's a pregnant pause before Angie replies, "I'm sorry. I didn't hear you. I believe I had a piece of crazy in my ear."

"Just listen. I found a store that did tea ceremonies but they don't just let you pay to learn. They want you to taste stuff you'll buy, which is fine."

As soon as I walked into the shop, an ancient little woman pounced on me, shouting *"Youli'tea!"* and started wildly gesticulating at all these tin canisters lining the walls. I immediately froze, thinking, "Shit, she's going to steamroll me into leaving here with a Mogwai. What am I going to do with a Mogwai? I just know I'm going to screw up time zones and feed the damn thing after midnight because if I'm having a snack, it's not like I could resist giving him some, too, because I hate for anything to be hungry ever, and also my house is already chaotic enough with two huge dogs and four cats and I can't even imagine what's going to happen once I accidentally unleash monsters, and . . . Wait, oh, she's asking me if I'd 'like a tea.' Yeah, that probably makes more sense. My bad." Eventually, she and I worked out a system of sign language—which mostly consisted of her pointing and my nodding—and we finally got the process under way.

(Sidebar: I hate when I encounter a language barrier. It's not that I'm all hard-line conservative and believe if you're going to be in this country, you need to speak the language and go get me a flag to hug, while you're at it. I mean, I'm descended from immigrants; I'd be pretty hypocritical if I thought others didn't belong here because they don't yet speak proper "Murrican." Rather, it's that my life and my work revolve around words; I get very frustrated when I can't use the tools of my trade to communicate with someone else.)

I continue. "This little Chinese lady took me around the place to find some teas to sample in the ceremony. I picked a jasmine tea—"

Angie interrupts, "I love jasmine tea!"

"Great! Because I have a pound of it, which, incidentally, costs eighty dollars. I'll send you some. Anyway, I said I liked jasmine, so she pulls out this container, and they aren't just leaves—they're little, tight balls of jasmine and they smell amazing, like the most exquisitely delicious perfume. I didn't know if I wanted to drink it or roll in it. Then, from what I can determine from her really broken English, she tells me she's got jasmine tea with rose petals, too."

"That sounds nice."

"Yeah, I walked out of there with eighty bucks' worth of that, too. I'll put it on the list of stuff to send you. So, we sit down at this gorgeous wood table in the back that looks like it's been carved out of a single tree. She starts to do the tea service, only I can't understand a frigging word coming out of her mouth, and she doesn't really understand me either. So I start talking slower and louder because part of me secretly believes that everyone understands English if you talk slowly and loudly—"

"Isn't that a Fletch quote?"

"No, he says everyone speaks English at gunpoint. Anyway, I'm trying to ask her about the steps she's taking and what everything means, but she just smiles and nods. Pretty much she just poured hot liquids into one little cup and then another and back into the first one, so I have zero clue about rituals.[126] However, the tea she serves me is way better than anything to come out of a box. Wait. . . . taxi! TAXI! Shit, there was a cab but he drove right past me."

"Maybe if you keep going in the direction he went, you'll find more cabs," she suggests. This? Right here? Is why Angie's kind of a genius.[127]

"Good call. I'm off." I begin to hike across the hill, rather than up or down it. "Anyway, I start to ask the lady about other kinds of tea. I tell her my favorite is English Breakfast because it's bold enough to put milk in. She nods like maybe she's starting to understand me and scurries over to this enormous inlaid apothecary chest—which Wendy would kill for, by the way—and starts opening tiny drawers. She pulls out some small containers and begins the whole boiling-water-cup-cup-cup dealie over. I try other varieties and they're all nice. But it's tea and not wine, so I'm not losing my mind over them or anything."

"Like when you didn't have any protein and you joined all those wine clubs last year?"

"Exactly. So, because I feel like we're finally communicating, I ask her all conversational-like what their best stuff in the store is and what's the most popular and it's cup, cup, cup again. And the whole time, she's smiling and saying, *'Youli'?'* and I yes, I do like, thank you. But at this point, I've had about all the tea I can hold, so I'm ready to make my purchase and get out. I kind of gesture to the register and she gets my drift."

"Oh my God, you spent over a hundred dollars on tea? Is Fletch going to murder you?"

....

[126] And now I'm never going to be America's Next Top Model.

[127] Now I don't have to face the shame of her Google-Mapping my coordinates.

A bitter laugh escapes me. "He's not going to kill me for spending a hundred. He's going to kill me for spending FOUR HUNDRED GOD-DAMNED DOLLARS!"

"Holy shit! What did you buy?"

"I told you I somehow agreed to buy a pound of each of the jasmine pearls. But apparently when I was trying all the other varietals, my *'I like'* translates to *'Yes, I shall take them all, many pounds, please.'*"

"What, you got ten different kinds? Are you going to have tea parties every day with your dogs?"

"No, just four. Two jasmine, one breakfast-type tea, and apparently a bag of their 'finest,' which was a hundred and eighty dollars a pound! And I'm all *'What is this?'* and she says it's organic bird tongue and then she fucking winks! What does the wink mean? Did I just accidentally ugly-American-loud-talk my way into buying heroin or something? Or am I actually drinking a tea made from the genuine inside of bird's mouths?"

Angie clucks her tongue. "Jen, you're being a dumb ass. Why didn't you just say no?"

"Because she didn't understand me! I couldn't say no in Chinese."

"You realize you could have called Wendy or Jen at that point. Both of them know conversational Chinese." Stupid show-off multilingual friends.

"Yeah, thanks. That would have been really valuable information to have, like, five minutes ago."

"Then you should have shaken your head to mean no."

Quietly, I admit, "I thought if I protested too much, she'd send me home with a gremlin."

"And now . . . you've lost me. What does that mean?"

"Not important. What IS important is that my credit card was an instant Berlitz course. As soon as she had an authorization number and a signature, she became fluent! Like she spoke transactional English only."

"Seriously?"

"Yeah, it was a little mind-blowing. After I signed my slip, she was all, *'Hey, thanks for coming in. I hope you enjoy everything.'* Like the second she had my money she was allowed to break character. She still had an accent, but nothing like what she'd had twenty minutes earlier."

"Do you feel gypped at all?"

"Honestly? Not really." I recently found out the guys who row the gondolas at the Venetian in Vegas aren't actually Italian, even though they speak with a heavy accent; it's just part of the act. I'm betting that's what happened here today, but I can't say I mind because I *felt* like I was really having a cultural experience in the middle of it. Maybe this is why places like Disneyland are so successful—everyone pretty much gets that it's just a sweaty college student in a Mickey suit, but in the moment? It's magic.

"Great. But, um . . . at what point did you purchase the drugs?"

"Shoot, I almost forgot! The lady starts to put my various teas into these metal containers, and in my head I'm all *'Why do these look familiar?'* and I realize these are the exact canisters they found in Claire Danes's backpack in the movie *Brokedown Palace*! Filled with drugs! And I'm all *'Holy shit, the TSA is going to think I'm transporting drugs— which may or may not be the case because what the fuck is bird tongue and why was she winking? I'm going to get sent to a Thai prison!'* So I ask the lady, *'Hey, am I going to have trouble taking these on the plane? Won't someone think these big containers of leaves are drugs?'* Then she says, *'Oh, just put my card with them. They'll know they're from a tea shop.'*"

"Ha! Right! You won't get hassled because you have a *business card*!

It's the perfect crime; Colombian drug lords do it this way all the time. I know because I watched a special about in on the Discovery Channel."

"Really?

"No, dumb ass! I'm kidding. And why would you go to prison in Thailand? Do they have a special dumb-ass extradition deal with the U.S.?" Angie's laughing so hard she's practically choking, but I can hear that she's trying to be supportive.[128] "Listen, if you're so worried, why don't you just FedEx the stuff back home instead of carrying it with you to . . . ? Where are you headed next?"

"Los Angeles."

"Instead of carting your drugs to LA, you mule."

"They aren't drugs![129] You're right, though. Shipping is a smart idea. I've already done it a couple of times. Actually, on Monday I bought Fletch a jacket in Portland, and I sent the package to his office since he's not home during the day to get it. The thing is, I included some of my laundry in the box because I'd overpacked. And when he got it yesterday, he was all 'Thanks for sending your dirty underpants to my office. That wasn't weird to show the guys in security *at all*.' But since he works in the Sears Tower and they screen every box pretty closely, I'll just send it to my house. Excellent call. Oh, hey! Taxi! Taxi! Yay! A cab is stopping!"

"Okay, I'm going to let you go. Where are you off to? More shopping?"

"Oh, God, no. I can't spend any more money. Seriously, I just bought all the tea in China."

"No, you bought all the tea in China*town*. Travel safely, see you soon, and go have some protein!"

....
[128]But FAIL. Massive fail.
[129]I think.

"I will. Thanks! Bye!" I hop into the cab, placing my bag of canisters on the seat.

"Where to, miss?"

I quickly run through my mental Rolodex of all the enriching activities left to do in San Francisco. I could check out the MoMA or the DeYoung Museum or, if I want to keep with today's Oriental theme, I could hit the Asian Art Museum. I could stroll in the Yerba Buena gardens or I could explore any one of the dozens of art galleries. I could buy a classic book and read it in one of a hundred picturesque settings. I could do an architectural tour or visit Dave Eggers's learning center at 826 Valencia. I could have any cuisine I want at some of the world's best restaurants. All I have to do is tell my driver where I want to go.

"Can you take me to the place with the sea lions?"

Don't judge me.

I had as much culture as I can handle for one day.

Besides, I'm sure they don't sell gremlins on Pier 39, and I could really use a corn dog.

To: stacey_at_home

From: jen_at_home

Subject: Whitesnake

Still haven't gotten the hang of these stupid extensions yet.

I just tried to let the hair go all curly, and when I was done drying it, I was all, "Hey! I look just like Tawny Kitaen!"

Then I went downstairs to show Fletch and he was all, "Wow, you look just like David Coverdale."

Argh.

Shear Jenius

"Tell me everything!"

"I don't even know where to start," I say. Stacey and I are seeing each other for the first time in six weeks. "Then again, nothing I've done was nearly as cool as what you were doing."

Stacey and her friends are back from a three-week trip of a lifetime, going back and forth between an uncle's villa in the south of France and Paris. Her days were filled with scouring local farmers' markets and cooking gourmet meals with the ingredients, reading great books poolside, walking all over Paris, and visiting churches and museums and other famous landmarks. Basically everything she did in France would have dovetailed perfectly into my Jenaissance, and it's a shame she's already plenty cultured. Then again, I wonder if I wouldn't have spent the whole time eating at Mr. Donut and complaining about French toilet paper, like I did when I was sixteen.

Stacey sits back on the couch and crosses her arms. "You are a complete dork. I want to know what you've been up to, so start talking."

I scrunch my eyes closed and try to think. "I can't remember what I e-mailed you last. Did I tell you about the black tar heroin I bought in Chinatown?"

"You did. Ever find out what organic bird tongue was?"

I bob my head, causing an avalanche of all this stupid hair. Did I mention these extensions are making me mental? First, I had no clue how much upkeep they'd take. Every night when I sit down to watch television, I have to spend an hour separating them, or else they'll turn into dreadlocks.[130] I have to use special shampoo and only boar-bristle brushes because plastic ones would yank out the bonds. But I forgot one morning when I was on tour and accidentally pulled out four sections, thus giving myself a heart attack because I thought I was going instantaneously bald.

I left the pieces on the counter because I didn't know if I should save them or what, and when I got back to my room, housekeeping was there. And the poor cleaning lady was all, *"Does missus have the cancer?"*

Now that I've got a couple of inches of growth between the glue and my scalp, the extensions are more like a whole headful of tiny bear traps. My hair's kind of like a small utility belt and would come in handy if I wanted to, say, carry batteries or a small flashlight or something up there.

(Sidebar: On the bright side, my sunglasses always stay firmly in place.)

....

[130]Suddenly I have a lot more compassion for all those terrible shots of Britney's weave. It'd be impossible to take care of all that hair and two kids, y'all.

Every time I try to run my hands through my hair, my fingers get tangled up. I spent fifteen minutes in Target last week trying to extricate my bracelets from my ponytail. Mortifying.

I never realized walking around with an extra head's worth of hair would be the equivalent of wearing a woolly cap all the time. I'm constantly sweating, and I've taken to carrying napkins so I can blot my face whenever needed. Which is often. Somewhere there's a Hindi chick with a sleek, sassy bob who's thanking Shiva daily that she's rid of all this foolishness.

Personally, I'd take every bit of it out myself right now, except I'll be damned if all the big hair doesn't make me look almost exactly like I did in college.

"Bird tongue is definitely a leaf, not a drug." I slip a pencil out of my purse and surreptitiously begin to scratch. Did I mention the itching? Oh, yeah, there's itching. So much itching, I want to tear my scalp off. "I did some research on bird tongue and supposedly it's all fancy and gourmet, but the tea it makes isn't anything spectacular. I thought it might give me super *strongs* or be like an organic amphetamine or something, but pretty much it's just green tea. Maybe it's making my immune system all tough, but in terms of flavor, eh. I'd rather have the hundred and eighty bucks."

"At least you got a great story out of the experience."

"No, pretty much I just confirmed how much more work I need to do on myself."

Stacey pulls a face. "Well, I strongly disagree, but what else?"

I got done with my tour two weeks ago, but it feels like forever. "Um, oh! Check this out—I'm in Los Angeles—"

"After San Francisco?"

Scratch, scratch, scratch. I dig deeper with the pencil, and I think I feel the lead break my skin. That can't be good. Maybe I should have used the eraser side?

"Right. I'm in LA and I'm in this car driven by a complete maniac. Traffic was brutal, so my schedule was beyond tight. To make up for it, my driver, Richard Fucking Petty, was taking shortcuts, like, on the sidewalk, no joke. Thank God no one walks there, or we'd have left a trail of bodies in our wake. I was in such a state of terror every hair on my arms was standing up. I kept demanding he slow down and he was all *'You want to be on time or not?'*"

"Nice. *'Would you like to die a horrible death on this canyon curve or would you prefer to be ten minutes late? 'Cause I'm cool either way.'*"

"Exactly. We finally get to a street where the traffic's at a crawl, and I'm all *'Whew! Not dead!'* And we were out of the canyon, where there's spotty cell reception, so I wanted to call Fletch and see how he was doing. While I'm talking to him, I see something out of the corner of my eye. There's some idiot in traffic next to me, and he's waving his arms wildly and shouting to a bunch of people eating out on the sidewalk. Plus, he's this huge guy in a tiny convertible. Like, he could never put the top up because he was too big. Seriously, he was like a monkey driving a Matchbox on YouTube or something. All he needed was a fez. I tell Fletch about it and I'm all *'What's with that asshole?'*"

Stacey grits her teeth. "I *hate* Los Angeles. Every time I go there, I hope it'll be the last time."

"Yeah, I've been saying it should just break off into the sea for years.[131] I just don't get that place. I mean, the weather's beautiful, but I would never, ever put up with the hassle of trying to get from point A to point B. It's as crowded as New York, but lacks New York's panache.

....

[131]Because it bears repeating, Nevada needs a coastline!

Like, New York is elbow to elbow but it's because the city's so filled with exciting stuff. All I saw in LA was tattoo parlors, cosmetic surgeons, and strip malls. Also, everyone wearing Ed Hardy? No." I feel claustrophobic[132] just thinking about LA and that makes me itchy again. I put my pencil back to work. "Anyway, we drive past the arm-waggling jackass, and I turn around because I want to see what kind of mutant he is."

"What was wrong with him?"

"What was wrong with him was that he was *Vince Vaughn*." Stacey's eyes widen. "And, *poof!* Just like that the crush I've had on him since *Swingers* vanished. The way he was carrying on in that car was like he really believed he was money, and it was gross. But it's fine because I've totally already transferred my crush to Denis Leary."

"He is a beautiful man. People don't always see that because he's so damn funny. Also, he's really tall!" Stacey worked as a roadie back in college[133] and met him a few times. "What else is going on?"

"Oh, you know how I wrote a lot about my college roommate Joanna in *Pretty in Plaid*?"

Joanna and I were BFF until she graduated and moved home to Chicago. We never fought or had any kind of falling-out, except for that one time when we were freshmen and I was stupid[134] and decided to divide the room in half with a giant piece of duct tape like on some sixties sitcom. Otherwise, we were more like sisters than friends. Over time, though, our lives led us in different directions, and we lost touch. I hadn't even talked to her for about twelve years; then a few months ago, I found her on Facebook and we reconnected.

....

[132]And possibly a little dirty.

[133]Seriously, does she not need to write a memoir about this?

[134]Read: drunk on California Coolers.

"I'm at my Chicago signing, reading a piece about her, and way at the back of the crowd, I see a hand go up. And the person says, *'I'm Joanna, and I just want to say how proud I am of you.'* Honest to God, that was the very best moment of the whole tour."[135]

"Aw, that just made my heart smile," Stacey says, hugging her arms into her chest.

"Doesn't it? We've been hanging out lately, and it turns out she's the exact same person I always loved. We promised that we're never going to lose each other again. She was such a positive influence on me, always countering my cynicism with happiness and joy. I feel really lucky to have her back in my life."

"I suspect she's got some great stories."

I snort in an unbecoming fashion. "You think I'm a dumb ass now? You should have seen me at seventeen. Anyway, the best part is Fletch and I went to Joanna's house last week, and I got to hang out with her husband and kids. She has kids! I'm all *'How can you have children? You're still eighteen.'* Her ten-year-old looks exactly like the Joanna I met when we were freshmen and has the same kind of ebullience, too. I told Joanna, *'All this kid needs is a pair of Keds and a bottle of Little Kings and I'd swear it was 1985 again.'* Now I feel like I should send Facebook a thank-you note."

"I love when Facebook's more than just a place to play Mafia Wars."[136]

"Or to be stalked by creepy high school boyfriends," I agree.

"Anything else we need to cover, or are we all caught up?"

....

[135]You ladies who tailgated at my Atlanta event? You come in a very close second.

[136]When Stacey invited me to join her crime family, I named myself the Lacoste Accoster.

"I guess that's it, except . . . um, can you help me get this pencil out of my hair?"

With my updates complete—and once Stacey stops laughing—we launch into a long discussion of *Project Runway*s past. We should be watching it right now, but with the Lifetime/Bravo legal battle over which network will get the show still not settled, all show fans are temporarily auf'd. As we're reminiscing about Santino's brilliant Tim Gunn impersonation, I suddenly snap my fingers. "Oh, my God, I didn't even tell you my big news! I wangled my way into being invited to Authors Night!"

"Which is?"

"A fund-raiser for the East Hampton Library in New York. But your question should be *who's that* because you're going to die when you hear who the honorary chairmen are. Brace yourself. . . . I'm talking Jay McInerney, Candace Bushnell, and Alec Baldwin! Plus, there's going to be a hundred other authors there, now including me! And the best part? Bethenny Frankel from *Real Housewives* is going to be there! Could you die?"

"I could die!"

"You should come!" Yes! That's brilliant!

She gives me a wry grin before saying, "I spent enough on vacations for a while."

"Okay. That makes sense. Anyway, after the big book-signing cocktail reception dealie, there are private dinners for some of the featured authors at mansions all over the Hamptons. I'm not a featured author— and why would I be?—but to go to a dinner all I have to do is buy a ticket. No one knows who's hosting which dinner until all the parties are assigned, but one of the hosts is Rudy Giuliani! I could go to Rudy Giuliani's house! How surreal is that? I mean, six years ago my electricity's being cut off and my car's getting repossessed and I'm being evicted from my apartment,[137] and now I'm all, *'Yeah, havin' dinner with Rudy in the Hamptons, what of it?'"*

"That's absolutely crazy. How will you make sure you get his party?"

"I went through the list of authors and tried to pick which one he'd most likely want. There's a dinner with this general who was in charge of the armed forces in Iraq. I looked him up on Amazon, and his book was paired with a bunch of conservative books, so I figure that's my best bet."

"Smart. And hey, that dinner can be your goal."

"Exactly!"

As I've been forwarding my cultural education, I've lost some steam because I couldn't figure out an end goal. When I was working on *Such a Pretty Fat*, my objective was to be healthier, and I had ways of calculating that. I could step on the scale, measure my cholesterol, check my blood pressure, et cetera.

"Be less of a lazy dumb ass" is kind of amorphous in terms of goals. How do I measure that? Count all the times I don't get pencils caught in my hair? Not poisoning myself every couple of days? Actually getting off the couch to find the remote control instead of watching yet another Snuggie infomercial?

Now, "Be able to carry on a conversation at Rudy Giuliani's dinner table without breaking into terror sweat," that's concrete. Plus, at the book event, I'll see Candace Bushnell and I can honestly tell her, *"Oh, yeah, Baudelaire? I've been reading him for a while now. Big fan."*

This event will really be my test, my version of the Empire Ball. This will be my chance to move among figurative royalty and see if I can blend in with them.

....

[137]Want to know more? Buy *Bitter Is the New Black*, available at fine booksellers everywhere.

For some reason, I've always linked the idea of being cultured with the notion of having class. I realize they're two separate entities, yet in my mind they're inexorably tied. I feel like one can't be classy if not first cultured. I liken this concept to Maslow's hierarchy—sure, it's possible to be self-actualized even when one's physiological needs aren't met, but I suspect it's way easier to reach that point on a full stomach.

In my mind, culture is one of the building blocks of class. And I admit my logic could be specious at best, but that's what's guiding me.

"This couldn't have worked out better. I'm so happy for you."

"The thing is, there's one problem. I want to look my best at the event, which means I have to keep this stupid hair on all summer."

"Hey, sorry I missed your call last week. I was out having an adventure." I'm in the kitchen, on the phone by the counter.

"Adventure? What kind? You weren't out chasing down the homeless again, were you?" Angie sounds awfully concerned on the other end of the line.

I let out an exasperated sigh. "Why do you people always assume the worst of me?"

"Because it's usually true?" Angie teases.

"Well, then maybe that guy shouldn't have flipped me off when I told him if *he's* allowed to throw my garbage around the alley, then *I'm* allowed to hit him with my car.[138] And it only happened once," I concede.

"If you ever move to the burbs, you realize the homeowners' asso-

---

[138]You'd be surprised how fast a crackhead with a shopping cart can move when properly motivated.

ciation will frown on your attempts to run over children with your riding mower."

"Then they should stay off my lawn. Anyway, I had an adventure!"

"Are you going to tell me about your adventure, or shall I just turn on the news?" Angie asks.

"No, no, it was nothing like that." Seriously, you threaten one vagrant with vehicular manslaughter, and suddenly everyone thinks YOU'RE the jerk. "Last week Gina and I went up to Little India on Devon."

"Cool! You plan to ditch the Lacostes for saris?" Actually, saris come in the most gorgeous fabrics, and if I could figure out how to style a preppy outfit out of one, I would.

"Not exactly. Whenever it gets warm out, Gina goes up there to get a henna tattoo. And then she gets Indian food afterward. She invited me to join her because she thought it sounded cultural. But I told her, *'I'd love to join you but I hate Indian food.'* And then I thought about the whole 'diving in' business and said, *'Although I'm not a hundred percent sure I've ever even had Indian food.'*"

"Wait a minute. I remember when Fletch went through an Indian-food phase last year. You kept bitching about how your downstairs smelled like grad-school housing."

"Heh, I completely forgot! You're right. Hey, you're a really good listener." Last year Fletch bought a bunch of Indian simmer sauces at Trader Joe's because he got on this whole *"I'm going to bring my lunch to work"* thing. He kept taking these sauces and trying to create dishes around them. Except he's not familiar enough with the cuisine to improvise anything, and nothing he produced was edible. I tried to tell him it was terrible but he insisted, *"No, it's fine,"* and a few days later I caught him sneaking the leftovers into the garbage disposal. We had a little come-to-Jesus meetin' about it, and I made him promise never to cook Indian again or else I'd make him eat the results.

"Anyway, before we even got to the restaurant, we stopped in this salon so Gina could get hennaed, which was fascinating. The girl did this whole elaborate design on Gina's shoulder with lots of dots and paisleys. She did it completely freehand, and it was beautiful. I wanted one, but I couldn't figure out a place on me to have it done. Not so much my style. But I figured, hey, I'm here, I should do *something*, so I decided on threading."

"Remind me what that is. Central Michigan's not exactly the threading capital of the world."

"Most people say it's an ancient technique using two twisted pieces of string to remove hair in lieu of tweezing or waxing. And yet I maintain it's an Indian torture device. Remember those horrible Epilady things from about fifteen years ago that ripped each individual hair out from the root?"

"I'm shuddering just thinking about it. The Epilady was as bad as childbirth." She corrects herself. "No, worse; I had drugs during my C-sections."

"With threading, instead of tearing out a tiny strip of hair at a time, it yanks a million out. Hard. I had my eyebrows done and it hurt like a bitch."

I'm not sure if threading's technically supposed to cause pain or if somehow my extensions and the threader were in cahoots. I get the feeling the woman operating the thread was somehow avenging her distant pilgrim cousin's sacrifice. In which case, who can blame her?

I continue. "Thing is, she used cuticle scissors to trim down the thicker part of my brows first, so now I look like frigging Carrot Top."

Angie barks with laughter. "Excellent!"

"And then—then! Because I'm a genius, I told the lady to get all the peach fuzz off my cheeks. But you know what? Those tiny golden hairs serve a purpose. Apparently they act as your skin's version of pressed powder, dulling all the little lines and imperfections. Now my face is completely naked, and for only seven dollars, I look ten years older."[139]

"So you don't recommend threading. Noted. Was lunch any better?"

"Fortunately, yes. When I told Gina that Indian food kind of scared me, she was this total voice of reason about it. She explained that I'm familiar with ninety percent of the ingredients in most Indian dishes; they're just combined in a way I've never tasted."

"Isn't it superhot?"

"See? That's what I asked. I'm the biggest baby in the world when it comes to anything spicy. I don't mind the flavor, but my colon is delicate from years of accidentally poisoning myself, and I don't enjoy crying on the toilet. Anyway, Gina said there are a ton of nonspicy dishes. Do you know much about Indian food?"

Angie guffaws. "We went to Culver's last night for butter burgers; what do you think?"

"Your seven-year-old isn't begging for curry in his lunch box?"

"Don't get me started. I just turned the younger ones' room into Guantánamo Bay. I spent a week telling them to clean it up because it stank, and they refused. I finally go in there to do it myself because the smell was unholy. Turns out those little bastards had been stuffing their skidmarked undies behind the dresser for weeks, so no wonder I've been washing the same three pairs over and over."

....

[139]Which shaves off the ten-year benefit I get from the frigging extensions. I can't win.

"So you're waterboarding them? Kind of harsh for someone who doesn't spank."

"Ha, no," she laughs. "But I stripped their room bare. I took out every single item except their beds, a chair, and their dressers. If they can't keep it organized, *I will organize it for them.*"

"How'd they react?"

"Don't know. I'll tell you when they get home from practice. And I'll tell you what, if they keep it up, I'm putting them in jumpsuits, too. Anyway, enough about my household terrorists. What'd you eat?"

I glance down at Maisy spread across my feet. Once in a while when Angie tells me heartwarming stories about her kids, I wonder for a minute if we didn't make a mistake by opting for pets instead of children. Then I hear a word like "skidmark," and I get real comfortable with our choices.

"Um . . ." I try to recollect all the delicious tastes and scents from that day. "We started with samosas, which are these deep-fried dumplings filled with veggies and spices. I made Gina order everything. She said the rule of thumb was to stay away from anything 'vindaloo' and stick with 'tandoori.' Then I got this mixed-grill thing that had lamb and chicken—no beef, by the way—done a bunch of different ways, and it was served with this phenomenal bread called naan. Speaking of bread, you know how when you go to dinner, you get a couple of rolls in the beginning, and then it's never really thought of again?"

"Not at Culver's, but yes, I understand the concept."

"Well, it's a whole different ball game with Indian food. This place had something like fifteen different kinds of bread—some of it filled with herbs and spices, some of it with vegetables, some of it with meat. We got a mixed basket, so I got to try a bunch of stuff. And you know what? In a country with bread that good, I can see why it would be easy to be a vegetarian. That's probably why they're all thin."

Angie snorts. "Uh-huh. *That's* why. Not dysentery or cholera or, you know, poverty."

"Oh. Right. Anyway, I brought a ton of leftovers home, and when Fletch tasted it all, he was incredulous. '*This isn't at all like the stuff I made.*' No shit. But the best part is, being there gave me a brilliant idea."

"You're going to stop eating beef?"

"*Pfft,* what am I, Gandhi? No. Consider *My Fair Lady* for a minute."

"Certainly, guv'nah."

"What did Eliza Doolittle have to do to pass herself off as a lady? Think about it. She had to shake her accent, right? But remember when she's having tea for the first time with Henry Higgins's mom and friends? She had the accent down, but her conversation was way inappropriate. She kept talking about her dead aunt and how someone had 'done her in.'"

I pause so Angie can drink in the genius of what I'm saying.

She neatly fills in the gaps. "And then they all went out for tandoori chicken. And had their eyebrows threaded before getting hair extensions. The new version's a smash hit on Broadway. People say it's better than *Cats.*"

"Shut it, smart-ass. I wasn't done. I said I wanted to include a fine dining element as part of my whole cultural Jenaissance, but that may be shortsighted. Sure, I'd like to use the right knife when buttering my bread in public, but that won't resolve how picky and narrow-minded I can be about food. With a couple of notable exceptions, I ordered the same exact meal in restaurants until I was eighteen years old—a cheeseburger, fries, and an orange soda."

"Kids like burgers. They prefer simple. That's why you see fish sticks on the little menu and not smoked salmon."

"Yes, but eventually *they* grow out of it. I'm not sure I did. I just

upgraded my love of burgers to steak and of fries to au gratin potatoes.[140]
But I don't want to be Miss Mayonnaise McWhitebread of the Connect-
icut McWhitebreads, getting all grossed out or throwing a fit if I don't go
to a steakhouse. I don't want to be the asshole ordering chicken fingers
when everyone else is having chicken tikka."

"Makes sense. You can only claim that you're 'allergic' to food that
scares you for so long."

I love how Angie gets it even when I'm not sure I can explain it.
"Exactly, and from what I've seen, dining's becoming more of an art
form. With food, the envelope is perpetually being pushed. I mean, people watch shows like *Top Chef* and *No Reservations* and a million other
programs on the food networks, and they're constantly trying new stuff.
Me, I've always been so afraid to taste anything I haven't already had, but
really, what's the worst that can happen? I miss a meal? I'm a little hungry? I get food poisoning? Not like *that* hasn't happened before."

I hear her trying to muffle a giggle. "Yeah, weekly."

I'd argue but she's not really exaggerating. "My plan is to open my
mind and palate to different cuisines exactly like I'm trying with the arts
and literature. So . . . I'm going to EAT THE WORLD!"

I wait for her to shower me with kudos for this breakthrough. She
doesn't. "Meaning?"

"I've looked up every kind of ethnic restaurant in this city, and I'm
going to hit them all. Do you know how much I've never tasted? I mean,
there's Serbian and Colombian and Malaysian and Afghan and Armenian,
and I have to look at my list for the rest of them, but you get the gist. And
maybe this isn't keeping with *My Fair Lady* word for word, but it defi-

----

[140]And orange soda to a nice, citrus-y sauvignon blanc.

nitely is in spirit. The bottom line is, if Eliza hadn't learned to dance at some point offscreen, she'd never have sold her total transformation at the ball. So, what do you think? Sublime or ridiculous?"

"Sublime. Definitely sublime."

"Cool, because first up, I'm slated to go out for Ethiopian food with Gina and Stacey. Which is weird because, not to be an asshole, but it didn't even occur to me that they had food."

"Is it too late to change my answer to ridiculous?"

AltgeldShrugged Twitter:
Never in the history of ever has one person stuffed so much crap in a single carry-on bag.

C·H·A·P·T·E·R T·W·E·L·V·E

Wickedly Imperfect

*W*orld, prepare to be eaten!

When I ran my "eat the world" concept by Fletch, he was not without questions. Or doubts.

"You're going to write a book about food right after one on weight loss? How does that work?" he wondered, running his hand down his face.

"Number one, opening myself up to new flavors isn't exactly the same thing as deciding to *'SuperSize Me,'* and number two, there was a book in between this one and that one, so . . . shut up. Plus, I'm trying to broaden my palate, and maybe other cultures have really delicious foods that are also superhealthy?"

He grudgingly admitted, "I guess it's possible."

"You don't sound convinced."

"I'm not."

I waggled a finger at him. "Listen up, mister. The next time *Top Chef* is on, watch it with me. You'll see that almost every single gourmand on that damn show is thin. Plus Padma? The host? Is like one of the hottest women on the planet, and she eats everything![141] Way I see it, there's got to be a correlation between satisfaction and not overdoing it. If so, I intend to find it."

"Okay . . . but so you know, I have visions of this turning into some kind of International Donut Taste-Off."

Oh.

That's kind of a good point.

I'm already a fan of Cuban sandwiches, Cuban coffee, the smell of smoke from illegal Cuban cigars, and all things Desi Arnaz, so Cuba feels like a fine[142] place for my maiden solo dive into the ocean of World Cuisine. Plus, there are so many Cuban restaurants by my house, I'm not sure how I've avoided them thus far.

I decide to try a restaurant called 90 Miles Cuban Café not because it's well reviewed or the menu seems appetizing, but because when I looked it up on Google Maps and selected "street view," I discovered they had a parking lot.

For me, taste and value and service are pretty much always trumped by convenience. One might offer the best product in the universe, but if I have to make a bunch of left-hand turns without benefit of traffic arrows

---

[141]Even her scars are sexy.

[142]Read: safe.

or need to parallel park once I get there, your business may as well not even exist. Offer me a small lot with well-spaced yellow lines or, even better, a valet, and you'll win my patronage for life.

I decide to brush up on my (essentially nonexistent) knowledge of Cuban food before I go. I pull up Wikipedia[143] and read that Cuban food blends African, Caribbean, and Spanish cuisines, which is exactly zero help, as I'm unfamiliar with most of those flavors. I also learn how Cuban food uses some ingredients common in Mexican food, but the spices and cooking methods are different, so again, I have no real map of what's to come. Basically I want to know if I'm accidentally going to bite into a flaming hot pepper so I can have a ramekin of ranch dressing ready, but my research proves inconclusive. I do find out that the bread in Cuban sandwiches is made with lard, which explains my affinity for it.

I get to the restaurant, park easily,[144] and enter. The place is packed, which I take as a good omen, particularly since it's almost three o'clock on a weekday. The air's perfumed with the scent of grilled beef and caramelized onions, another excellent sign. The aroma reminds me of the time my mom wanted to make our old house smell nice for a real estate open house, so she cooked a bunch of peppers and onions right before people arrived.[145]

I take my place in line and try to make sense of the menu board. Everything sounds tasty and uses innocuous ingredients, such as beans, rice, vegetables, and nonoffal cuts of meat, but I'm still perplexed.

There's an employee standing next to me, wiping the soda cooler. He observes, "You're confused."

....

[143]Is there anything Wikipedia can't tell us? I mean, if you're somewhat flexible on accuracy?

[144]Yay!

[145]In somewhat related news, the house took almost three years to sell.

"You're right," I reply. "I need help figuring out what to order. I want the most 'authentically Cuban' item on the menu. What do you suggest?"

He places his towel on the counter and takes a step back to scrutinize the menu board with me. "I'd suggest either the bistec—it's flank steak grilled with Cuban spice—or the ropa vieja—shredded beef slow-cooked in a tomato base. I'd also do one of these." He opens the cooler and pulls out some kind of Spanish-language soda. "You like pineapple?"

"I adore pineapple." Not long ago, I bought a gorgeous fresh pineapple and left it sitting on the counter. For some reason, all the cats made friends with it. They nuzzled it and elbowed one another out of the way in order to sit closest to it. They loved that damn pineapple, and I have no *idea* why. But I never even got to eat it, because every time I went to cut it, they'd swarm me. Eventually, I had to toss it out when it went bad.

Wait, that's not the whole truth.

I cut off the top, made the cats pose for pictures with it on their heads like a bunch of tiny little Carmen Mirandas, and then I threw it away.[146]

"You'll want this." He hands me a brightly colored can of Jupina. "I'd also get one of those." He points to something toasty and golden in an encased plastic case next to the cash register. "It's like a croissant, and it's filled with guava and cream cheese. It's called a—"

"Sold!" I shout. He's a bit taken aback, so I explain, "You had me at croissant." He grins and goes back to his cleaning.

I decide on the bistec, not because it necessarily sounds better, but because I'm wearing a yellow polo shirt, and I don't want to dot it with ropa vieja splatters. The meal comes with rice, black beans, and plantains, and I'm interested to taste their slant on these dishes.

....

[146]Suck on that, PETA.

I place my order and pay, then wait on a stool by the window. The waiting area's festive, full of photos of palm trees and sparkly beaches and happy fishermen reeling in giant swordfish.

When my food's ready, I have to grip my carryout container by the bottom because it's so heavy. But that doesn't mean I'm going to eat it all, *Fletch.* Even if the smell practically intoxicates me on the way home and I have to struggle to keep my hands on the wheel and out of the bag for fear of getting a DWI.[147]

Once home, I arrange about a third of the meal on a plate. I lay down a bed of rice, top it with a piece of the bistec, and wedge my plantains in next to it. The black beans are the consistency of soup, so I put those in a ramekin. I tear off half of the pastry, and guava cream cheese oozes out. My intention is to save it for dessert, but I might not be able to wait.

I'm tentative at first because I can't guarantee the meat wasn't basted in kill-the-gringo chili peppers. But a few chews in, I realize the seasoning evokes a nice, smoky taste. There're garlic and sweet peppers and onions, and nothing sets my mouth on fire. The rice is just right—not too hard, not too mushy, and the same can be said about the beans. The plantains aren't sticky-sweet like they can be when they're too ripe, and overall, the meal perfectly balances flavor and texture. The pastry's creamy, tangy, and flaky—three of my favorite adjectives—and I wolf down the entire half, finishing it first.

Maybe there will be a little bit of International Donut Taste-Off in this. Shut up.

I take my time and savor each bite. I try pairing different things together—the tender rice is even better combined with the beans' rich broth, and the mellow saltiness of the beef is enhanced by a chunk of

....

[147]Driving While Ingesting.

plantain. And I realize everything's more delicious when followed by a swig of Jupina, which is so magical, I have to call Fletch and narrate my lunch.

"Why has our country never created a pineapple soda?" I demand.

"Are you looking for a dissertation on America's taste in nonalcoholic carbonated beverages, or are you being rhetorical?" he inquires.

"I mean, what's wrong with us? We invented lightbulbs and telephones and the sixty-nine Mustang, but no one ever thought, '*Hey, why don't we throw a little pineapple juice into this here can of 7-Up?*' I tell you what, if I lived in a place that sold Jupina, I'd never leave."

He snorts. "You do; it's called Logan Square."

"*Pfft*, you know what I meant."

"Yeah, and yet with all that free and clear access to pineapple soda, can you believe some Cubans still float over here on doors and inner tubes? Sure is a mystery."

"Don't patronize me; I'm just saying the soda's really good. Also, the country looks beautiful. I mean, Hemingway spent *all* that time down there, right? And on *Road Rules: Semester at Sea*, they visited Cuba because oily Veronica needed to meet her grandmother, which was totally emotional, and for the first time that season, I didn't want to kick her until she was dead. Anyway, the landscape was nothing but lush greens and hot pinks, all surrounded by palm trees[148] and an endless blue ocean."

"That sounds great," he concurs.

"The whole scene was lovely—lots of tropical birds and big-game fishing."

Fletch adds, "Think of how tan you'd get if you lived there. Plus, you could drink all the pineapple soda you wanted on the beach."

....

[148]I'm the biggest sucker in the world for palm trees.

"Tell me about it! That stuff's meant to be consumed with a little sand between the toes. And what if someone served it in an actual pineapple? Ooh, or a coconut? Heaven! By the way, did you know Cuba used to be a huge hot spot for American tourists? It was like Florida Jr."

"You're right. Sounds like a terrific place. And perhaps when you move to Havana in search of your precious fruit soda, Fidel will ask you to write his newsletters."

"Wait, are you mocking me?"

He is the very model of innocence. "Not me."

"Whatever. My point is the food was delish and there's a ton left over, so I'm saving it for your dinner."

"I look forward to it. But hey, do me a favor," he requests.

I reply, "Sure, what do you need?"

"Try not to become a Communist before I get home, okay? Bye!"

Pfft. Communism is based on egalitarianism and the equal distribution of resources.

And I'm totally going to violate those principles when I eat Fletch's share of the pastry.

I spend the next week toggling between random cuisines. So far, I'm a huge fan of Mediterranean food. Who knew the humble chickpea was so versatile? And much as I love pork and beef, suddenly I'm all *lamb, where've you been my whole life?*

The one regional cuisine I haven't enjoyed is Swedish. I figured I'd be all over it, considering how much I adore the meatballs and lingonberry sauce in the IKEA food court. But when we ate at a Swedish joint, they served us a dish that was scary enough to change my opinion of the entire country. Fletch ordered potato sausages, which sound great, right? We imagined thick country pork sausage, nicely seasoned with sage, blended into a chunky patty, studded with red potatoes, and browned to perfection. Maybe they'd even come with gravy!

What we got was a bowl of two-inch-long glistening pink tubes. They were so phallic that we had to cover them with a napkin. Gina remarked that we'd been served a side of castration. Fletch spent the rest of the meal with his legs crossed, and I was so nauseated that I couldn't eat at all. Do me a favor, Sweden—please just stick to affordable flat-pack furniture and food court meatballs.

(Sidebar: Okay, I ate my cinnamon roll, but that still doesn't make this an International Donut Taste-Off.)

Between meals, I've been watching edifying opera DVDs. Surprisingly, opera appeals to me. I didn't expect it to be so engrossing! I thought it was going to be a few single people slowly trolling across stage wearing bustiers with Viking horns over their long blond braids. And then I realized my expectations were based on Bugs Bunny's *What's Opera, Doc?* and I had a Shame Rattle reoccurrence.

I really enjoy how many folks can be onstage singing at some points, in all kinds of costumes.[149] I really connect with the storytelling element, too, so I'm glad some of the DVDs have subtitles. Because I've been able to follow along, I've learned that operas are *dark*, dude. Honest to God, every single one of them's filled with betrayal and lust, and people are always getting stabbed and dying in one another's arms. Reality television—or soap operas, for that matter—have nothing on *this*.

So far *Carmen*'s my favorite, probably because I know the music best. Seems like every fifteen-year-old figure skater ever has performed

----

[149]I haven't seen a Viking helmet yet!

to "Habanera," all painted up with smoky eyes, wearing latticed Gypsy outfits and big flowers in their baby-fine hair. Considering that "Habanera" *is* about Carmen choosing who she wants to take as her next l-o-v-e-r, the inappropriateness of a child doing a triple axel to it boggles the mind.

I love how opera music is as rich and complex as a good bowl of carbonara. When I listen, it booms throughout the media room, and I practically swoon every time the tenors sing. I think with opera I feel the music as much as I listen to it.

The problem is, as much as I'm enjoying the DVDs, I'm only watching them on DVD. I haven't been to a real opera yet, but not for lack of will. Chicago's opera run is limited and currently out of season, which is a shame because if I want to truly experience opera—and I do, desperately—I must be there live.

I need to put on a ball gown[150] and sit with everyone in the audience while they stir in anticipation. I want to use my funky little binoculars[151] to watch the orchestra as they prepare. (By the way, is there any sound that quickens the pulse more than an orchestra warming up? Whenever I hear the random strings and woodwind instruments all discordant, I just know something great's about to happen.) I want to see if a wineglass[152] actually cracks when the soprano hits her highest note.

In short, I want the whole meal.

....

[150]First I need to get a ball gown.

[151]Then I need to get funky little binoculars.

[152]Sure they let you bring drinks into the opera, right?

My opera and World Cuisine educations are on temporary hold since I'm on my way to New York! I guess I shouldn't have mocked Stacey last year when she entered all those crazy recipe contests, because that's why we're on a plane right now. Stacey's one of three finalists in a cocktail competition, which is hilarious, considering she's never been a bartender.[153] But I'm not laughing because she got an all-expenses-paid trip to the city, and I'm her plus-one.

When we land, we're going first to her hotel and then to mine. We've learned over the years that the very best vacations include some alone time, so we're not sharing her free room. When I tried to reserve a room at her hotel, it turned out they were fully booked. I checked out all the hotels in one square mile of hers and had the requisite sticker shock upon seeing New York hotel prices. I guess I've never been to New York *not* on business, so I've never paid for myself.

I end up choosing the Four Seasons, partly because I was able to find a sweet deal on the Internet, and partly because I'm extremely loyal to any organization that turns my book into chocolate. The price is still higher than what I'd pay at a Westin or a Hyatt, but I can justify it because the rest of the trip is free, and I've earned a little luxury after hauling ass all over the country for a month.

Of course, Fletch was less easy to sway. I finally changed his mind by convincing him (a) it's only two nights, (b) I'm sure to get a funny experience out of it since my staying there smacks vaguely of a *Beverly Hillbillies* episode, and (c) if I do get a good story, we can write it off.

Our flight's without incident and traffic from LaGuardia's surprisingly light, so we get to Stacey's hotel before we know it. When I checked it out online, I saw a twee little European boutique hotel. But when we

------

[153]Or made the actual drink.

enter, I learn something very important about photos on the Internet: things are not always as they appear.[154]

The lobby manages to feel both empty and crowded, which I assume has something to do with the cracked, barely-more-than-six-foot-high ceilings. The carpet runners are threadbare, and the furniture's old and shoddy. Turns out the ambient glow from the photos was not mood lighting—rather, it was most likely an imperfection-masking dollop of Vaseline on the cameras lens.

The walls are empty of any kind of adornment, but the good news is there are plenty of random nails still sticking out, should one suddenly muster up a painting or framed photograph.

While I hang behind with our bags, Stacey heads to the check-in desk, where most of the staff is busy either spraying one another with juicy sneezes or hacking into Starbucks napkins. I make a mental note not to touch anything in the lobby, because I'm fairly sure this is Ground Zero for the swine flu.

Key in hand, we take an elevator so small that we're the only ones who can fit in it. "Stace," I say, so close to her, my breath moves her hair around, "I got a baaaaad feeling about this place."

"Eh." She shrugs. "I've seen worse. It's free and I'm pretty much just going to be sleeping here."

The elevator lurches to a stop and we exit on her floor. We weave down narrow, confusing catacombs of hallways and finally get to her door. Stacey places the electronic key in the lock, the green light flashes, and she turns the handle . . . yet the door doesn't open. She tries again, with the same result. She tries fifteen more times and the door remains

----

[154]Perhaps if Match.com had been around when I was single, I'd have already known this.

closed. I cannot currently assist her, as I'm (a) sticking my clenched fists in my armpits in order to avoid any germs and (b) attempting not to laugh out a lung.

Finally, in a move worthy of Agent Jack Bauer himself right before he finds/stabs an insurgent in the thigh, she inserts the key and hurls her entire self against the door. She flies in the air, feet leaving the floor, and body-checks the door, resulting in a thump heard round Midtown. The wall surrounding the door gives a bit, yet there we stand in the hallway.

"Hey, what if you pull the handle up?" I gasp, between guffaws.

"That's ludicrous. When have you ever seen a door handle open up instead of down?"

I counter, "When's the last time you stayed in a hotel where the entire staff was infected with the bubonic plague?"

"You make an excellent point." Stacey yanks the handle up and, like magic, the door opens, revealing the majesty of the accommodations and thus prompting me to double over once and for all.

The carpeting's an unnatural shade of green and sprigged with big bouquets of peach roses, which was probably the height of style when it was installed in 1982. Coincidentally, that's exactly when the television was manufactured, so it's nice to see they found a theme and stuck with it. I wonder if when we turn it on, we'll see nothing but *Dukes of Hazzard* and *Cheers* reruns?

There are two beds in here, which is one bed too many for the available square footage. As I make my way over to sit on the tiny horseshoe-shaped chair across the room, I soundly slam my hip into the sharp edge of the writing table, as there's only about a six-inch passage between it and the first bed.[155]

....

[155] And yes, this makes me a tiny bit nostalgic for the old house.

Once I finally stop hyperventilating, I suggest, "Maybe you have a nice view?" pulling a sheer curtain back only to come face-to-face with the building's industrial air conditioner. Then I realize her room is dark not because of cloud cover, but because the HVAC unit is blocking out all available light. "By the way, I would check those sheets for stray p-u-b-i-c hairs right now."

"Think you'll ever be able to say any vaguely sexual words without spelling them?" Stacey asks as she turns back the paisley bedspread.

"Probably not." What can I say? I'm m-o-d-e-s-t.

To be fair, the crucial parts of the room are clean—sheets, toilet, floors, et cetera. The bathtub is spotless, but I imagine it's not hard to sanitize something that's only three feet long. "You could wash an Oompa-Loompa in that tub!" I exclaim.

"Well, not a full-sized Oompa-Loompa," Stacey disagrees, before pointing out the sponge painting on the bathroom walls, composed of both the yellow color found exclusively on roads dividing traffic and the safety cone orange.

Stacey throws her bag on the spare bed, and the window catches her attention. She points to the oddly shaped pleated valance hanging over the sheers. "It would appear that Paris Hilton has lost her skirt."

I break out into fresh peals of laughter. I'll be damned if that thing doesn't look exactly like a skirt's been cut in half and then stapled into the wall.[156] "Well, I really like the art in here."

Stacey swivels her head to inspect the naked walls. "But there is no art."

"Aha! That's where you're wrong," I disagree. "You're not taking into account the chair rail of dirty footprints over there." Stacey pales for

----

[156]Yeah, you read that right. Stapled.

a moment as she sees the ghosts of the feet of hundreds of travelers past all over the far wall. "Seriously, I can get a bigger room if you want to stay with me."

Stacey shrugs philosophically. "Listen, if I can live in a mud hut in Kenya for three months, I can handle a less than ideal hotel room.[157] This'll be fine. No misunderstanding, I'm ready to get the fuck out and hit the Four Seasons, but it's fine. If I stay elsewhere, it'll just screw up all the pickups and drop-offs for the cocktail competition tomorrow, and I don't want to come off as ungrateful."

"All right, but if you change your mind, you tell me."

Stacey gathers the few things she'll need before returning tonight to sleep, and we make our way to my hotel. We could probably walk there from here, but why would we walk when there are so many cabs? I mean, sure it's a little bit lazy but I'm trying to stimulate an economy here, people—if you think about it, I'm kind of a hero. (At least that's what I'll tell Fletch.)

When we arrive, a doorman's at the cab and grabbing my bag out of the trunk before I'm even finished paying the driver. With a courteous bob of the head, he says to me, "Good afternoon, Miss Lancaster. Welcome to the Four Seasons."

"Holy shit, Stacey! They know my name!"

They know me here?

They know me here!

How cool is it they know me? I mean, I just made my reservation online like everyone else. Maybe for a minute I thought about calling the concierge and pretending to be my nonexistent assistant to see if it would get me preferential treatment, but that felt wrong and undeserved. Plus,

---

[157]Memoir! Memoir! Memoir!

if I need to explain to someone who I am, then that pretty much confirms I'm only important in my own head. I never, ever want to turn into "Do-you-know-who-I-am?" girl because . . . *ick*.

Yet the doorman knows me. How can that be? What if a reader works here and she saw my name on the reservation and was all, *"She's an author!"* which I guess would mean I actually am kind of a celebrity and . . .

Wait. That can't even be a little bit true. And this is the exact type of arrogance and delusion that got me in trouble so many years ago. There's got to be a better explanation.

"How do you know my name?" I ask.

"I'm afraid I can't reveal my secrets," he says with a sly grin.

Then I glance down.

Oh. He read my goddamned luggage tag.

Argh, I really am Jethro Bodine.

The doorman whisks my bag away, and Stacey and I pass through the stunning three-story lobby. We admire all the Asian art and inlaid tiles and massive stone columns, topped with a modern yet elegant skylight before we get to the reception desk. I rarely bust out this adjective, but it's totally appropriate here. Swanky. This joint's swanky. (Wonder if they have a ce-ment pond out back?)

A competent professional who appears to have no communicable diseases whatsoever greets us at the two-story reception area. "Welcome, Miss Lancaster." I made note of the fact that the doorman had a headset, so I spare myself the whole embarrassingly self-involved thought process.

While I check in, we tell the desk clerk about the nightmare of Stacey's room and soon all three of us are cracking up. "I don't care if I'm on a higher floor, but I am interested in a room with a dirty footprint chair rail," I say with a straight face. "Might you have any available?"

"Possibly with a two-thirds to scale bathtub? We have a small, dirty Oompa-Loompa in need of a good scrubbing," Stacey adds.

"I'm sorry. I don't; we just ran out of the last of those," the clerk apologizes, trying to keep the corners of her mouth from turning up. "However, I'm able to offer you a complimentary upgrade to the next class of room, and it's a corner so your views will be much better. It's quite spacious. But if you prefer, I can have housekeeping rearrange the furniture to make sure you bump into it."

"That shan't be necessary," I reply in a fake-haughty voice.

I complete the check-in service and thank the clerk again. When she says it was her pleasure, I believe her. I bet none of the dignitaries or the *real* famous people who check in here every day try to make the desk clerk smile. And I ended up with a better room not by pulling the (faux) important card, but just by being myself.

And speaking of the room . . . wow. This is larger than the apartment I lived in after college, and a thousand times nicer. A bellman shows us all the amenities as I stand there openmouthed. Not only is the room equipped with stuff like a five-function printer and a PlayStation, but there's a section with a private bar, already stocked with ice.[158] There's a luxurious sitting area buffeted by fourteen-foot-high windows, and on the opposite side, there's a huge walk-in dressing room leading to a massive marble bathroom.

While the bellman sets my suitcase on a rack in the closet, I rush to the tub. My Internet friend Melissa—who I'm meeting for the first time tomorrow—told me the rumor is the tub fills completely in sixty seconds. I intend to test this myth, desperately hoping it's true. Although I wonder

----

[158]LOVE!

how busy and important their usual guests must be if they only have sixty seconds to draw a bath.

As I take it all in, I suddenly feel like every single cast member of *The Real World* on the day they move into their glorious, albeit temporary, homes. Unlike them, I won't be hosting any threesomes in this tub.

After my bag's in place, the bellman shows me how to work the myriad window treatments. There are thick sheers and elaborate draperies on one wall of windows and a sturdy roman shade on the other. Because they're so long and heavy, everything's been automated, and I can control them with the electronic panel next to the bed. I can see this being an endless source of amusement for the next few days.

As I tip the bellman, he mentions my tub's about to overflow. Time elapsed? Fifty-five seconds!

I've said it before, and I'll say it again: Four Seasons, there's nothing you can't do.

"How do you like your hotel?"

I'm sitting at a bistro on the Upper East Side having lunch with Melissa C. Morris, who, aside from being possibly the preppiest girl in the world[159] and a devoted dog owner and a clever writer, is a real-deal New York Social Diary socialite. We started e-mailing each other a few years ago because I'm a huge fan of her Web site. She lives this amazing life full of benefit dinners and international travel and cultural activities and just *dolce vita* in general. She chronicles it all on her Web site, but

....

[159]She told me where to find the argyle socks for the cover of *Pretty in Plaid!*

instead of it being all exclusive and show-offy, she manages to make you feel like you're walking around in her Wellingtons for a while.

Melissa has the best manners I've ever witnessed. Graciousness emanates from every word she writes. Ever see those old Emily Post books where she says the hostess is responsible for making everyone feel welcome? And if someone at the table drinks from the finger bowl by mistake, the hostess must follow suit? Melissa would absolutely quaff her bowl.

When I mentioned getting together, I unabashedly told her I wanted to spend some time soaking up her social graces. And so impeccable are her manners that she didn't even laugh at me.

I'd planned on working with an etiquette coach at home, and I contacted a ton of places but not one of them ever called or e-mailed me back, which, if you ask me, is pretty fucking rude. Charm school FAIL. I figured I couldn't learn anything from places so lacking in basic social niceties, and decided to do things on my own, ergo Melissa.

Today's plan is to first have lunch and then check out the sculpture garden at the Met, where she's a member. I quietly make note that while eating our salads, we pretty much handle our utensils and stir iced tea and work our napkins the same way.

I suspect my baseline table manners are fine, and no one will automatically assume I'm a member of the Clampett family, should they see how I eat soup. It's the more advanced parts of etiquette I don't quite get. Like, I've had people over for dinner before, but I don't really understand how to make a party flow smoothly. Pretty much I just pump everyone full of cocktails, they get drunk, food ends up being served hours later than anticipated, and on occasion, if Fletch is working the grill, he sets his pants on fire. At my last dinner party, Gina came into the dining room and said, "Hey, did you want your cats on the counter? Because they're licking the chicken." Mind you, this is after I demonstrated how the cats beg at the table and how sometimes I chew up bits of my meat and feed it to them and . . . actually, that veers dangerously into Elly Mae territory, doesn't it?

Obviously Melissa and I aren't going to cover how to throw a dinner party that doesn't descend into an episode of *Jerry Springer* or, in Fletch's case, *ER*, but I'm interested to see her social graces in action. I guarantee Melissa's never once given anyone the impression she was only a breath away from giving them a solid punch in the neck, no matter how annoyed she felt inside.

"The hotel's awesome! Big thumbs-up if you ever want to recommend it to out-of-towners. And I can confirm the business with the bathtub, too. My room has everything anyone could ever possibly need, except an iron. Instead, they have a twenty-four-hour valet and pressing service. But I'm not paying thirty bucks to iron a pair of shorts that cost twenty, so I'm going to be wrinkled while I'm in New York."

She stirs her iced tea and assures me, "No one will notice. By the way, how was your evening out?"

"So much fun!" I tell her. "You were right; Buddakan was a blast." Last night, Stacey and I staked out a community table in the front bar of this funky Asian fusion place in Chelsea. I can barely talk today because I'm so hoarse from all the shouting and laughter. "Good call on where to sit, too. Our friends drifted in and out, but at one point, we were a group of, like, ten chick lit authors. We had this total Algonquin Round Table moment, except we spent most of our time mocking the *Real Housewives of Orange County*."

"Talk about your Vicious Circle." She grins.

Okay, hold the goddamned phone—I just unintentionally referenced something both historical and somewhat literary, which means . . .

My Jenaissance is working!

Today's pretty much been the best day ever. After Melissa and I finished lunch, we headed over to the Met, where at no point did I squeal about seeing the very steps where Blair Waldorf held court every day at lunch.[160]

What took me by pleasant surprise was that Melissa was fun. Before today, it never occurred to me that impeccable social graces and joie de vivre weren't mutually exclusive. I knew I'd enjoy her company, but didn't expect to laugh so much while I was in it. She's like some kind of F. Scott Fitzgerald heroine who'd behave perfectly at the society ball, but wouldn't be above spiking the punch bowl if the mood suited her.

After our museum excursion, I had to go back downtown to support Stacey at her cocktail contest. The three finalists were having a mix-off and the winner would leave five thousand dollars richer.

Stacey totally left five thousand dollars richer.

And I will never mock her recipe-writing prowess again.

After we got done with contest stuff, we went back to my room before heading out to the sponsors' dinner. Having been inspired by Melissa's fine manners, I ordered us a cheese plate and offered Stacey a beverage.

I leaned into the fridge under the private bar and began to pull out bottles for her approval. "Okay, looks like we've got tons of sodas, including Orangina. Um . . . there's also water and white wine and a whole bunch of little airplane boozes and, oh! There's this!" I held out a large plastic Voss water bottle, halfway filled with a creamy taupe liquid.

....

[160] At least not out loud.

"That's not water," Stacey observed.

"Okay, you know how sometimes hotels leave that menu that you hang on the door if you want something? Well, I ordered breakfast last night and under the hot beverages section, you could pick all kinds of stuff—coffee, black tea, herbal tea, et cetera. I picked the giant latte. Then after that section, there was a part where you could select what you wanted with your beverage, you know, like honey or lemon or two per-cent milk. There was an option for half-and-half, so I asked for some, thinking I'd add it to my latte to lighten it. I mean, coffee can't be too creamy or sweet for me."

"Basically, you want it to taste like melted coffee ice cream."

"Exactly! So breakfast came this morning and I immediately poured my latte, only when it came out, it was super thick, and I'm all *'What's with this?'* Then I sweetened it and took a sip, and holy cats! They'd misunderstood my instructions and made *the entire latte out of cream!"*

Stacey was appalled. "*Blech!* Did you send it back?"

"Hell, no, I didn't send it back; it was the most delicious thing I ever tasted! I drank as much as I could, and then I took what was left in the pitcher and poured it into this water bottle so I could pour it over ice later! Plus, it was fifteen dollars and I was not about to let that go to waste." I waved the bottle at her. "You want some?"

Stacey tried hard to hide her smirk. "I'll pass, thanks."

"Your loss," I replied, making a mental note to order the same thing for breakfast tomorrow.

After cheese and ice-cream lattes, we had an amazing Italian din-ner[161] and ended the evening with cucumber martinis in the bar at the Four Seasons, possibly the greatest place on earth to people-watch, as

....

[161]During which I made a note to schedule an angioplasty.

everyone looks quasifamous. I wanted to go up to each table and ask, "Are you someone I know?" but mustered enough self-control not to.

We noticed one particularly handsome man at the bar, drinking coffee and reading a book. There was a pair of flashily dressed, completely cosmetically enhanced, ridiculously blond gold-digger-type girls making rounds in four-inch heels. They'd been sitting with a table of foreign businessmen, laughing uproariously at everything they said. "Those Japanese guys must be really funny," I said, to which Stacey replied, "Oh, honey, no."

Then Stacey and I were the ones to laugh uproariously when the Japanese businessmen left without them. We watched as the girls regrouped and then homed in on the man at the bar, circling him in a cloud of perfume and expectations. They flirted and cajoled and tossed their magnificent manes of hair. They carried on, subtly shoving their silicone in his face until he finally scowled and pointed at his wedding ring, scattering the skanks like scalded apes.

We may or may not have cheered . . . hip-hip-hooray for the handsome man who loves his wife!

Stacey went back to her place a while ago, and I'm up in my room, reading in bed. I tried to watch television, but after thumbing through something like six hundred channels, I turned if off. I don't do well when I'm presented with too many choices.

I begin to monkey with the curtains. If both sets of drapes are closed, the room's too dark, and if they're both open it's too exposed. I settle on shutting the sheers but I'm still not comfortable.

It's odd how much more at ease I am in my own skin on this trip than I was at the Colony Club last year. The same kind of crowd frequents both places, but now I don't feel like I'm from a different universe. I'm not—and will likely never be—one of *them*, whoever the faceless, hatboxpurchasing patrons are, but the little voice that kept telling me I didn't belong here last year seems to be silent. As I survey where I've landed, I can't help but be pleased.

And yet, happy as I am with my progress, my million-dollar problem remains. This room's too big to be cozy. Although this is the perfect spot to share cheese with my bestie, I need an ambient glow to fall asleep. Last night this wasn't an issue because my desire for an ambient glow had taken a backseat to nine tickled pinks—a blend of pineapple juice, coconut rum, and sparkling wine. But tonight I took it easy, sipping one cocktail for hours, and because of my pot o' latte, sleeping might be a challenge.

I try flipping on the television again, but even turned all the way down, it's distracting. I click it off and flip on the little banker's light on the desk, but I can see its pinprick of white in my peripheral vision, and it annoys me.

Then I spot the answer. In the corner, between the windows, is a large framed lithograph. Above it is a picture light. If I turn that on, it should provide the ideal amount of ambience. I scan the wall for a cord and a switch, but the light is hardwired into the wall.

I turn my attention to the bronze hood over the two tiny halogen bulbs. There's no switch, so maybe this is just one of those things you touch to light. I tap it in random spots but nothing. So I begin poking at the bulbs, and suddenly I'm swimming in a pool of mood lighting. Awesome! The bulb on the right fizzles out, but it's fine. Lefty provides all the glow I need.

I cross the room and climb back into bed. As soon as I reposition myself with my book, I realize that Lefty's letting off a blinding beam of light. I shift around to the right side of the bed. No luck. The glare is slight, albeit bothersome. I shift again.

Frustrated, I slam shut my book and cross the room. With my index finger, I jab at the offending light and immediately recoil because JESUS CHRIST, THAT'S HOT! I shove my finger in my mouth to cool off the singed flesh.

And then I poke at the bulb again because I am not nearly as smart as I'd assumed I'd become.

BURNING!

Well, now I have two problems. Not only have I seared off my fingertip, but now the fixture smells vaguely hot. Or of hot dogs. Which may just be the aroma of my flesh roasting on the bulb. I don't really want to call down to the front desk and give them the impression I'm a dumb ass, and yet I also don't want tomorrow's headline in the *Post* to read "Big-Ass Author Burns Down Luxury Midtown Hotel."[162]

Think, self, think.

Okay, I've got this. All I need to do is pull out the halogen bulb. Yes. Genius!

But wait, self, wait.

I've already burned my finger twice. What I need is a tiny oven mitt to place between my tender flesh and this searing-hot bulb. So I grab what's closest, wrap it around my hand, and go for it.

The second my wrapped finger hits the heat, the fabric, my flesh, and the bulb fuse into one entity.

And this is how I set the curtain on fire.

Apparently these are not hot-lightbulb-and-dumb-ass-retardant curtains. Instead, they're the flame-briefly-melt-and-leave-two-silver-dollar-sized-holes-in-them kind.

----

[162] They like puns. Which are funny, when they don't reference the size of my backyard.

I do manage to turn off the light, though.

So there's that.

We're having breakfast in my room as I tell Stacey my tale of woe.

"I'm sure it's not nearly as bad as you think," Stacey cajoles. "This must happen all the time."

I purse my lips and glower at Stacey, saying nothing.

She backpedals. "Fine. Maybe it doesn't happen all the time, but perhaps they won't notice?"

"Oh, yeah? You don't find this a little obvious?" I pull out the sheer and demonstrate the holes' girth by thrusting my thumbs through both of them.

Stacey sizes them up, turning her head first to the left and then to the right, before declaring, "Yeah . . . you're screwed."

Stacey carefully selects a piece of honeydew from the fruit plate while I say, "My only hope is they won't cost so much. I mean, the sheers in my house were only about five bucks each."

"Are yours fourteen feet high? And twenty feet long? And custom-made?" she prompts.

"What are you talking about?" I ask, spearing a giant piece of pine-apple. "You've been to my house a hundred times and you've seen my windows and . . . Oh. I get it."

"What are you going to do?"

I mull over her question before replying, "I plan on being a complete coward. I'm going to leave them as they are, and I'm not going to have a mortifying conversation when I check out, and when they send me the bill, I'm going to pay it."

Stacey moves the piece of melon around on her plate. "They'll probably just put it on your credit card."

"Even better."

"This could only happen to you."

"I'm aware of that."

"Are you still glad you came?"

"Absolutely!" I exclaim. "But I've learned something on this trip."

"What's that?"

I sigh. "I may not be wearing a rope belt, but somehow I'm still channeling Jethro Bodine."

To: melissacmorris_at_home

From: jen_at_home

Subject: Daisy Buchanan

Hey, Melissa,

I've been meaning to drop you a note to tell you how much I enjoyed spending the afternoon with you. Later that day I found myself trying to describe what you were like to my friend Stacey. I wanted to get across that you had perfect manners but there was something just a little bit, I don't know, precocious or naughty beneath the surface, in the most delightful, let's-go-swim-in-the-fountain-in-our-formal-wear kind of way. So I said, "She's just like an F. Scott Fitzgerald heroine!"

However, as part of my culturing-up process, I just reread *The Great Gatsby* and, oh my God, all the women in it are JACK-ASSES.

So you're not like an F. Scott Fitzgerald heroine. You're better.

Anyway, hope France was lovely!

Jen

Nightmares, of the Nonkitchen Variety

"How's the little patient?"

Air rushes out of me like I'm a deflating balloon. "Not great."

Fletch and I are at brunch with Gina, who's asking about Maggie, our elderly calico cat.

Gina knits her brow. "I'm so sorry; what's going on?"

"We've been hitting the cat hospital weekly and we're trying desperately to get some weight back on her. Since the only thing she'll eat is ten-dollar-a-pound shrimp from the Whole Foods raw bar and she likes it fresh, I'm constantly driving there to pick up supplies. I kind of know what a soccer mom must feel like now, as it seems like all I do is load everyone up in the backseat and drive them around. Did I mention I have to keep taking the dogs in to their vet because somehow the staff can't take a proper sample from Maisy and her weird cyst. I guess it's hard to wield a needle when a pit bull's trying to French-kiss you."

Gina squeezes some lemon into her green tea. "Maisy can't help being such a love bug. What's Maggie's prognosis?"

I sigh again. "She's almost seventeen, and she's lost more than a third of her body weight. She has pancreatitis and there's a real possibility of intestinal lymphoma. Breaks my heart to say it, but she's not long for this world. But every day I get up and determine how she's feeling. So far, she's still spry and content and greets me at the top of the stairs, where she demands her breakfast."

With a somber expression, Fletch adds, "She's a happy little cat. Her spirits are high, so she doesn't seem like she's suffering in any way. But the minute we feel like she's no longer enjoying her life, that's it."

"*Ack* . . . these decisions," Gina says, laying down her fork. "This is the worst part of being an adult."

"Tell me about it," I reply glumly.

"Listen, this may be a bad time to bring this up, but yet another slutty alley cat has brought her family of kittens to live in my backyard. I've been in touch with every shelter and apparently it's 'kitten season,' so I can't get any of them to take them. I've been feeding them every day—they're so cute, by the way—and I keep pestering rescue organizations. So far no luck," Gina tells us.[163]

"Any possibility you'll keep them?" I ask.

"Oh, please, you've said it yourself—as long as I'm single, I'm one feline away from becoming the crazy cat lady. There's no way I can add another to the mix; I don't have enough spare bedrooms." Gina has an

---

[163]Somehow every stray cat on the South Side finds its way to Gina's yard. Maybe because she's yet to not rehome them?

upstairs cat and a downstairs cat. Upstairs Cat loves Downstairs Cat but Downstairs Cat pees on everything whenever she comes into contact with Upstairs Cat. After four years and a number of consults with behavior specialists, Gina's pretty sure they're never going to find détente, so the cats live separate lives in the same house.

I toy with the uneaten part of my pancake. "You know, Fletch, all of our cats *are* between fourteen and sixteen years old. They aren't going to be around forever. Maybe we should—"

Fletch sets his coffee down harder than necessary, and it sloshes out the side and into the saucer. "Absolutely not, no way in this world, don't even entertain it as a possibility," he asserts.

"But—" Gina and I both blurt at the same time.

"I'm sorry, this is nonnegotiable. We have two dogs and four cats. We can't have any more."

"Why not?" I persist. "Our house is plenty big."

"Square footage is not the issue; the issue is not being reported to the authorities for pet hoarding."

I grumble, "Hardly hoarding. They live like kings; they're allowed to sit on or scratch up whatever furniture they like and have all the treats they could want and sleep in bed with us and . . . That's probably your issue, isn't it?"

In my defense, I come from a long line of fanatical animal people. When I was in college, my parents got this overbred Great Pyrenees named George. He was, for lack of a better description, bloodthirsty. He had an overdeveloped urge to guard, and the object of his obsession was my father's blue leather chair in the family room. He wouldn't let anyone but me and my dad get within five feet of that thing, and God help you if you tried.

We all loved George, but really couldn't have him attempting to assassinate every guest in our home, particularly since he weighed in around a hundred and thirty pounds. Desperate to accommodate him, my parents spent twenty-five *thousand* dollars on an addition to the house, where George could hang out when anyone visited.[164] But apparently a room of his own didn't fix Georgie's problems, so my dad's secretary found a doggie psychologist.

Every Saturday morning as I'd get ready to head to one of my two jobs, I'd hear my parents and the dog shrink downstairs training with George. We had to call the dog guy "Uncle Kent" so George would believe he was family, a member of our pack. The Saturday-morning pattern was always the same. George would bark and lunge, his electronic shock collar would go off, he'd yelp, and then the smell of singed fur would waft up to my bedroom.

Sadly, all their effort was for naught, as George tried to murder my mother one night when she sat in my father's chair, and then George—who, frankly, was always sweet with me—was no more.

In retrospect, there's a chance Uncle Kent was taking my parents for a ride, because who ever heard of a dog psychologist, particularly in northeastern Indiana at that time?

George was followed by Ted, an overbred hundred-thirty-pound Newfoundland. Apparently my family did not learn the lesson of buying a purebred from the least expensive breeder the first time.[165] Perhaps they figured we'd have more luck with a behemoth creature if they picked one that was, say, black and not white this time.

It might stand to reason that since the former guard dog made guard-

---

[164]And yes, I was paying for school myself at the time and living at home. Don't get me started.

[165]Amish puppy mill? Yes, please!

ing his sole priority in life, the water-rescue dog would have a great deal of enthusiasm for water rescue, yet everyone seemed rather surprised when Ted would do things like dive through windows to "save us" when we were out enjoying the pool.

Poor old Teddy didn't even make it a year.

I returned to my college campus around this time and adopted a magnificent Malamute/Akita mix named Nixon. I made the mistake of bringing him home one weekend, whereupon he and my father fell instantly, madly, deeply in love. I can't say my dad stole my dog so much as I simply ceased to exist when my father walked into the room.

Essentially, Nixon resigned from being my dog.

Nixon lived for more than another decade, far longer than most of his size and breed[166] largely because my dad's world revolved around him. He spent his life driving around with my father, perched in the front seat of his tiny Toyota, his enormous head pressed against the car's ceiling, on their way to get him his daily sausage biscuit.

Anyway, the fact that I'm far less insane than my family in all matters regarding pets is moot because if Fletch says we can't rescue a kitten, then I need to defer to his wishes.

The funny thing is, I'm with Fletch because of these very cats. When we met fourteen years ago, my cats were the arbiter of who was and wasn't worthy of my attention. I'd never date anyone who my pets didn't like; I mean, they're instinctive like that. My rationale was if someone wasn't nice to my pets, eventually, they wouldn't be nice to me, either.

When Maggie met Fletch, she immediately climbed on the couch and curled up on his shoulder in a fluffy little ball of calico fur, and I knew he was a keeper.

....

[166] And WAY longer then the life expectancy of most of the Lancaster dogs.

When I wake up this morning, two days after our brunch with Gina, Maggie isn't waiting for me at the top of the stairs for the first time ever.

When I find her lying on the counter, she's encircled by all the other cats, who normally never gather together.

She refuses her shrimp.

And then she looks up at me with her big, round, wise eyes that so enchanted me almost seventeen years ago, and her message is clear.

This is it.

She's made her decision.

She's ready to go.

I wish I felt more ready to let her go.

When we get home from the vet, Maisy goes directly into empathy mode, and there's no point for the rest of the day when she isn't resting her head or paws or whole body on me. Over and over, I kiss the broad, flat part of her head between her ears and nuzzle her powerful neck. She gazes up at me with so much concern in her chocolate brown, black-lined eyes. Her beautiful tan-and-white face is all wrinkled in worry.

Maisy's one of the biggest reasons I worked so hard to become a writer. I wanted to have a job that would let me be home with her every day. I miss her every second that we're apart. I couldn't bear the idea of being away from her fifty to sixty hours a week at some office job.

I don't know what I'd do without this dog. I look back on every stressful moment in our lives over the past seven years—and there've been plenty—and there was never a second that Maisy wasn't right by my side, grinning her wide pit bull smile, desperate to make me happy.

Other than my sweet baby, the one thing that helps me take my mind off how heartbroken I am is, surprisingly, *The Real Housewives of New Jersey*. I've been so busy pursuing cultural activities that I've had neither the time nor desire to watch this season. Plus, I recognized Housewife Dina from her over-the-top nuptials on *Platinum Weddings*, and it sort of felt like pop culture was eating itself.

But lying in my basement in the dark, pit bull snuggled up to me, cold nose wedged in the crook of my shoulder, I crack my first smile of the day when Teresa flips out, calling Danielle a "prostitute whore" before upending the dinner table.

Sad as I am, I still recognize awesome when I see it.

Fletch and I head to Las Vegas for Fourth of July weekend. With Maggie being sick, we'd planned to cancel the trip, but she was gone before we had to make that decision. Given the option, I'd rather have my cat and be home.

Normally I'd be beside myself, but it's been a rough week. I don't feel in much of a holiday mood, particularly since when we land, it's raining. In Las Vegas. Which is the *desert*. In the summer. This trip already feels like a bad omen.

The crowds and the sound of slot machines and whole 24-7 nature of the city fail to charm me this time. The lights are too bright and the colors too garish, and if one more person blows smoke in my hair in the casino, I'm going to pull a Teresa and start tipping over tables.

And this is exactly the mood I'm in when we get to the restaurant for our requisite one fancy vacation dinner. My ill humor only worsens when we're given a shitty table directly between two ten-tops of screaming assholes from St. Louis, all done up in jean shorts and Cardinals jerseys. "I'm sorry, but I thought this place had a dress code," I fume to Fletch.

We specifically picked this restaurant because it has a view of the fountain, but all we can see is the wait station, full of water pitchers and sugar caddies and the POS order-entry computer.

The service is terrible because our waiter is too busy being run around by the Cardinal fans, and we sit with dirty plates and empty glasses for far longer than is acceptable, particularly at a four-star restaurant.

I begin seething, taking the whole experience personally. And when Fletch goes to the bathroom and sees all the empty tables in the back with the primo fountain view, his mood darkens as well.

Foul and slighted as I'm feeling, I decide it's time to fight back. Surreptitiously, I pull out a small notebook and pretend I'm jotting down notes, which leads the entire staff to believe I'm reviewing the restaurant. And then I begin to take notes for real when I discover the potatoes are bland, the lobster potpie one big crock of gluten, the Kobe beef tough, and the foie gras double-plus un-good.

When the waiter tries to bring us the last course in our tasting menu, we tell him we've had enough and are ready to leave right this minute, check, *please*.[167] As we're leaving, the maître d' says something along the lines of "I hope we'll see you back again," to which I reply, "Not in this lifetime." We stomp over to see a Cirque du Soleil show, and I spend the entire performance grousing about the terrible meal and poor service.

---

[167] And yes, I overtipped. I'm a pathological overtipper. It's one of my few saving graces.

When we return to our hotel, we recount the whole experience to the concierge in righteously indignant detail before going to bed. By the time we're back from brunch, the manager of the restaurant has called our room twice to apologize and invite us back for a dinner on the house.

That's when it hits me—I pulled the "don't you know who I am" card. I'm suddenly mortified by my privileged, officious behavior.

Somehow over the course of this project, I've managed to twist what I've learned over my cultural Jenaissance into flat-out, unearned elitism. I mean, just because I've now had Kobe and foie gras doesn't exactly make me an expert, yet there I was, acting as though I was. My Shame Rattle sounds again and again. In the past two days, I've behaved with the exact amount of arrogance and egotism that cost me my job so many years ago, which means I'm missing the point of everything I've been working toward since winter.

This isn't how I want to be. I don't want to turn what I've learned into a weapon. I want to be a better me, not a bigger ass.

There's a scene in *My Fair Lady* where Eliza goes back to hang out with all the other flower girls, and they don't even recognize her. She still wants to be friends with them, but she's changed so much, she makes everyone uncomfortable and has to leave. She finds herself trapped between two worlds, unable to feel real belonging to either. While I based some of my Jenaissance on the play, that wasn't the part I'd hoped to emulate.

If I want to make a good impression at Authors Night, my renaissance needs to be genuine, and I have to stop worrying about the class part of the equation. I mean, I'm not going to outclass a bunch of millionaires— particularly with eight dollars in my purse—and trying to would be an exercise in futility. I need to find a way to be a kinder, gentler, more articulate me. I want to be the kind of me who doesn't have to recount a reality show moment to best capture my feeling on a particular subject. And I don't want other authors to roll their eyes after it's over, saying, *"What was up with that Lancaster chick? Obnoxious!"*

So over the next month, I need to figure out how to better myself without losing what defines me.

I can start by not benefiting from my own bad behavior.

I decline the opportunity for a free dinner and later, when it's time to eat, we end up at In-N-Out Burger.

It's one of the best meals I've ever had.

When we get home from Las Vegas, I set my bags down by the back door and check the voice mail. There's a message from the vet, who in a very matter-of-fact voice tells me that Maisy's cysts—you know, the ones they'd been saying for years are nothing and they only aspirated at my insistence—are cancerous, and I should probably make an appointment to schedule surgery.

I feel like I've just been kicked in the heart.

While I take to my bed in hysterics, Stacey helps Fletch find a new vet, one who won't blithely write off a spate of cancerous tumors as "Eh, just doggie zits" for three years.

Honestly, it's a good thing it's Sunday and my vet's office is closed, because I'm not sure I can trust myself right now not to do something stupid. I mean, I always joke about stuff like bludgeoning the contractor and punching bad drivers in the neck, but I actually feel like I could commit physical violence right now against a doctor either too lazy or disconnected to take proper care of my baby.

The worst part is the kennel's closed, too, and we can't even pick her up until tomorrow morning. Fletch tried to contact them about getting the dogs early but kept getting the answering machine.

On our last night in Vegas, Fletch and I sat by the hotel pool and split a bottle of wine while we watched the fireworks. We were both pretty melancholy about Maggie, and somehow over the course of the conversation, Fletch agreed that we should take one of the kittens from Gina's backyard.

But I wondered how we'd take just one kitten out of three. How would we go about deciding who's going to get spoiled rotten with all the ottomans they can shred and who might perish on the streets? And wouldn't they miss one another?

While Fletch decided he'd get us another bottle of wine, I decided we'd take all three and sent Gina a tipsy e-mail saying as much. Fletch eventually agreed to my idea, but since I first plied him with liquor, I'm not sure his acquiescence would hold up in court.

My face firmly planted in my pillow, I beg Fletch to call Gina and find out when we can get the kittens because I desperately need something else to occupy my thoughts. We make plans to stop by tomorrow night.

I spend most of the next twenty-four hours hugging my dog and crying. I also Google Canine Mast Cell Disease and almost throw up when I find out the typical life expectancy after diagnosis and with treatment is one to two years, if we're lucky.

Suddenly, my baby dog, my best friend, the greatest gift I've ever gotten other than my husband, comes with an expiration date.

While I'm waiting for Fletch to get home from work so we can pick up the kittens, I furiously start scheduling cultural activities to keep me occupied. I sign up for foreign cooking classes, wine appreciation courses, and cheese seminars. I buy tickets for dance recitals and theater performances and book dinners at molecular gastronomy restaurants. I'm trying to be as show-must-go-on as I can, but I wonder if I'm going to be able to focus on anything in the near future.

Gina greets me with an enormous hug and a million words of encouragement. She's baked us one of her world-famous pound cakes, too, which really touches me. I'm not close to my family anymore—let's just say big, fat, thoughtless mouths are a genetic trait—so it feels really good to have friends filling these roles.

Gina leads us down to the basement, where the kittens are currently being kept. "How'd you catch them?" Fletch asks. When we saw her a couple of weeks ago, Gina told us the shelters instructed her not to touch them, as her scent might turn their mother against them. As far as we know, no one's ever laid a human hand on them.

"I lured them into my gingerbread house," Gina replies. "I opened a can of Trader Joe's tuna, set it in the cat carrier, and then shut the door on them. Then I brought them into the basement and essentially dumped them into this." Gina points at the largest dog carrier I've ever seen. Both our old dogs George and Ted could have fit in there together. Nixon, too. Possibly even Spiro Agnew.

"Why do you have this? Did you have a Malamute I didn't know about? Or a pony?" I asked.

"No, when I brought Bailey in,[168] he needed to be separated and contained while the abscess on his leg healed, so I bought this for him to live in. That is, until he took over my whole guest room."

The plan is for Fletch to reach in the enormous doggie condo, grab the kittens, and deposit them in our more portable cat carrier. Before we do, I want to take my first peek at them. I peer into the doggie condo, which we've tipped on its side so the kittens can't escape through the open door. There are three tiny gray bundles of fur, all hunkered together in the very corner of the carrier. "Oh, my God, they're adorable!" I squeal.

"I've been calling them the Cherubs because they're so stinking cute," Gina replies.

"We're going to call them the Thundercats until we figure out what to name them. Also, that'll help me not get too attached in case they test positive for feline diseases, you know?"

Gina muses, "I was really surprised to get your note Saturday and then to hear from you, Fletch. I thought when we were at brunch, you made your thoughts on new kittens pretty clear. You're really behind this?"

With an entirely straight face, he says, "Absolutely. This is the very best idea I've heard since you, Lucy and Ethel, got all the cats together for a playdate. I mean, what could possibly go wrong incorporating three feral kittens into our household?"

"You'd prefer I start crying again?" I challenge.[169]

"No, no, certainly, let's collect our precious kittens and go home.

....

[168] AKA Upstairs Cat.

[169] Emotional blackmail—I plays it.

Maybe we'll find some stray dogs on the way and bring them, too." The thing is, he argues, but if he didn't want to be here, too, even a little bit, he'd never have agreed to this.

Fletch bends down and places his hand in the condo to retrieve the first kitten. I can't wait to get a closer look at them! They seem so tiny and perfect, cuddled together. One's all gray and white and extra fuzzy, one's sleek and small with black tiger stripes on slate-colored fur, and one's a blend of stone and tan colors, spots and stripes. Their eyes are huge in shades of blue and green, taking up most of their tiny faces. I'm not sure I've ever seen anything cuter or sweeter or . . .

"*AAAHHHH!* I'm bitten! One of them bit me! Look at this—blood!" Fletch shouts.

"What? That can't be," I say. "Their teeth are tiny."

"Their teeth are tiny *razors*," he snaps.

"Try it again," Gina suggests. "Go in more slowly this time. You probably just scared them."

Resigned, Fletch takes a deep breath and slowly lowers his hand back into the condo. He lingers with his arm in for a second before yanking it out and flailing backward. "OW! Jesus Christ, ow! They're like piranha in there, a carrier full of fucking piranha! They just tore the shit out of my hand." Fletch holds up the bloody stump attached to his wrist.

"Oh, no!" Gina exclaims. "I have rubbing alcohol; we can put it on your cuts."

"Yes, because THAT will stop the rabies," Fletch responds drily.

At this point, Gina finds a gardening glove that barely fits over his fingers. We try to help him retrieve the kittens, but it's kind of impossible, considering how hard she and I are laughing.

Every time Fletch thrusts his hand in to grab one, a different kitten attacks. At some point, one of the kittens begins to panic and sprays diarrhea, and then Fletch has to navigate through that, too. He shoots me the world's dirtiest look, to which I reply, "Hey, I can cry again," and he continues his mission.

We finally get them all gathered up, and while Fletch gets a bleach-and-antiseptic bath from the elbows down, I eat some pound cake. (It's delicious!)

As we drive back up the expressway, I feel hopeful.

I figure nothing that starts out this bad can end any worse.

Gina had never gotten a real look at the little guys, and when we finally do see them up close, we notice they're in rough shape. Sneezy, rheumy, wheezy, itchy, and one of them has what appears to be a giant pink balloon attached to his butt.

This can't be good.

I bring them to our cat vet first thing in the morning. Turns out the poor little guys wouldn't have made it for more than another day or two. They have eye infections, upper respiratory infections, dehydration, ear mites, and fleas. Ten percent of their body weight is worms. And one of them has a prolapsed rectum, which essentially means the little guy had such bad diarrhea that he blew out his o-ring.

Fortunately for Fletch, they don't have rabies, nor do they have any of the fatal cat diseases, so we authorize treatment, thus incurring the first pet surgery to repair Thundercat One's bunghole.

There's an issue with Thundercat Two's eye and we're referred to a feline ophthalmology clinic.

Nope, I didn't know such a thing existed, either.

I find out that Thundercat Two needs to have his third eyelid sewn over the eye if there's any chance he'll able to keep the eye. I confirm that even with one eye Thundercat Two will have an excellent quality of life, so I sanction the surgery and name him Odin.[170]

Thundercat Three makes a complete recovery. There's nothing additional wrong with him, except that he's an asshole. He's such a jerk that the vet's office has to spend the whole week weighing him in a trash can. The nurse tells me she holds him up in the window of his incubator so everyone can get a glimpse of his "mean face" whenever the staff needs a lift.

Naturally, we name him Chuck Norris.

As for Maisy, our new doggie vet refers us to "the Mayo Clinic for pets" in the suburbs, where Maisy's operated on by a board-certified surgeon and her follow-up chemotherapy will be taken care of by a canine oncologist.

Yes, *canine oncologist.*

Apparently they exist, too.

Maisy comes through her surgery like a champ. In the meantime, Chuck, Odin, and Angus[171] finally get to come home.

One might think the kittens would show a little bit of appreciation for the people who wrote enormous checks on their behalf.

One would be wrong.

For the first few weeks, they actively hate us, and every time we go into their room, they cower and hide. At one point, Fletch asks me if someone couldn't get sweet, socialized, nonferal kittens for twenty-five dollars at PAWS.

....

[170]Come on, it's the perfect name for a one-eyed cat. And if we ever get a three-legged dog, we're naming him Tripod.

[171]Thundercat One was named Angus once his swelling went down enough to determine his sex.

"Um, yeah," I reply, "but only if they don't like a *challenge.*"

We're slowly winning them over, one can of kitten food at a time. Now their hissing and cowering is cursory at best.

Maisy's in fabulous spirits, too, although I have to try to keep her from leaping, cavorting, and frolicking until her stitches come out. She acts like everything was like the season on *Dallas* that turned out to be Bobby's bad dream.

As for me, yesterday was the first day in a couple of weeks that I didn't have to spend hauling pets to specialty clinics or having panic attacks.

That was nice.

Which means now I can get back to the business of culturing up, a task made less easy by being stared at by seven and a half sets of eyes.

To: stacey_at_home

From: jen_at_home

Subject: why you bring home tiny devils?

I'm in the process of rearranging the furniture in my office. As it's my desire to jam every inch of living space full of as much furniture as humanly possible (at least according to Fletch) there are still some unhomed items floating around the middle of the room. Presently I have a rolling office chair pulled up to the front of my desk and Maisy's climbed into it.

She's sitting upright on her haunches and facing me.

We appear to be having a meeting.

I keep cracking up while I consider what we might need to meet about, e.g., "Items on Maisy's Agenda."

1. Why U No Give Maisy More Cookies?

2. Maisy Prefer Make Poops in Front Yard and Care Not If U Think It Kind of Ghetto.

3. Maisy Never Forget Time U Drop Pork Chop on Floor and Maisy Quicker Than U.

4. U Hurt Maisy Feelings When U Call Her "ArmpitBull." Maisy Not the One Too Lazy Give Baths and Maisy Tongue Only Capable of Clean So Much.

5. Maisy Beg to Differ—Guest DO Want Maisy Jump All Over Them.

Speaking of Maisy, she's doing really well. Her stitches are healing up nicely and she's in her usual high spirits. She was extra-snuggly the first night she came home, but outside of that, it's business as usual.

Now what we need to work on is keeping her from sharting herself every time one of the Thundercats hisses. . . .

ALTGELDSHRUGGED TWITTER:

Watched Singing' in the Rain *today for the first time.*
Note to self: BUY TAP SHOES.

C·H·A·P·T·E·R   F·O·U·R·T·E·E·N

Either You're In or You're Out

*B*ack in the dot-com era, the big thing for newly minted executives was to join superexclusive private clubs. Previously these clubs had been the bastion of old Chicago families and businesses.[172] But because everyone was caught up in the glamour of the dot-com lifestyle, these staid old institutions began opening their doors to new members. In fact, they started bending their own rules about income and selection, offering specials to those of us in certain industries.

Fletch and I snapped up a membership at a club housed in the Sears Tower. Instead of making us pay something like five thousand dollars, they let us in for a discounted rate of five hundred dollars. Nothing made us happier than to put on our finest clothes and pop on down to the

----

[172]Read: old money.

Tower for some drinks and a quick bite. Didn't matter that we had to eat at the club because we were both a week away from payday and had no cash for groceries; we could just sign for everything and pay later.

Eventually the dot-com bubble burst, and we didn't have the means to settle up, so we defaulted on our membership. I suspect we weren't alone.

My guess is our chichi private club went back to being a quiet place for lawyers and bankers to enjoy a quick lunch before returning to their office to work another ten hours. And I'm willing to bet they don't miss us and our raucous conversations when we'd prattle on about our go-to-market strategies and sticky content and oh-my-God-how-cool-would-it-be-to-have-an-IPO. I suspect they used to look at us over their reading glasses and think, "Kids, when you stop selling air and start doing real business, y'all be sure and let us know."

There was one club I particularly wanted to join because they had an enormous outdoor pool surrounded by a giant sundeck. Unfortunately, I didn't know any members who'd sponsor me—or have good enough credit—to get in. For ten years, it's been my goal to wield the means and wherewithal to join.

As it turns out, the membership application takes two minutes, it only a costs a couple bucks more than my old gym, and I don't even have to be friends with anyone to sign up. No one does a credit check or makes me go through any kind of awkward interview process. Pretty much they show me the pool, explain where to park, and that's it.

I'm not sure whether to be disappointed or overjoyed.

But either way, I'll finally be tan.

Today's my first day using the pool. I pretty much fly out of bed and change directly from my pajamas to my swimsuit. Then I whip my hair back into a bandanna and throw on yesterday's gym shorts and I'm on my way.

When I get to the club, I toss all my stuff in a locker, grab my well-loved old Lands' End boat-and-tote bag, and rush up to the pool.

I'm delighted to finally have a place to wallow, yet the second I walk out onto the sundeck, I realize I'm doing it wrong. Apparently no one got the memo that this club is no big deal, and everyone's dressed to impress.

Ladies sport the kind of bikinis that are so intricately beaded they'd fall apart if they touched water. And their hair's done and their makeup's perfect and no one's wearing a ratty old gym shirt as a cover-up. Unconsciously, my hand goes to the small patch on the side of my suit where the chlorine destroyed the elastic last year as I work my way over to the corner of the sundeck.

I settle into the chair and spend a few hours swimming and sunning, yet I never quite seem to enjoy myself.

I feel awkward and out of place here, and I can't figure out why, particularly since I didn't even fake my way into this membership.

After a week of torrential rain, Chicago's finally graced us with a sunny day. Today I feel a little more ready to hit my pretentious pool. Instead of wearing my usual gym shorts over my bathing suit, I've got on a snappy new gauzy tunic.[173] Instead of my usual bandanna do-rag, I'm protecting

---

[173]It's from Target, but it's totally adorable.

my hair with the same kind of awesome woven straw cowboy hat you always see the *Real Housewives* wearing to the beach.

I set aside my old Ray-Bans and am instead sporting flashy sunglasses with sparkles all over the stems. I've donned some heeled sandals in lieu of Crocs and I'm carrying a little bag from the Four Seasons and not my tote.[174] When I hit the sundeck, I note with satisfaction that I'm done up exactly like every other woman at the pool, except I'm not wearing a spangled bikini, which . . . no. Instead I have on a new understated black miracle suit, with the tiniest bit of decorative trim.

I choose a chair with the best angle to the sun and observe how everyone else spreads out their club-owned towels. One goes on the top of the chaise, one covers the bottom, and the third is folded up into a little pillow until it's used to dry off after a dip in the pool. I follow suit, sit, and like everyone else in a thirty-foot vicinity, I pull out my Kindle to read my Lauren Conrad book.

And yet, once I'm settled into my little corner between the hot tub, tiki bar, and lifeguard stand, I still feel like a poseur.

Granted, I may look like everyone here, but I have the sense that I don't belong here. I mean, no one's saying anything to or about me or in any way making me feel uncomfortable. In fact, nobody's paying me any attention whatsoever.

I try to get to the root of my discomfort because I don't want to ruin another day at the pool. Why do I feel this way? I don't have sorethumb syndrome—I took special pains on wardrobe today.[175] It's not a fitness thing because I'm happy with my current level of *strongs* as I've incorporated exercise back into my life. And every body shape is repre-

---

[174]A lot of women have their actual handbags up by the pool. I find this very odd.

[175]Screw up one sorority rush and it stays with you for the rest of your life.

sented here, so even though I'm not the thinnest, I'm not the fattest. I'm also not the youngest or oldest or ugliest or prettiest. Seriously, I'm the median in every outward aspect. So whatever's going on right now is internal.

This has got to be some manifestation of the cognitive dissonance I felt back in our Sears Tower club. I knew deep down we couldn't afford what we were doing, but I figured if we kept it up long enough, everything would fall into place. You know, fake it till you make it. Only we didn't make it.

That's not the case now, though. I mean, I didn't even sign for anything from the snack bar because we have a full pantry and fridge at home.

Maybe it's the vitriolic feedback I sometimes receive. Some people get all pissed off when they come to my blog and find out I'm no longer stuck in a terrible apartment and cashing in coins to pay my electric bill. They accuse, "You've changed!" Which I have, because change is inevitable. No one's exactly who they were half a decade ago. Plus, I never pledged to live like a monk. I have no issue with anyone having nice things, myself included. My lesson was never "You can't own a Prada bag," it was "Your Prada bag can't own you."[176]

Eventually I found a way not only to live my life on my own terms, but also to live within my own means. Sometimes those means include a trip to Vegas or new shoes. I'd be lying if I said this didn't make me happy. Not being broke[177] is a hell of a lot better than being broke.[178]

....

[176]And why would you carry it to the pool? This still has me scratching my head. The lockers here seem quite secure.

[177]And bitter.

[178]And bitter.

Yet there's a huge part of me burdened with survivor's guilt. Not everyone bounced back from the dot-com era. A lot of people who were devastated stayed devastated. Or they managed to get their shit together, only to be redevastated by the current economy. My heart aches for them. I feel so guilty that Fletch and I made it out—although not without struggle—when others didn't.

I wish I could make things right for them, too.

Yet I know it's not my responsibility.

But you know what?

I do have a responsibility.

I made a commitment to try to improve myself. So I guess the root of my problem today—and what's making me feel like a phony—isn't this situation. The club members aren't at fault, nor are the flashy sunglasses. The issue isn't that I drove here in my own car, instead of having to take the bus like I did back in the day.

The problem is that I'm sitting here mindlessly reading a book by a reality television star instead of taking this time to listen to an opera or watch a classic film or take in a new museum exhibit. I was doing well in my cultural pursuits, but the Maisy news threw me so much that I got off track. I didn't want to go to see the new exhibit at the Field Museum; I just wanted to lie on the couch and hug my dog and watch *So You Think You Can Dance*.

In so doing, I've gone back on my promise to *try* to expand my mind, and that's the problem.

Fortunately, the fix is simple.

I close my Kindle and place it back in my bag. Then I pull out an old paperback copy of a novel from my classics reading list, and I turn to page one.

Hours later, I'm rock-lobster-red from the sun and totally dehydrated, yet I haven't been able to pull myself away from what I've been reading. I found my old copy of *Brave New World* recently, and I haven't looked at it in twenty years. I kind of want to kick myself for not doing so sooner.

Huxley's novel is sort of like Virginia Madsen's character's description of wine in *Sideways*—it's living and constantly evolving. For example, if you drank a particular wine now and then resampled the same vintage ten years from now, you'd taste entirely different things, even though the contents are exactly the same. Reading this book at forty-one is a whole different experience from what it was when I read it in college.

I must inadvertently let out a contented sigh because the male model two chaises down turns and smiles at me. Even though I've been engrossed in this book all day, I haven't been completely unaware of my surroundings. I noticed when this dude sat down and took his shirt off because all the women around me let out a collective gasp. He's been getting in and out of the pool at various points, and I can tell whenever he leaves because all the girls exhale and stop sucking in their tummies. I can see why they're so into him; this guy with his sculpted abs, cornflower blue eyes, and chin-length, tousled golden mane would make Bradley Cooper look like an ugly stepbrother.

Of course, my type is of the taller, louder, fatter, bigger-headed variety, and Fletch prefers I keep my dating to a minimum, which means I'm one of the few chicks who doesn't spend the afternoon either blatantly ogling or walking next to him and "accidentally" dropping her towel. I admit it's been fun to watch, kind of like visiting the monkey cage at the zoo.[179]

I get back to my reading and I hear a male voice say, "Hey, great book." I glance up and see NotBradleyCooper is addressing me. And then he lifts his book, which is a much newer hardcover edition of *Brave New World*.

I can feel fifteen sets of eyes boring into me. "Cool! Have you read it before?" I ask him.

"Only like a dozen times," he says and turns up the wattage on his Ultrabrite smile. One of the gals behind me actually moans.

"I can't get over how current it still is even though it was written, when? The forties?"

He flips to the front of his copy. "Huh, it was actually the early thirties."

"Wow."

As flattering as it is to have the pretty person's undivided attention, I'm at kind of a crucial point, and my eyes keep drifting back to the bottom of the page.

"I'll let you get back to what you're doing," he says. "Happy reading!"

And my reading is happy. Because I finally feel like I'm back on track.

Over dinner, I recount today's stories to Fletch. I finish by saying, "Five bucks says all those chicks will show up with Aldous Huxley tomorrow."

---

[179]Really, they should advertise the floor show in the membership brochure.

"Yeah," he replies, "but it won't matter."

"What do you mean?" I ask.

"Well, you said he looked like a male model and he ignored all the slutty girls and he told you 'happy reading.'"

"So?"

"That means he's gay."

Which is awesome.

I mean, come on, I'm reading Oscar Wilde next.

Of course, I may have to tell him I was the lady reading Huxley. He may not recognize me in my do-rag and old gym shorts.

The forecast this weekend is dismal, and I won't be able to do any of my Utopian reading series[180] by the pool. My foul-weather backup plan involves viewing classic musicals, and I've been happily ensconced in the world of Gene Kelly every time it's rained, but I forgot to return my latest batch to Netflix and I've got nothing new. So, when Stacey offers me a last-minute invite to a live-theater marathon, I readily agree.

I've attended just about every kind of production at this point—huge budget shows with crazily elaborate sets; small, intimate productions where I sat close enough to determine which actors needed a shave; moderate-sized, painfully artistic shows; showy song-and-dance fests, et cetera. The one aspect I've yet to cover is the workshop, and I'm doing that today.

Stacey and I are going to a media day for the Steppenwolf Theatre's First Look Repertory of New Work, which involves three brand-new

---

[180]Next up? Orwell, lots and lots of Orwell.

plays being shown to an audience for the first time. The playwrights and actors use a scaled-down set, taking this opportunity to figure out what does and doesn't work before the play goes into formal production. What we're going to see is three shows in their most raw form. Stacey says sometimes the work is genius . . . and sometimes the play will never see the light of day again.

Today all three plays, which normally rotate nights throughout the run, are performed in a row for the press. I'm kind of excited about having a theater marathon, as the closest I've ever come to anything like this is the time in college my friends and I went to see the movie *Assassins* and then immediately drove across town to watch *How to Make an American Quilt*. (Actually, all I can remember from that night is Sly Stallone running around in a bloody white suit and making myself sick on popcorn, so perhaps it's not the greatest comparison.)[181]

I asked Stacey if I had to prepare in any way, but her only advice was to wear comfortable pants. Done. The shows are being performed in the Steppenwolf garage, which confused me because I couldn't figure out if they had to move the cars or what. But apparently there's a whole theater built within the parking structure, which I find vaguely disappointing. I mean, what's more stripped down than workshopping scenes in front of an old Astrovan with an oil leak?

The stage is set up as a square between two seating sections, each accommodating about forty people. I imagine this'll be a challenge for the actors, as they'll have to be superconscious to make sure they're always properly in profile, lest half the audience stare at the back of their heads. Now that I'm a bit of a theater veteran, I know to make a beeline for the chairs in the last row in the back corner because (a) no one can

---

[181]P.S. I kind of miss Winona Ryder. Come back!

cough on my neck there[182] and (b) I'm not sharing an armrest with any strangers.

The first show is called *Honest*, which is about a James Frey–type author who may have taken liberties in retelling his life's story. I immediately connect with the subject matter, and I'm so impressed that the playwright actually learned not only how publishing works but also what it's like to write a memoir. I'm on the edge of my hard plastic seat for the whole show. When it's over, I happily engage in the postproduction discussion and praise the playwright on his uncanny accuracy.

Stacey and I break for lunch, returning for the four o'clock show. The seats we'd been in are empty, so we settle in there again. The second show's called *Sex with Strangers*, and it's about a male blogger who catapulted to Internet infamy for detailing all his sexual exploits online.

During the first scene change, I lean over to Stacey. "This play is totally about Tucker Max!"

"Who?"

"Um, he's a male blogger who catapulted to Internet infamy for detailing all his sexual exploits online." Then I go on to describe a host of similarities between the protagonist and the real guy.

Stacey gives me a little moue of disapproval. "There's an actual man who behaves like this?"

"Yeah, he wrote *I Hope They Serve Beer in Hell*. It's been on the *Times* list, like, forever. I think every fraternity guy in America has read his stuff. What's funny is that for all Tucker's success, not one of these fancy theater people has any clue that Tucker exists. What's even funnier is Tucker would probably be pissed if he knew there was a play where a character based on him was secretly a nice guy."

---

[182]Seriously, cover your mouth. Were you raised in a barn?

Despite strong performances, I don't love this play, and when it's over, we dash across the street for dinner, figuring our time would be better spent eating pork chops and not struggling to find something polite to say.

When we return, our seats are taken, so we walk around the stage to sit on the opposite side. The row in the back is completely empty when we sit. This time, Stacey gets the corner; it's only fair.

Not more than two minutes later, I'm checking my BlackBerry for the hourly Shit the Thundercats Broke update. *Aw, man,* I frown to myself, *I loved that potpourri bowl.* While I try to tally up this week's damages, I notice a shadow over me.

"That's my seat," says the shadow.

"I'm sorry?" I reply, glancing up to see a pale, disheveled man, clad in ill-fitting clothing.

"I was sitting there." He points at my lap, which causes me to giggle inadvertently. Seems like if there were a homeless guy sitting on my knees, I'd have noticed, right?

When I realize he's not joking, I ask, "Did you leave something here? There was nothing on the chair when I sat down."

"No," he responds. "But that's my seat."

What is this, second grade? "Oh, I apologize; I didn't realize there were assigned seats for the third show," I say, knowing damn well there aren't. I turn rather obviously to glance at all the empty chairs to my right. Then I return my attention to my BlackBerry—*Oh, no! Not the frog statue!*—while he continues to hover and glare. I can see Stacey concentrating intently on the playbill.

Mr. Homeless clears his throat and ups his glower factor.

I ignore him.

He does not sit in any of the empty chairs next to us, all of which have a better vantage point due to being closer to the center of the stage. He simply stands, anxiously shifting his weight from one leg to the other.

Dude . . . rude much?

I realize this man is not going to give up, so I finally ask, "Do you need me to move?"

"Yes, please."

Seriously? I glance down at Stacey, who's now trying to cover her laughter by coughing. Wait, I thought *I* was supposed to be the bad wingman? I scoot over a seat and the man plops down between us. Then I make a point of having a conversation around him for the next fifteen minutes until the play starts.

When *Ski Dubai* begins, I forget the petty turf war and pay attention to the stage. The only bit of set is a large piece of Samsonite luggage, which is used not only to haul clothes, but also as a bed, a shopping cart, and a desk. There's a dreamy, almost surreal element to this production, and between key scenes, a woman walks the length of the stage carrying a huge photograph of Dubai at night, studded with hundreds of tiny LED lights.

Even though there's literally nothing onstage but a bag, the writing and acting are such that I can imagine the oppressive desert wind of Dubai and also the cold crunch of snow in the indoor ski slope. I spend an hour and a half completely immersed on the other side of the world. I find myself being glad for the empty stage, as any scenery might have interfered with my imagination.

When it's over we rush to the garage to avoid the postshow traffic jam. "Hey, what was with the creepy homeless guy who insisted he sit between us?" I ask. Stacey looks as though she's dying to tell me something, but simply holds up a finger and doesn't say a thing until we're in her car with the doors closed before she bursts out laughing.

"He's not homeless!" she snorts, slapping her hand on the steering wheel, trying to catch her breath.

"Then who was he?"

Still laughing, Stacey sputters, "He's the theater critic for—" and then she drops the name of a great big newspaper.

"Oh . . . so *that's* why you didn't tell him to pound sand when he was trying to bully me out of my seat."

"Exactly."

"*Hmph*," I snort. "You know what? Maybe Mr. CriticPants should spend a little less time analyzing what everyone else does wrong and a little more time figuring out how to come across as less of an asshole."

Wait a minute, that? Right there? May just be my thesis statement.

Earlier this week, Fletch and I were at the bookstore, stocking up on beach reads for the Hamptons. When we passed a poetry display, he gestured toward the stack and asked, "You need any of those for your project?"

I replied, "No freaking way."

"Really? You've been complaining about wanting new cultural activities. Seems like if you drank wine, read poetry, and listened to classical music in one sitting, you'd hit the high-culture trifecta. You could even do all of it poolside."

I pondered this for a second before replying. "You're probably right, but I can't bring myself to read poetry. Something about it gives me a primal urge to beat up the author and steal his lunch money."

To backtrack, I haven't been exposed to any classic poems since my twelfth-grade English class. I detested the poetry portion of the semester and didn't see the point of agonizing over every verse, talking each line to death as we dissected meanings. I could pretty much sum up every poem we ever read in one of four ways:

(a) Love is rad.

(b) I am sad.

(c) I feel mad.

(d) War is bad.

Done. Now, let's have another in-class viewing of *East of Eden*, shall we?[183]

I do have to give the poets we studied credit for taking the effort to make their stuff rhyme. Seriously, there are only about seventy words in the English language that don't pair up with something else, so if this is an issue, simply don't end the line with "twelfth" or "almond" or "orange" or "penguin." Easy-freaking-peasy.

Point?

Any poetry I've stumbled across since AP English comes from bloggers who occasionally take a break from spilling all the intimate details of their lives to categorize their pain in verse. Should you think I didn't secretly mock them before, you should see how hard I laugh when gifted

---

[183]James Dean is *so* the original Robert Pattinson.

with one hundred free-form lines about the dead daffodils of despair, with no regard to cadence or meter. It's all I can do not to leave notes in their comments sections, saying stuff like, "Iambic pentameter, bitch!" and "Would a couple of couplets kill you?" and "Hey, e. e. cummings called—he wants his lowercase letters back."

I'm laughing as I recount my past brushes with poetry to Stacey on our way to lunch at Lula Café.

"The way I see it," I tell her, "I'm giving myself a get-out-of-jail-free pass on whatever activity seems the most unpleasant. I hate poetry; ergo, I get a pass."

Stacey cuts her eyes away from the road to glance at me. "You realize this is exactly why you *have* to study poetry now."

"Um, no," I reply.

"You say you want to challenge yourself, and poetry presents a challenge, so why are you completely dismissing it out of pocket? I'd be willing to bet there are poets you'd enjoy. Poetry's one of those things people write off without giving it a chance because it can seem boring and scary."

I nod vigorously. "Exactly my point."

"You don't have to embrace it all; rather, it's that you should keep looking until you find the piece that speaks to you. Poetry's like anything else you've worked on—you haven't loved every opera, but once you found *Carmen*, your whole perspective changed."

"Your voice of reason intrigues me, and I would like to subscribe to your newsletter," I mutter.

"You're saying you've never read anything that appealed to you? Nothing? I don't believe that."

She's got me there. "I'm okay with Robert Frost," I admit. "You sort of know what to expect when you read him. Like, he's totally reliable and unswerving. He's kind of the McDonald's of poetry; I mean, his poems aren't the best burger you'd ever eat, but they're consistently tasty." I think about some of my favorite work, like "Fire and Ice" and "The Road Not Taken." "Or no, wait, he's not that pedestrian. He's more like . . . the In-N-Out Burger of poetry."

Stacey says nothing, so I continue. "Also, I always connected with 'If' by Rudyard Kipling. Back when I was my sorority's rush chairman, I memorized all the words. When we'd all be up late getting ready for the next day's party, and everyone would be bitching about how hard I was making them work, I'd quash their complaints by reciting stuff. I'd be all, *'If you can make a heap of all your winnings and risk it all on one turn of pitch and toss and lose and start again at your beginnings and never breathe a word about your loss.'*"

"They hated you." This comes out as a statement, not a question.

"Absolutely!" Years later, their animosity is still a source of pride. All good rush chairmen are despised.

"Maybe you need a mentor?" Stacey suggests. "I didn't really know which poets I loved until I studied under the resident poet at my college."

I bark with laughter. "Your college had a *resident poet*? Ha! How often did his place get tee-peed? Daily? Hourly? Did he ride around campus on a recumbent bike with a jaunty orange safety flag flapping in the breeze? Did he carry a valise? Did he wear an ascot? Or was he a she, and did she wear long hippie skirts and never shave her legs, ever?"

"I bet your school had a resident poet, too."

"Doubtful."

"Not doubtful. I bet they have one, and you just don't know about it."

"Well," I muse, "if my school does have a resident poet, he's not to be found in the Phi Delt house."

"Just do me a favor, after lunch, go home and Google 'famous poets.' A lot of their stuff is online. Read through some of it. I'll make you a deal. If you don't find something you like, I won't harass you about learning more."

"What do I get if I do find something I like? Then what do I get?"

Stacey purses her lips and pulls her brows together. "You get the pleasure of reading something amazing."

"*Pfft,* that sucks." Stacey gives me her thousand-yard death glare and I relent. "Fine. I'll do it."

But I won't like it.

When I get home, I dutifully sit down at my computer and Google "famous poets."

Okay, fine. It's actually three days later when I finally work up the motivation to input this particular search string. And then I make a typo and accidentally search for "famous pets."

I'm surprised at how many presidential dogs I know. There's Millie, Barney, Buddy, Checkers, Manchu, and Sailor Boy. I wasn't sure of LBJ's dogs' names, but I did know he used to pick them up by the ears.[184] What's funny is I'm not sure I could name all their respective vice presidents.

I'm interested to read that Winston Churchill had a cat named Margate. I find this curious; I never pictured him as a cat person. I see him more as someone who'd have had dogs, like maybe English bulldogs.

....
[184]Jackass.

That seems so veddy, veddy British, doesn't it? Personally, I want a pair of bulldogs someday, and coincidentally, I'd like to name them Winston and Churchill, but I'd probably call them Winnie and Chilly for short and—

Ahem.

Famous *poets*.

I decide the fairest way to do this is to research what people consider to be the top one hundred poems of all time. I run across a good list, and luckily, it links to everything I need to read.

I plow through work by Ezra Pound and Oscar Wilde. Nothing they have to say speaks to me much. Neither Stephen Crane nor William Butler Yeats does it for me, either. I hit a string of Robert Frost work, and I like all of it, but it doesn't count because I already admitted an affinity for him. Robert Burns does not write in a language I even remotely recognize, so he's out. Sylvia Plath makes me want to stick my own head in the oven, and Allen Ginsberg needs to set down the bong, man.

I'm completely confident in my poetry-hating stance until I read "The Raven" by Edgar Allan Poe. I know many lines from this one because of that "Treehouse of Horror" episode on *The Simpsons*, so I'm giggling to myself as I picture Bart as the raven. I finish The poem fairly quickly and figure this is as good as any stopping point.

I feel as though this poem has no effect on me, yet while I'm walking down the hall to throw a load of laundry in the dryer, I notice a pigeon staring at me from my neighbor's window ledge.

And I almost have a frigging heart attack.

"How's it going? Anything speak to you yet?" Stacey and I are in the car, on our way to our weekly Whole Foods shopping expedition.

"Other than 'The Raven'[185] scaring the bejesus out of me, no," I reply.

"You can't hate what you're doing, or you'd have quit by now."

"I'd admit to being intrigued, but that's it. I'm not yet fond of any work, but the observations are interesting to me. First, who knew how much poetry had worked its way into pop culture? Like the speech the president gives in *Independence Day* that always makes me tear up? Bill Pullman uses a line from a Dylan Thomas poem when he talks about not going quietly into that good night. Cool, right?"

"Cool that you recognize it now," Stacey adds.

"Also, how come Shel Silverstein's considered one of the greatest poets of all time, yet no one's said shit about Dr. Seuss? Not only did he rhyme, but he drew! I mean, come on, let's give credit where it's due. And, wow, did Sylvia Plath have daddy issues or what? And Emily Dickinson? Jesus Christ, she makes me want to stab myself in the eyes and then shove handfuls of Prozac in the empty sockets." I slump back into my seat, exhausted at my own diatribe.

Stacey's nodding after I finish. "I never loved Dickinson. But want to hear something that might make her work a little more enjoyable for you? Almost everything she wrote can be sung to the tune of 'The Yellow Rose of Texas.'"

"No!" I exclaim.

"Take a listen—'*Because I could not stop for death/He kindly stopped for me/The carriage held for just ourselves/And Immortality.*'"

"That is AWESOME! Did she do that on purpose?"

"She wrote in running meter, so her work lends itself to songs with

---

[185] And the pigeon.

the same beats. Lots of her poems work with the theme to *Gilligan's Island*, too."

I let that sink in for a minute. Actually, that's not true. I silently sing those lines, Gilligan-style. "Cool as that may be, I'm giving this part of the project one more afternoon to find something I love before I officially give myself a pass."

Stacey seems a bit smug as we pull up the parking ramp at Whole Foods. "You'll find something."

Pfft. Not bloody likely.

Well, hell.

Stacey was right. Again.

Turns out there's a whole genre of poetry I like . . . and some of it doesn't even rhyme!

I started reading Maya Angelou, and hers are the first words that actually reached up from the page and said, "Hey! Pay attention!" From Maya Angelou, I moved on to Gwendolyn Brooks. Those women can give entire books' worth of a story in twenty lines.

The site I used to research them suggested I'd like Robert Hayden, too, and damn if I'm not moved by his work. And Langston Hughes? His "Let America Be America Again" poem gives me chills, even though it paints a picture of this country that I hate to think could be true. I probably connect more with these poets now that I have a little background in the blues. There are common rhythms and themes between their work and the lyrics I've heard.

I'm not yet sure how to articulate why their poems speak to me, and I'm completely green when it comes to figuring out various interpretations. But I know now that poetry is capable of holding my interest, and I want to learn more.

I want to get some of their books, but . . . I probably won't read their stuff by the pool at my club. Somehow that seems to go against the spirit of what they've written.

By the way, if anyone wants to beat up Maya Angelou for her lunch money? They're going to have to go through me first.

ALTGELDSHRUGGED TWITTER:

Expert: Most plastic surgeries are performed on the middle & lower-middle classes. Me: Duh, how else are they going to get on Rock of Love?

Have Fork, Will Travel

"Hey, you like cheese."

I say this to the back of Fletch's head, prompting him to look up from his mammoth plastic storage bin of cords. He recently got a new desk[186] and has been busy rearranging his office to accommodate it. Somehow in moving things, he's unearthed a number of yet-to-be-homed power cords and computer cables. He carefully winds each one in on itself and secures it with a zip tie so he won't find it in a Christmas-tree-light-string snarl when he needs it. And yet I'd be willing to wager all the money in my purse—again, about eight dollars—that he will never, ever need it because we have *no* powerless appliances and *ten thousand*

---

[186]Yes, courtesy of a late-night Ambien shopping spree.

spare cables. The dove gray one he's oh so lovingly laying to rest right now probably belongs to the dot-matrix printer we owned in 1996[187]. Or maybe an Atari Pong console.

Cautiously, he replies, "I do like cheese. But if you're hinting at another one of your 'Let's have cheese for dinner!' ideas, count me out. That's not a balanced diet."

"*Pfft*, it's totally balanced if you have grapes, olives, and crackers. Anyway, that's not my point. I signed up for a class on wine-and-cheese pairing tomorrow night, and I want you to come with me."

I've done an awful lot of work on my Jenaissance so far, but most of what I've done has been with Stacey or Gina or my college roommate Joanna. This project isn't driving us apart, but not much of it's brought us together. Now that's about to change.

His expression is vaguely stricken. "Wouldn't you rather take Stacey?"

I shake my head vehemently. "Stacey already *knows* how to pair stuff. Don't you remember when she told us about her 'cheesemonger,' and I kept giggling because it sounded dirty? She's the main reason you and I have progressed past cubed cheese. Plus it's being taught at the Chopping Block, and you said you wanted to take classes there."

"I said I wanted to take a grilling class there, not some mincing wine-and-cheese class."

"Well, you're in luck! I signed us up for lessons on making Brazilian and Indian food, too. But tomorrow night, we learn wine and cheese."

Fletch then puts on an expression I call his "Muppet face." He wrinkles his brow and flattens his lips so hard that his chin begins to curl up

....
[187]And replaced in 1997.

toward his nose, like he's a sock puppet and the fist inside is clenching. "Any chance I can get out of this?"

I consider his request for a moment. "Tell you what—you find the office machinery that goes with the cord in your hand, and I'll rope someone else into going with me."

Fletch and I arrive at the Chopping Block with a few minutes to spare. We check in at the front counter, and I locate my sticky paper name tag. When I signed up I wasn't quite sure who'd join me, so I simply wrote "guest" on the form. I pick up a blank name tag and a Sharpie and hand them to Fletch. "Fill this in."

"Why?" He's been antagonistic about tonight ever since we got in the car. I swear he Googled every road under construction and made sure to take them, so our three-mile trip took forty-five minutes.

If I had to guess why he's uncomfortable, I'd say this is one of those instances in which he's worried people will assume he's gay, like when I ask him to hold my purse while I tie my shoe or suggest he might enjoy whipped cream in his mocha.

(Sidebar: I blame Judd Apatow for Fletch's sensitivity. Had he not written such a great scene in *The 40 Year-Old Virgin*, Fletch and I wouldn't have spent the last few years telling each other, *"You know how I know you're gay?"*)

I massage my temples. "Because you *have* to. Everyone else is wearing name tags."

"Can't I leave it blank? Or just fill in 'guest'?"

Barely containing my annoyance, I hiss, "Or maybe you can draw one of those round-trumpet-arrow symbols, and we'll have the rest of the class call you Prince?'"

He gives in. "Fine. But you fill it out. I have the handwriting of a serial killer."

We pass all the upscale kitchen accessories and cookbooks[188] and settle in on chairs around the big butcher-block counter filling the center of the room. Each place is set with a plate of seven cheeses, two wineglasses, one of which contains champagne, a cup of water, a pencil, some paper with descriptions printed on them, and a butter knife. We sit at the end, and I can see Fletch tense up when he notices every other person at the counter is female.

As I am having none of his tomfoolery, I take a closer look at my plate. I'm delighted to recognize some of what's there. There are a couple of pale, hard offerings that I'm sure are Manchego and Gruyère.[189] I'm willing to wager the big white dollop is goat cheese and the soft, double-rind-covered one is Brie. Brie was my gateway cheese—I tried it for the first time some years back, and I loved it so much it gave me the courage to realize that not all cheese is rectangular, individually wrapped, and the color of Paris Hilton after a spray tan.

Most of the offerings look delicious, save for the pile of debris sitting in the middle of it all. This heaving, yellowing, blue-green mass is lumpy and loose and crumbly. This is less "cheese" and more "gangrene."

As if this mass of unpasteurized unhappiness weren't gross enough, it also reeks.

A lot.

If someone wanted to spread the taste of death on a crostini, this is

....

[188]Martha Stewart's book on cupcakes, I'll be back for you!

[189]See, Stacey? I totally pay attention to you.

what they'd choose. If I accidentally stepped in this, I'd find the nearest garden hose to remove it, as the sidewalk edge might not get it all off and I'd fear it would eat through my shoe.

I point at the glob. "This one is terrifying."

"Yeah, but maybe if you understand it, it won't be so scary," Fletch counters.

"Really, now you choose to be the voice of reason? Really?"

Before he can reply, a late-coming couple takes the two remaining seats next to us. They appear to not only be heterosexual but also married. The husband catches Fletch's eye, they both grimace and nod, and finally Fletch's shoulders relax.

The class begins and I'm so busy shooting daggers in Fletch's direction that I completely miss the instructor's name. The literature we've been handed calls her "the Wine Goddess," so I decide to go with that.

Wine Goddess instructs us to raise our glass of champagne so we can toast to good wine and to not being lactose intolerant but I already drank my champagne because no one said not to.

Seriously, I paid sixty bucks a head for this; I will suck down whatever's placed in front of me.

Wine Goddess's assistant refills my glass, and after strict instructions on how to swirl and sniff, we proceed to toast and I drain my cup. Nice. Very dry. Or not very dry. I'm not entirely sure I know the difference. Perhaps I should listen instead of mentally skewering Fletch with the kabob sticks that are now twenty percent off?

Wine Goddess makes some kind of soften-up-the-room joke about how her job is about making pairings accessible to the proletariat, which causes Fletch to grab my sheet and scratch, *"The proletariat don't take wine-and-cheese classes."*

We're instructed to hold up our glasses and swirl again. I follow suit and drink all I have. This is tasty. I can't tell you why it's tasty, but it is.

Then again, I never met a glass of wine I didn't like.

We're sampling something called Gruet Brut Blanc de Noirs. I'm unsure of the literal translation, but I will verify that it's vaguely less burp-inducing than other champagne.[190]

Before we nibble on the first offering of cheese, we're instructed to have another sip. I have to motion to Wine Goddess's assistant for yet another refill, and she shoots me a murderous glance. Hey, you in the apron, listen up—when I am sixty dollars' worth of drunk, *then* you're allowed to get snarky. Till then, shut up and pour.

Wine Goddess instructs us on the proper way to hold a wineglass, which is by the stem only. The reason for this is you don't want the heat from your fingers to alter the wine temperature. Frankly, I've always held my glass by the stem because I don't like smudgy fingerprints, so I'm pleased to have been inadvertently right about something. Apparently the true wine snobs grasp nothing but the flat base of the glass, yet when I try this hold, I almost dump the rest of my champagne in my lap.

(Sidebar: The next time you watch any lowbrow reality show, pay attention to how all the girls hold their glasses. I guarantee each of them clasps it by the bowl. It's crazy-making.)

We huff and swirl, huff and swirl. Wine Goddess quizzes us on what we smell, but all I can come up with is that my champagne smells like champagne with a few undertones of rage emanating from Apron Girl. Other people at the table suggest they taste sour apples and yeast. How the hell do they taste that?

We take our first bite of cheese, and ding, ding, ding, score! I was

---

[190]I wonder if that's its selling point?

right! This is Gruyère, also known as Comté.[191] We're told these pair nicely because both are delicate and mellow. The champagne is acidic and acid is BFF with all the salt in the cheese. The cheese has a bit of a crunch to it, which is a relief because the last time I served Gruyère, I thought I might have sliced it on a dirty cutting board.[192]

We learn that the crunchy bits aren't salt (or crumbs from a sandwich two lunchtimes ago) but sugar crystals known as lactase. "Sometimes there's sugar in cheese?" I ask and Wine Goddess confirms this.

I poke Fletch. "See? The Swavery Grilled Cheese totally *was* a good idea."[193]

"Keep working the stove in the middle of the night and I *will* make you sleep with a bell around your neck," he replies.

Next up we sample the pairing of sauvignon blanc with goat cheese, but I already know how well they complement each other. However, Wine Goddess almost ruins this pairing for me as she makes us swish and hold the wine under our tongues to see what our sweet-tart receptors do. (Hint—saliva's involved.) I fear I won't be able to help myself from teaching everyone how to make themselves drool at my next party.

We come to the chardonnay–lump of infection pairing and my palms begin to sweat. I don't want to be the only asshole at the counter who's afraid of cheese, and yet I really, really don't want to put this hideous concoction anywhere near my face.

Wine Goddess explains how the weird residual stuff left in your

---

[191]Make a panini out of this cheese, adding a slice of Granny Smith apple and some Dijon mustard. You'll totally thank me.

[192]To think I did all that surreptitious cheese-wiping for nothing.

[193]One Ambien-induced night I tiptoed down to the kitchen and melted cheese, toasted bread, and coated the whole thing in sanding sugar. I dubbed it "swavery" because it was both sweet and savory. And it was delicious! (I think.)

mouth after you sip some chardonnays is oak sap and tells us it's best to serve the wine with food, as that will help get rid of the resin. Then she prompts us to taste the Roaring Forties Blue. I hesitate.

Okay, I've had bleu cheese before, and I like it just fine on my chicken wings and in my Cobb salad (provided the chunks are small and white), but this is . . . so far outside my comfort zone. I did mention it looks like a bruise, yes? Yet I'm fascinated to find out it originated from the cracks in a cheese mold. I love knowing that some industrious French farmer looked at the blue veins and said, "Pairhaps ziz vill bee delectabulll and not jus' garbaaaghe?"

Taking the tiniest, least-in-need-of-an-antibiotic-looking bit on the tip of my knife, I break off a big piece of bread and spread it. Then I pop it in my mouth and force myself to begin to chew, and I realize it would be my great pleasure and honor to pair this with a chicken wing, for it truly *is* delectable.

Who knew?

I mean, except for the professional at the front of the room who specifically picked it, the fine cheesemakers at the Roaring Forties company, and the original Frenchman who wasn't afraid to let a little penicillin ruin his *fromage*.

After a quick discussion about how screw caps eliminate "cork taint,"[194] we move on to a bottle of Regis Cruchet Vouvray, which may as well mean "purple monkey dishwasher" to me. Wine Goddess explains that this is the "nerdiest" of wines, and if you ever encounter a wine snob, this is the one about which he or she will go on. I guess it's because it's kind of weird, it's an acquired taste.

We huff and swirl and I take a sniff and all I smell is dark and fore-

---

[194]Which also makes me giggle.

boding and . . . wait, I think I caught a whiff of something other than "wine." The nose on this is like a . . . Fig Newton?

Wine Goddess asks, "What do you smell?"

I blurt, "Figs?"

"Very good!" she exclaims. HA! Yes! In your face, imaginary person against whom I was competing! I win!

I take another taste and realize that I don't actually *like* figgy wine. Huh. Apparently I have met a wine I don't like. Considering how many boxes of pure swill and bottles of Boone's Farm I've happily quaffed in my lifetime, this feels like a tiny victory.

But I don't dump my Vouvray into my heretofore-empty spit bucket because I still haven't tasted it with the Brie. Except, this isn't Brie at all—it's a Brie impostor called Robiola Due Latte. As with each cheese, we're instructed to pick up a bit on our knife and give it a solid whiff before tasting.

"What do you smell?" Wine Goddess asks.

"A farm," one girl replies, wincing.

"No, it's like sheep poop," her friend corrects.

"Eau de sweat sock?" asks the wife beside me.

Apparently because the Roaring Forties was so stinky, I didn't even notice the stench wafting off the Robiola. The scent is indescribable unless you've had a mouse expire under your fridge and couldn't get maintenance to pick it up all weekend.

I'm terror-struck about the possibility of this passing my lips, but Wine Goddess has been spot-on in almost every other instance. So, on blind faith alone, and despite my olfactory protest, Fletch and I give a quick "cheers" by tapping our knives together.

I watch as Fletch recoils and tries not to gag, which is kind of weird because there is a frigging *choir of angels* sounding off in my mouth right about now. They're up there singing *Ave Maria* and rolling around in this stuff. I take a much larger portion and savor it before sipping the Vouvray.

Yeah, that still kind of sucks.

But it sucks less with a cheese chaser.

I deposit the rest of my glass in the bucket and swirl around a quick water rinse before declaring that figs belong in cookies, not beverages. Then I scoop up the Robiola left on Fletch's place and marvel at how smooth and creamy it is and how the flavor swing-dances with every single one of my taste buds.

After the Robiola we have Tempranillo with a sweaty slice of Manchego[195] and Shiraz with Dutch Gouda,[196] both favorites and which I expected to love. Yet I can't get the thrill of tasting Robiola out of my mind or my mouth.

I have been ruined by stinky cheese.

Our last selection is Parmesan paired with an Italian red wine called Avignonesi Vino Nobile de Montepulciano. Alone, both are fairly nondescript, but once I taste them together, I suddenly want to rush out of the store and whip up a big batch of pasta and marinara and serve it with tumblers full of this wine to my whole family, which is odd because I don't even particularly like red sauce.[197]

Wine Goddess tells us that Italian wines aren't cocktail wines, meaning they're not something you should sip while watching *The Bachelor*. (Noted.) They're specifically made to pair with food, which is kind of genius.

At some point in the evening, Fletch stops being so taciturn and

---

[195] The "sweat" is actually expressed oil.

[196] Deeply yellowed because it's aged five years.

[197] Or most of my family.

begins to enjoy himself. Maybe it's the wine, maybe it's the cheese, or perhaps he stopped worrying that people would think he was gay.

Nah, it's probably mostly because I promise he can buy a new ten-inch chef's knife at the class's conclusion.

Regardless, we likely just made cheese for dinner less of a fantasy and more of a reality.

Now, if only I could get him to toss that stupid box of cords.

"Hello, hey, Fletch? Ohmigod, you're going to die! You're SO going to die! Guess where I got us reservations?"

"Conference call."

"What? Where's that?" I haven't heard of Conference Call. Is it new, I wonder? I'm doing my best to keep up with all the latest eateries in *Time Out Chicago* but these places keep popping up like mushrooms and they all have such odd names.

"Clarification—I'm on a conference call," Fletch says.

"Oh." That makes more sense. "But then why are you talking to me if you're on the other line?"

"I only picked up because I saw caller ID flash fifteen times in the last two minutes and I assumed you were bleeding."

"I'm fine—actually, I'm better than fine because I got us reservations at Moto! How incredible is that? It is beyond impossible to get in there." I am seriously gloating over snagging a reservation. Moto specializes in molecular gastronomy. The chefs eschew burners and ovens, opting instead to create food using blowtorches and liquid nitrogen, all of which I learned from watching Marcel and Richard compete on *Top Chef*.

Fletch is a tad curt. "Okay, (a) that you got a reservation proves it's not impossible, and (b) can I call you back? I can't keep my other call on hold much longer."

"Well, make sure you brag to your little friends at work. They'll be duly impressed."

"I doubt that because I'm sure they don't care. And if it's so hot, how'd you get us in? Did you tell them who you are or something?"

I don't have the heart to tell him we got in because I went to a free reservation-finding Web site and didn't have a specific day or time in mind.

So with great conviction, I tell him, "Yes. Yes, I did."[198]

We arrive at Moto about fifteen minutes early. Our table isn't ready yet, so the hostess invites us to sit at the bar, which apparently is right in front of us. This bar is the antithesis of any bar I've ever seen before. Instead of being decked out with mirrors and tiny lights illuminating shelves full of call brand liquors, it's a simple counter with a couple of stools. The wall behind it is blank and unadorned except for a couple of framed prints. When I sit down, I bash both my knees against the bar.

The bartender hands us drinks menus, and while we're trying to decide, we watch him place a handful of eyedroppers filled with colorful liquids bulb side up in a rocks glass full of ice. They remind me of those little paraffin bottles full of sweet-flavored syrups I used to have as a kid.[199]

"What was that?" I ask as a waitress whisks the glass into the dining room.

....

[198]Oh, come on. Every marriage can use a little mystery, right?

[199]I vaguely recall swallowing the wax from time to time. This is probably why I can't do long division.

The bartender explains, "That's our Martini Library. The individual pipettes hold different-flavored martinis, so you can mix and match them."

"How do you drink them?" Fletch asks.

"*Why* do you drink them?" I add.

"How about you see for yourself?" The bartender reaches under the counter and presents us with a glass containing two fuchsia pipettes. "On the house. This one's raspberry."

I pick mine up and I'm completely flummoxed as to how to get its contents into my mouth. Maybe this really IS one of those Nik-L-Nips from my childhood. Maybe I'm supposed to bite it, drink it, and then chew the container till my jaw hurts? I kind of don't want to suck on it because I have a small phobia.[200]

Before I begin tearing it with my teeth, Fletch demonstrates the proper technique. He lifts it to his mouth, tilts his head back, and squeezes it from the bottom. He considers it for a moment before proclaiming it, "Nice."

I follow suit, taking care not to squeeze it so hard I drown, or so lightly it dribbles on my dress. Raspberry-flavored success! Tasty though it may be, I figure if I get a whole cupful of these, there's bound to be an accident, so I decide on a different cocktail. We watch as the bartender assembles our drinks. Mine contains a mixture of gin, white grape juice, lime, and brandy. Fletch opts for something made of rye and grapefruit juice—gross—but the bartender assures us it's a crowd-pleaser.

Assembling each beverage takes a couple of minutes and a lot of concentration. The bartender pivots back and forth behind the bar, grab-

-----

[200]I can't bring myself to drink anything with a n-i-p-p-l-e on it. This is why I almost drown every time I get a bottle of Evian Sport water. I tend to aim it at my mouth and then squeeze too hard, and it hits my throat like a garden hose.

bing ingredients and measuring apparati. "Sure are lots of moving parts to this operation," Fletch notes and the bartender nods serenely while he pours and mixes. I can tell Fletch is itching to hop behind there to fix it himself. When we were in college, he always prided himself on his speed as a bartender. His cocktails were never good, he'd make customers jump when he slammed empty bottles into the trash, and he made waitresses cry, but he was fast—I'll give him that.

The bartender tenderly stirs each of our drinks before using eye-droppers to add the last bits of ingredients. "Enjoy!" he says, placing the chilled glasses in front of us. As soon as we taste them, we understand these were worth the wait.

Grudgingly, Fletch admits, "Yeah, I probably couldn't have done this myself."

"Check it out," I say. "The grapes on my swizzle stick are frozen."

"Mine's got a cube of frozen grapefruit juice in it," Fletch tells me.

"That's so *Schoolhouse Rock!*" I exclaim. "'They had a fun time making sunshine on a stick!' Remember that?" Before Fletch can agree, the hostess informs us our table is ready. She suggests we leave our cocktails at the bar, and someone will deliver them to us.

"I'm already impressed," Fletch whispers to me. "That's great service."

"Oh, please," I say. "We used to do that when I worked at the Olive Garden."

We enter a minimalist dining room, dark save for the few pools of light coming from candles scattered on ledges. One wall is lined with padded banquettes in a neutral color and a large, light curtain masks the wall across from it. Tables are small and close together, and each is covered with a simple white tablecloth. There are no centerpieces or art anywhere.

There's nothing on our table except a napkin, a water glass, and a piece of paper describing the wine pairings for the two tasting menus. When a hostess called to confirm my reservation, I had to choose between the ten- and twenty-course option, as there are no other dinners here. I went for the ten when she informed me the twenty takes over five hours to serve. Who has that kind of time?

After the waiter confirms our order and wine pairing, he returns with two bowls. "This is your menu," he tells us, referring to the thick piece of printed parchment. "All of your upcoming courses are listed on it. In the bowl you'll find a balsamic reduction and ramp butter. You can begin your meal by eating your menu. Enjoy." And with a slight bow, he backs away from our table.

I run my fingers over the menu, which is actually a piece of herbed crostini printed with edible ink. I break off a piece and cautiously dip it in the butter. This feels so wrong, but the second I catch a whiff of the fragrant spices, I change my mind. I take a bite, savor for a moment, and exclaim, "Wow . . . this menu is delicious!"

"Can't eat the menu at your precious Olive Garden, now, can you?"[201] Fletch teases me. Then he takes a bite of his menu heaped with butter. "Hands down, this is the best menu I ever tasted." He chews thoughtfully. "You've got to give them props for coming up with such a clever way of dealing with bread service, which is generally pretty pedestrian, no matter how nice the place is."

"I know! I'd love to have some more. I'm all, 'Excuse me, waiter, can I get another basket of menu for the table, please?' Seriously, between this and the drinks, I've got a feeling this meal's going to be an adventure."

Our plates are cleared and our first wine match arrives. We receive

----

[201]DO NOT BASH THE OLIVE GARDEN.

our first course, Moto's take on a Denver omelet, which is served on a long, narrow white plate. We get what appears to be one Tater Tot, a spoonful of scrambled eggs over a pile of tiny diced vegetables, and a small, buttered English muffin. But I'm quickly learning that nothing is as it seems. The Tater Tot's actually a cube of deep-fried shrimp, and the eggs are a deliciously fluffy powder that evaporates the second it hits my tongue. And the bread's a big puff of meringue topped with something sweet and peachy.

The whole time we're eating our first course, we're laughing. I mean, Tater Tots are supposed to taste like grease, salt, and potatoes. There's no shrimp involved. Eggs are, well, they're eggs. Except here, they're totally not. We both agree we like the first wine pairing. "How on earth did the sommelier figure out what best pairs with cartoon food?" I muse.

As a nod to where I've come from, I begin to record my reactions to each wine in Lolcat. *Wine Spectator* may give this bold New Zealand sauvignon blanc an 89, but I rank it a "nom."

Our second wine pairing arrives, and Fletch and I have a small spat over it. It's a Moscatel Secco, which Fletch swears is what Fred Sanford drank on *Sanford and Son*. I argue that can't be true because his yard was filled with old toilets and stuff and there's NO WAY that Fred's "muscatel" could be related to this fine (nom plus one) Portuguese offering.[202]

"This is instant risotto," the waiter says, setting two small square bowls in front of us. "Take your spoon and mix the sauce with the grains, and it will instantly 'cook' them." We follow our instructions and stir our servings until all the rice and the pieces of fresh scallop are covered. Even

---

[202]Bite me, Wikipedia. And don't tell him I was wrong.

though the "rice" is more like a dried noodle,[203] the result is both al dente and creamy, exactly like real risotto.

At this point, neither Fletch nor I can contain our giggles. Even though we've not consumed one whole cocktail each, we feel euphoric. Maybe it's something about finding comedy injected in a situation that, although it's often pleasant, isn't usually funny.

Next up, we get what the waiter calls "deconstructed French onion soup." He presents us with an almond-shaped bowl that has golden Gruyère melted in an artful swoosh on the inside lip and a pile of sautéed, shredded onions placed in the corner. Then he takes a fragrant broth and pours it over everything.

The scent of the broth hit me while the waiter was ten feet away, so I already have my spoon ready the second he leaves our table. I dive in. "Everything I eat here suddenly becomes the best thing I've ever tasted," I remark. Fletch can't respond as he's heroically fighting the urge to bury his face in his dish.

Before the fourth course is served, I glance at my watch. "Do you realize we've already been here an hour and a half?"

Fletch's eyebrows fly up. "Really? I had no idea."

Our fourth course is Moto's version of chicken wings. "We've taken seared capon and served it on a bed of braised celery. This here"—the waiter gestures to a long swath of a creamy pinkish substance—"is your bleu cheese puree, because you can't have wings without bleu cheese, right? This"—he points at an angry red dot in the middle of the plate—"is our house-made wings sauce. And, finally"—he points to a plastic-wrapped bit of parchment bread with a photo printed on it—"this is a picture of your plate. You can eat this, too."

....

[203]Or maybe a Rice Krispie.

"How?! How does the chef come up with this?" I wonder out loud.

Fletch shrugs. "He must have *really* played with his food as a kid."

I imagine some guests bring their plastic-wrapped photo home as a souvenir, but not me. I rip that thing out of the packaging and stuff it in my mouth. This one's different from the other one. Instead of garlic and Parmesan, it's flavored with chili powder and tastes exactly like a wing. The heat gets me and I discreetly cough into my napkin.

"A little hot for you?" Fletch asks.

"Yeah, but it's more of a back-of-the-mouth burn, not so bad."

I try hard not to inhale my "wings," choosing to delight in all the flavor nuances. The colonel may use eleven herbs and spices, but this dish has, like, a million. I take meager sips of the Brut paired with it, anxious to draw out the pleasure of this experience as long as possible.

"Hey, did you taste the dot of sauce yet? It's . . ." Fletch pauses to find an appropriately epicurean term.

"I haven't." In one fell swoop, I spear a bit of capon, sop up the sauce, and pop it in my mouth. I wait to feel the buzz coming from perfectly cooked capon mixed with a delicately balanced sauce, but all I feel is . . . warmth. Or, rather, heat.

Hot heat.

Fire heat.

Burning, burning, BURNING heat.

". . . kind of spicy," he concludes as tears begin to pour out of my eyes. I'm trying desperately not to make a scene, but I'm sputtering and choking. I grab my water to attempt to quench the feeling that *I just French-kissed the devil.*

I cough and wheeze and try to furtively wipe my tongue with a napkin, but that just seems to make THE HOT angrier. "There's a bit of an after-burn, too," he helpfully adds. I slam the rest of my water, my champagne, his water, his champagne, which I practically have to wrestle out of his hand, and I only find relief once I place his melting grapefruit-juice cube in my mouth.

I'm quickly distracted from my seared mouth when I see what the table to my left is being served. They're getting mini-cupcakes baked with duck fat and filled with fois gras![204] The woman next to us groans as she bites into the cake, but no one pays attention. Everyone in here has cried out in joy and pleasure at least once over the course of their meal.

While I covet cupcakes, our fifth course arrives, and it appears to be a . . . a half-smoked cigar served in a dirty metal ashtray. Actually, it's a Cuban sandwich shaped like a cigar, and the ash is really just a bunch of mashed seeds, but it's almost too realistic. They've even created a cigar label out of some edible paper.

"I can't eat this," I say.

"I'm not sure I can, either," Fletch agrees.

My stomach begins to roil. "A dirty cigar-filled ashtray is exactly what I picture when I feel sick and want to make myself barf."

Fletch pokes at the pile of ash. "That's got to be the magic of this place. It fools your senses. Your eyes and your mouth transmit entirely different images, and your brain gets mixed signals."

"This whole meal has been some Alice in Wonderland 'eat me' kind of shit," I note. "And it's like there's a party in my mouth, and I want to send out a Twitter message inviting everyone to join me."

"That's quite the astute observation. Perhaps *Saveur* magazine will commission you to write down your thoughts for their next issue?"

"Okay then, how about this? Tonight this restaurant has taken some-

---

[204]Damn! Should have gotten the twenty-course dinner!

thing I've done every day of my life and turned it completely on its ear. They've redefined the whole concept of food for me."

Grudgingly he admits, "That's not bad."

I continue. "It just occurred to me that there are no paintings or posters or anything on the walls because this meal IS the art. And now I am going to eat some damn art." I lift my cigar, dip it in the ash, and take a big, confident bite.

And maybe I had my eyes closed, but it still totally counts.

To: fletch_at_ work

From: jen_at_home

Subject: my mother is a fish

I wrote that I enjoyed *As I Lay Dying* on my Facebook wall today and every girl I know who went to Ole Miss posted to say that the whole town of Oxford, Mississippi hated Faulkner. They said he was really just an angry old drunk.

But, seriously? He won the Nobel Prize for Literature! If that doesn't excuse you from having a few snorts before chasing lippy college students off your lawn, why even *be* an author?

The Real World: Middle Age

"**N**OOOOO!"

I'm sitting at my computer, Googling the name on the slip of paper in front of me. I glance at the screen and back down at the paper and bury my face in my hands. This can't be. This simply can't be.

With a trembling hand, I dial Fletch's office. He's been much better about picking up the phone since I stopped calling him to discuss what happened on my TiVo cache of *Big Brother*.

"Hello?"

"Bad news!" I gasp.

Fletch is instantly concerned. "Is Maisy okay?"

"What? Oh, yeah, she's fine. She's on her bed and Chuck Norris keeps ambushing her and batting at her tail."

"Did the Thundercats break another vase?"

I grit my teeth. "We have no more vases to break." The upside of saving three feral kittens is the satisfaction of knowing they're going to have a happy and safe life. The downside of saving three feral kittens is suddenly your house is filled with THREE FERAL KITTENS.

"Then what's going on?"

"You know how for Authors Night we had to select an authors' dinner? And I picked the one with the general because I thought it would be at Rudy Giuliani's house? Well, we got the dinner all right."

Fletch is excited because he really wants to meet the general and talk all about the kind of boring Army stuff that makes my eyes glaze. "Great!"

"Not great. Not great *at all*. I just got the host's name and address, and I did a little Google-stalking. Okay, not only are we NOT going to be at a lovely dinner party filled with like-minded conservatives—we're going straight into the belly of the beast."

I can hear him exhale. "Now you're starting to confuse me. Does this have anything to do with *Big Brother*?"

"No! The house where this thing's being held? Okay, not only is the host buddies with George Soros but her foundation helps fund Media Matters for the Left and her son works for the Obama administration! This is an unmitigated disaster."

"How so?"

"How so? HOW SO? I am going to crash and fucking burn the second anyone brings up politics. I won't be able to keep my enormous mouth shut! I'm going to end up getting kicked out!"

Fletch is the voice of reason. "Isn't the whole point of your project to push yourself to grow? Doesn't it stand to reason that figuring out how to behave at this party will be much more of an accomplishment than if you sat around with a bunch of Republicans?"

I can't argue with his logic, and yet . . . maybe I don't want to grow quite this much.

"What are you getting?" I ask.

Stacey scans the menu before replying, "Probably the wiener schnitzel."

I snigger. "Because it's fun to say 'wiener'?"

"No, I'm not *twelve*. I've had it before and I know I like it."

"By the way, speaking of being twelve? Fletch and I were at our knife-skills class[205] last week, and the instructor was talking about all these different types and brands of knives. The one that made us both giggle first was the boner by Friedr Dick. And then later, the instructor showed us this Japanese model of knife sharpener and said the only downside was you couldn't use it on German knives because the blade's not as thin. And then—then! She demonstrates and says, *'See? You can't put your ten-inch Dick in here because it's too thick and it'll get stuck.'* Fletch and I laughed so hard, we had to put our heads down on the table."

"Did everyone else laugh?"

"*No one.* They all just chopped their onions and looked uncomfortable, which pretty much puts the nail in my theory that class follows culture." Not quite cause for Shame Rattle, but close.

Stacey and I are having dinner at a German place. I decided to add this cuisine to my Eat the World curriculum even though I've technically had German cuisine before, having spent a few days in Germany when I

....
[205]Cooking, not stabbing.

was in high school. However, my memories are fuzzy at best.[206] I recall writing my name in mustard on my plate at some restaurant on the Autobahn although I can't tell you what I actually ate.[207] And when we were in Bavaria, my friends and I stopped into some chalet-looking place when we had a free afternoon. We couldn't read the menu, so we just pointed to the item that sounded most like soup. Whatever we got was fine, but it wasn't memorable.[208]

Since this restaurant is right next to where we're going later, giving German food another whirl made sense. The outside is adorably authentic-looking and I've wondered what the inside was like when I've walked by. Fletch is always saying we should stop in for some big sausages, which always makes me giggle since I apparently turn into Michael Scott whenever anyone says anything even resembling a vaguely double entendre. As part of my cultural Jenaissance, I'm working to change this, but it's so hard.[209]

Anyway, on the street, it's 2009, yet the second we actually enter the restaurant, it's 1976. I'm not sure why it feels so dated in here, but it might have something to do with the Fifth Dimension playing "Up, Up, and Away in My Beautiful Balloon" on the hi-fi. Or maybe it's all the faux-wood paneling, or the heavy carpeting and low acoustical tiled ceiling, or maybe it's just the weird built-in "architectural" arches that we all loved so much back during the Bicentennial.

Each table is surrounded by the chairs my Girl Scout buddy Donna had in her breakfast nook, and the restaurant's lit with the exact same caned, tulip-shaped hanging lamps I had in my fourth-grade bedroom.

....

[206]Thanks to delicious German wine and parents on the other side of the earth.
[207]Probably mostly French fries.
[208]Except for the bread. The bread was spectacular there, as it is here.
[209]That's what she said! Argh! I did it again!

Frankly, I'm surprised there are German beer signs on the walls and not Jimmy Carter campaign posters. Feels like a key party could break out in here any minute. We spent a solid five minutes gawping and looking for Jack Tripper before we even picked up our menus.

"What should I get?" I ask Stacey.

"You can go one of two ways with German cuisine. You can take the sausage route. . . ."

I shouldn't have to tell you what this statement's effect is on me.

Stacey ignores the interruption and continues. "Or you could go the braised-meat route." She pauses and raises an eyebrow, waiting to see if I can find an entendre. I can't, so she goes on. "If you want braised, probably the most traditional item here is the sauerbraten, which is their version of pot roast."

My stomach inadvertently heaves and I tell her, "Oh, I am *not* eating that. *That* I've had before. My dad is cuckoo for German food, and once for his birthday, he asked my mom to make him a sauerbraten. She cooked that damn thing for a week and our whole house stank of feet. I kept calling it sour-rotten. Even our dog was repulsed. She hid upstairs for three days. And then when my mom finally served it, the meat was awful and there were gingersnaps in the gravy!"

"To be fair, the recipe calls for gingersnaps. They go in the sauce."

"Are the cookies whole but soggy from meat juice?"

"No. They're ground up."

"Exactly." And then we both quietly shudder.

Stacey returns to her menu and her smile becomes a wry twist. "Perhaps you'd like a traditional German appetizer? Why don't you try this or this?" She points to the part of the menu that lists jalapeño poppers and buffalo wings.

"Laugh all you want, but as I kid I'd have killed for 'traditional German' poppers or wings, no matter how spicy, if it meant I didn't have to eat vinegar-cookie stew."

We decide to forgo appetizers because of the time constraint of hitting our friend's book signing in an hour. And something tells me we'd have struggled deciding between the herring in cream choice, the sausage salad suggestion, and the headcheese platter.

I order an iced tea because I'm driving, which is a shame because now that I've taken some wine courses, I actually understand why German wines like Riesling appeal to me so much. I like the floral notes and how sometimes the wine smells of green apples and fresh melons. I dig the mouth feel of a medium-bodied wine, and I appreciate that although it can taste sweet, the finish is crisp.

I decide on the rindsroulade, which is a strip of marinated sirloin wrapped around bacon and onions and served with a side of spaetzle, a homemade German noodle. Stacey, of course, gets the wiener schnitzel, an innocuous breaded meat cutlet.

Our dinners are served and there's nothing green anywhere near our plates. Or red or yellow or orange, for that matter. Stacey's dinner consists of a big beige patty with a scoop of something less beige, and mine entails a giant brown lump and some soft noodles, all swimming in a deep pool of gravy. If you eat with your eyes first, this is in no way appetizing. Suddenly I wish we hadn't refused our waitress's offer of more bread.

I take a bite of the spaetzle, which has the flavor and consistency of noodles in canned chicken soup. I slice a bit of my meat roll and taste it. I have a few more bites and proclaim, "You could serve this to people who've had stomach surgery. The rindsroulade could replace the rice in the BRAT diet."

"It's that bland?"

"Yeah. I mean, not bad, per se, if you're looking for comfort food. And I could see eating this and then having the energy to chop down the whole Black Forest. But it's superplain. And heavy. This? This is the polar opposite of Chinese food. You know, you have some and an hour later you're hungry? You eat this, and two or three days later, you're hungry again." I slice into the middle of my meat, splitting it up so I can take half home to Fletch. It's not that I'm such a doting wife. I'm just hoping a couple of bites will scratch any itch he had to come here for big sausages. As I cut, I hit something rubbery. "Wait, what is that?" There's a foreign object lodged in the middle of my meat roll.

"A pickle, I think."

"Okay, *now* I'm grossed out. I like a nice, cold dill slice served with a sandwich or piled on a burger, but a big, hot pickle[210] baked inside my meat? That's messed up."

Neither of our dinners hold our attention long, so we finish more quickly than we anticipated and we have time for dessert. Stacey gets more iced tea, and I order German chocolate cake.

Whatever the rest of the meal lacked is made up for by this dessert. The slice is multilayered and piled high with buttery, chocolate-y, nutty frosting, full of freshly shaved coconut. The cake itself is dense and dark and moist. I can't believe this came from the same kitchen as my entrée.

I make Stacey take a bite before I inhale the whole thing. She retrieves a fork and takes a small taste. "That *is* good. But you know what I don't get? If German chocolate cake comes from Germany, what's up with the coconut? Since when does coconut have anything to do with Germany? You see any coconut trees near the Berlin Wall? No. It's weird."

....

[210]Heh.

"That is pretty random," I agree. "Do you see that in a lot of German restaurants, I wonder?"

"I wouldn't know. I don't ever go for German."

"Oh, really? I guess I thought you did. I mean, you knew about this place and wiener schnitzel and all and maybe you grew up coming here."

Stacey gives me an odd look and slowly replies, "Um, Jen? We Jews tend not to congregate in places filled with Germans. Particularly places filled with Germans AND big ovens."

"Oh?" I think for a moment. "*Oh*, I get it." I mentally scroll through my Rolodex of other cuisines I need to try. "Then how do your people feel about Lebanon?"

Stacey cocks her head even farther to the left and narrows her eyes. "Does the word 'diaspora' mean anything to you?"

"Do you avoid their restaurants, too?"

She laughs. "Actually, no, Lebanese food is delectable! Wanna do lunch at Semiramas next week?"

"That depends. Has their dining room been updated since the Betamax was invented?"

"It has."

"Do they use any spices other than salt?"

"They do."

"Will their meat dishes make me titter like a twelve-year-old?"

"Depends. Do you find sheep funny?"

"Hell, yes!"

"Then they've got 'em."

I don't even hesitate to answer. "Consider it a date."

"Dance! You dance! Dance, girl!"

In the darkened theater, I reach for Joanna's wrist and squeeze it. She pokes me in the side in return while a ballet dancer *grand jetés* across the stage.

"Dance! Uh-huh! Dancin'! You're dancin'! Woo!"

Joanna and I are attending a fund-raising dance performance, and we're seated not only in the nosebleed section, but also apparently right next to a woman who has so much joy in her heart for dance that she can't help but let it out in quick Tourette's-like bursts. On my neighbor's last "Woo!" she shakes her head so enthusiastically that she pelts me in the face with a couple of her hip-length dreadlocks. Fortunately, it's not one of the beaded strands.

However, I'm fairly mellow about the whole thing, as Joanna and I had dinner at a Russian place beforehand, where we discovered the joy of flavored flights of vodka.

Traffic was obscene getting downtown, so I was almost half an hour late to meet her. While Fletch did his best to weave in and out of lanes to get me there quicker, Joanna sent me updates on her iPhone, telling me there's a damn good reason that Russia never became a superpower in regard to wine. "Imagine cherry cough syrup," she wrote, "only thicker." Given that description, how would we then *not* opt for vodka?

Some details of our dinner escape me[211] but I remember being first served a sampler platter heaped with colorful scoops of salads made of simple ingredients, like carrots and beets and mushrooms. This was followed later by another platter filled with hearty fare, such as stuffed cabbage and meatballs and Stroganoff. Our entrées were much heavier than German food, but also much more flavorful.

....
[211]See: Flavored vodka, flights of.

By the time we finished, we'd eaten ourselves sober again and were so stuffed that we could barely walk the few blocks to the theater. Okay, no offense, Russia, but if this is how you fueled up prior to battle, no wonder you couldn't beat Afghanistan.

Meanwhile, back in the nosebleed balcony, my neighbor is banging her armrest and screaming, "Spin, spin, spin!" while a ballet dancer performs a *fouetté en tournant*.

Yes. Shouting will absolutely help him spin.

Joanna's husband is with their kids, so we're not under any kind of time constraints. And, as this is the first time just the two of us have been on the town together in something like fourteen years, we're going to take advantage of the situation. We could stay out all night if we want. We won't, but I love having this as an option.

When the show's over, Joanna and I make a beeline for the nearest cab, heading directly to the most magical place in the city. On Friday and Saturday nights, the lobby of the Peninsula Hotel turns into something more akin to Willy Wonka's factory. Tiered tables fill the center of the room, and each of them is heaped with dozens of chocolate treats, like chocolate crème brûlées, chocolate truffles, chocolate cookies, chocolate cakes, chocolate tarts, chocolate-covered strawberries, chocolate donuts, and chocolate mousses, all served alongside melted chocolate for fondue and various flavors of hot chocolate. The spread is nothing short of obscene.

"I've never seen anything like this," Joanna says, eyes wide. "My girls would lose their minds."

Once seated, and after we select our treats and sparkling champagne–vodka cocktails, we begin our postmortem on the performance.

"Did the Happiest Woman in the Entire World wreck everything for you?" I ask.

"She didn't bother me. Judging from how muscular her arms were and her carriage, she had to be a dancer, too. She was probably just excited to see her friends onstage," Joanna replies. It's rare to get Joanna to ever say anything bad about people, despite having lived under my terrible influence on two separate occasions.[212] "How'd you like the performances?"

"Honestly?" I admit. "I didn't really understand most of them." The element of storytelling was seriously lacking in some of the pieces. Although I loved watching the movement, I couldn't always figure out the motivation behind it.

"Oh, thank God, me neither! I figured since you'd been studying about dance, you knew something I didn't."

I shrug. "I've been spoiled by *So You Think You Can Dance.* I mean, they have some of the best choreographers in the country working on that show, plus they explain what the dance is about before every performance. And maybe they're dumbing it down for the masses, but as a member of the masses, I appreciate the summary. As for tonight, I didn't expect a full breakdown, but a few hints as to plot might have been nice."

"Yeah, those couples in all the loose clothing in the fourth number with all the sticks? What was that about?" Joanna asks, taking a bite of her chocolate-cherry compote.

"*Pfft,* I couldn't begin to tell you. But if I had to guess, I'd say they were crows." I dig into my white-and-milk-chocolate mousse. "Oh, and P.S.? I could have done without the charity's president rallying against the evils of the Republican party in his speech, too. I mean, I'm here,

....

[212]Once on January 21, 1986, she said three mean things before lunch, and it was so out of character, we all marked the event on our calendars.

paying seventy-five bucks a ticket specifically to support *your* organization; can you not call me the devil, please?"[213]

"I noticed you were squirming at that point."

"That's also because Dreadlocks McShoutypants was having a conversation out loud with herself. Apparently she needs to remember to pick up some spirulina at Whole Foods on the way home. As for the dancing, you know what else bothered me? This is petty, but I didn't like the *sound* of people dancing. On my stupid show, they edit out the noise of the dancers leaping and landing back on the ground. At this thing, everyone sounded like a herd of cattle because we could hear every foot slapping the stage. I found it distracting."

She looks thoughtful as she picks at the pecans on her tartlet. "I guess I didn't notice."

"As part of my project, I've been watching a ton of old dance movies lately. They took out the stage noise, too, except in the tap-dancing scenes, which are supposed to be heard."

Joanna gives me a wry grin. "My oldest takes Irish-dancing lessons. I guess I expect dance to make a lot of racket. By the way, have you seen *Singin' in the Rain* yet?"

"Yes, and I loved it so much!" I exclaim. "What's funny is after seeing some old musicals, I told Stacey I thought the *SYTYCD* dancers are way more athletic than Fred Astaire and Gene Kelly. Maybe these kids don't have their charisma, but in a lot of ways, their technique is better. She countered by telling me after Michael Jackson moon-walked for the first time on the VMAs, Gene Kelly called to congratulate him. Then Michael told Gene if it weren't for him, he'd never have become a dancer.

---

[213]Seriously, my team is not without compassion. And we're not all out hunting moose or bombing abortion clinics, either.

Now a lot of the guys on *SYTYCD* attribute their love of dance to Michael."

"Maybe it's just as simple as that soda commercial—every generation inspires the next," Joanna remarks while stifling a yawn.

"Are you exhausted?" I ask, glancing at my watch. "You realize if we were still in college, we'd just be getting ready to go out now."

"A little bit, but I'm fine. Although tomorrow I've got to work our block party with a vodka-and-chocolate hangover; I may regret this then."

I laugh. "Twenty-four years later and I'm still a bad influence on you."

Joanna drains her glass and finishes her truffle. "What should we do now? You want another drink, you want more chocolate, or do you want to call it a night? I'm game for one more if you are."

I consider all our options. "You know what? As long as you don't hit me with your dreadlocks, I'm pretty happy with whatever's next."

Joanna just sent me a link to a review of the dance. Apparently the people in the loose clothes were supposed to be subsistence farmers.

And I still don't get it.

"If we go tomorrow, they'll have belly dancers," I say.

"Yeah?" Stacey replies. "Then let's definitely go *tonight*. Want me to see if the girls are free?"

Stacey and I are on the phone coordinating our outing to a Turkish restaurant, and I'm glad she's suggested our friends join us because I've discovered that the Eat the World portion of my project works better in groups. More people not only means more dishes, but it also increases the likelihood that SOMEONE there will want to discuss *The Real World: Cancún* with me.

I know.

I know.

I know.

If at any point you're compelled to mock me for still having the Bunim-Murray monkey on my back this deep into my cultural Jenaissance, feel free. No ridicule dished out could be equal to the embarrassment I feel for indulging in this urge.

My relationship with *The Real World* started at the show's inception. When the New York season premiered in 1992, I was twenty-four and stuck living in my childhood bedroom. After my parents stopped paying for college, I had no choice but to move home and commute to a regional branch of my university. Between classes, I worked two jobs in order to scrape together the cash I needed to get the hell out of my parents' house.

At the time, I was understimulated and in a funk, and I desperately craved the company of people my own age. In my hometown, anyone I'd have wanted to be around scattered the second we'd graduated seven years before. When I could arrange time off work, I'd scamper back down to the main campus, but those stolen days weren't enough to keep my loneliness at bay. I felt like my twenties were escaping me.

Sure, I was involved with a sorority, but with my work schedule I rarely got to spend time with my sisters. Most of them had apartments together off campus, but I lived thirty miles away. On the one hand I didn't have to share a bathroom with half a dozen girls, but on the other, no one was waking them up at six fifteen a.m. on Saturdays after their double shifts to "Use the stiff brush to scrub algae off the steps in the pool before you go to work, Jennifer."

I yearned for conversations that didn't revolve around the extent to which I'd fucked up my educational trajectory or why I'd mulched the lawn instead of bagged it.[214] I don't blame my parents for being hard on me; they were none too thrilled to have an adult chick back in the nest, either.

So when I saw the promos for *The Real World*, I was desperate for entertainment and, more so, fascinated by the premise that anything could happen on camera. I thrilled at the prospect of being around people my own age, vicarious as it might have been.

I had a rare night off when the show premiered, and I sat transfixed during the opening credits. As the cast members were introduced, I found that they lived in the kind of funky loft I'd always dreamed of living in myself.

Every participant had been hand-selected not because they were going to get naked in the Jacuzzi or punch random strangers in bar fights, but because they were pursuing their talents in New York.[215] Bunim and Murray filled that house with aspiring writers and musicians and dancers and models. And these individuals didn't spend their time trying to outdo one another with outrageous behavior; instead, they used the experience to try to understand their roommates, themselves, and their place in the world.

Of course complications arose, but nothing was manufactured back then. Apparently, Bunim and Murray originally kicked around the idea of scripting the program, but scrapped it. Occasionally you could see the hand of production encouraging the cast members to discuss certain topics, but they were important issues, like racism and sexuality and home-

....

[214]Coincidentally, both entailed a distinct lack of effort on my part.

[215]I had talent. Algae scrubbing is a skill, yo.

lessness. In one episode, Julie's mother came up from Alabama, and Julie poured her heart out to her roommates about how much trouble she had finding a connection with her mother. I knew exactly how it felt to have a mom whose idea of how a daughter should behave was diametrically opposed to her own. Julie's personal growth felt like my personal growth.

Did they have issues with one another? Of course. But the problems came about organically because you simply can't stick that diverse a group of people under one roof and not have them, you know, stop being polite and start getting real.

For me, *The Real World* filled a void and made me believe that I was hanging out with friends for half an hour each week. Even if we were in different places, I understood exactly where they were in their worlds. I was there, too.

The Real World: New York is, or rather was, the utopia of reality television. The next season in Los Angeles was a fine follow-up with another totally diverse cast. They dealt with issues of violence and alcoholism and politics. And everyone still had normal names like Beth and Glen and David, and not one of them had been surgically enhanced. My passion for the show remained, but when it premiered, I'd managed to move back to campus, so I didn't afford it the importance of season one.

I wondered if the show might lose a touch of its original magic in the third iteration, but then San Francisco premiered. There was an urgency to that season, as cast member Pedro passed away from HIV complications the night of the premiere. Conflicts were amplified by Pedro's looming illness, and relationships were shattered when common ground could not be found. The house was rife with misunderstandings, and everyone was on edge from the first episode. If New York was the utopia of reality television, San Francisco was the perfect storm.

By the time the London came on, I was dating Fletch, who'd developed a distaste for all things MTV. He claimed that the show held no value, but I suspect he was just jealous he'd turned twenty-five and missed the opportunity to audition.

When the Miami season rolled around, I'd graduated from college and was working my first professional job. I mostly caught up with the show during the weekend marathons. Suddenly watching a bunch of college kids lying around on couches and bitching about who had moved their stuff stopped being "must-see" TV.[216] With the exception of cast member Dan that season, the series ceased to interest me. I only kept watching because I was addicted.

I planned on quitting cold turkey when they went back to New York. I couldn't relate to any of the cast members. Yeah, I laughed at some of their antics, but the show was intrinsically different by then. The first season was almost the next generation of *The Breakfast Club*. They were people who'd been tossed together and who'd forged uncommon friendships. Were it not for an in-school suspension, you'd never see criminal Bender and prom queen Claire making out in a file room or Claire giving basket case Allison a makeover. And in real life, you'd never find the flamboyantly gay Norman befriending Julie, the repressed Southern virgin who was so naive she assumed Heather B. was a drug dealer because she was an African-American woman with a beeper.

The further the feel of the episodes got from the originals, the less voraciously I watched. My interest waned as the number of boob jobs on the show waxed. The return to New York should have been the last season I tuned in, but then the Chicago season took up residence in spitting distance of me, and I had no choice.

----

[216]If you want something to complain about, children, then try doing data entry for nine hours a day.

And then the *Real World* went to Las Vegas . . . and that season was so distasteful that its hold on me finally broke. I'm not sure how episodes went from Julie camping out in a "Reaganville" for the night to understand the plight of a homeless family to roommate threesomes,[217] but it did and I'd had enough.

I thought I'd successfully kicked my habit after the disease-infested, hot-tub-filled Las Vegas season in 2003, only to be sucked in by a snowy day, the appallingly amoral Denver cast, and the discovery of my cable box's on-demand feature in 2006.

My Shame Rattle at being back on *The Real World* bandwagon was palpable.

Fortunately, it was short-lived.

I had enough self-respect to avoid Sydney, Hollywood, and Brooklyn, and when this latest season rolled around, I really believed I was home free.

So, what broke my resolve? What lured me back into the fold? What got me up on the Bunim-Murray horse again? I knew the show would never be as good as it once had been, so quality wasn't a motivator. And I'd have laid money on the Cancún kids being the most vapid, self-indulgent group yet, wrapped in a cocoon of arrogance and ignorance and abs, none of which appealed to me.

What sucked me in this time?

Weather?

Weakness?

Want?

Nope. Welty.

Specifically *Eudora Welty*.

....

[217] Possibly to understand the plight of herpes and poor choices?

I've been diligently working my way through the classic novels list that my friend Jen put together for me. Mostly I've been reading them on my Kindle because classics are dirt-cheap that way.[218]

However, not long ago I found myself at the bookstore unexpectedly,[219] and there were a few titles I hadn't yet downloaded. I didn't have my list with me, so I tried to remember what I didn't have. I knew there was some book written by a woman with the initials E.W. but I couldn't remember who or what. I asked for help.

I located a clerk and said, "Hi, I'm looking for a classic novel but I can't for the life of me remember who wrote it. I can picture her name, though, and her initials are E.W."

The clerk immediately pointed me in the direction of a summer reading display. "You probably want Edith Wharton or Eudora Welty." Wow. Incidentally, I've yet to stump a bookstore clerk, video store employee, or wine shop cashier with what I always assume are out-of-the-ordinary requests.

(You have no idea how much this impresses me. They should probably make a reality show about this. I'd totally watch.)

Anyway, I bought both Edith Wharton and Eudora Welty and figured I had my bases covered. As it turns out, Jen meant for me to get Evelyn Waugh, who, I should mention, *isn't even a chick.*[220]

I immediately fell in love with Edith Wharton, toggling back and forth between *The Age of Innocence* on my Kindle and *The House of Mirth*

---

[218] These authors are dead. They don't need my dollar.

[219] Fletch made me take my car in for detailing at the shop across from my usual B&N as I accidentally spilled a whole container of kebabs in there. He said my car smelled like Afghanistan.

[220] Feel free to insert a "Jen continues to be a philistine" footnote here; it's justified.

in paperback. Her style is deceptively breezy because her wit is so biting. In her novels, she painstaking catalogues the messed-up social mores of the Upper East Side glitterati.

This, in Jen-speak, means I totally develop a girl crush on her.

Wharton prompts me to send gushing e-mails to my agent, saying stuff like:

> The strangest thought occurred to me today—without the vicious social satire of Edith Wharton, we'd never have had a Blair Waldorf. Personality- and circumstance-wise, they seemed to have an awful lot in common
>
> Also, I think this may be why *Gossip Girl* is so popular with you gals in publishing—it is RAMPANT with nods to all kinds of books. For example, having Lily marry Bart Bass? Lily Bart? Sound familiar? And isn't Newland Archer awfully similar to, oh, say . . . Nate Archibald? Same kind of character, too. And Wharton loved to make plays on names; ergo, Chuck Bass becomes Chuck Bastard in a minute. Or perhaps it's a wink to Faulkner, because Chuck Bass is a motherless boy? (She died and now his mother is a fish.)

After going on and on about my brilliant discoveries to Fletch, I mention how Kate sent me a link to a twenty-five-page comparison of a certain *Gossip Girl* episode to *The Age of Innocence*, which prompts him to wonder, "Is it that you discovered this literary connection, or is this maybe one of those cases when you're the last horse to cross the finish line?"

While Wharton helped me get in touch with my inner cognoscente, Welty made me want to slap babies. I specifically picked up Welty's *Delta Wedding* because I liked the title and the concept appealed to me.

According to the book jacket, this is a "sometimes-riotous portrait of a Southern family." Since there's almost nothing I dig more than some old-fashioned Southern dysfunction, full of mint juleps and creeping vines and creepy uncles and no-necked monsters, I figured I'd take to it like a kudzu to a telephone pole.[221]

What I didn't count on was my developing an urge to maim myself and others rather than read one more frigging description of spready ferns and golden-winged butterflies and skies the color of violets and snow-white moons and *can something please happen because oh, my God, enough with the descriptions stop already!*[222]

I did a Google search to see if I'm the only one to have such a visceral reaction to *Delta Wedding*. As it turns out, I'm not. The consensus is that once one gets fifty pages in, the pace quickens, but I wasn't sure I could make it that far without kicking my pets or something. Others suggested the reader take a piece of paper and draw a family tree to keep track of the sprawling cast of characters, which . . . no. If a book requires a Visio diagram to keep everyone straight, it's too damn complicated. And then I saw that a *Kirkus* reviewer had described little Miss Pulitzer Prize's prose as being "lucid yet tortuous."

Which, ha! I knew this book was fucking torture.

In short?

It's not *me*. It's *you*(dora).[223]

And then . . . I opened a dictionary.

I wasn't aware at first that tortuous means "full of twists and bends—

---

[221]This last bit sounds better if you say it in a Scarlett O'Hara accent.

[222]And yes, I know she won a Pulitzer. But I've been in *People* magazine. *Twice.* Suck on that, Eudora Welty.

[223]Get it? You(dora)? Like Eudora? Get it? Yeah, well, fine. SHE wasn't funny, either.

circuitous" and not "causing one to feel tortured." Yet I stand by my opinion.

After throwing my paperback across the room for the umpteenth time, I decided to rest my brain with a little television. That the television just so happened to be tuned into the premier episode of *The Real World: Cancún* was kismet.[224]

Which is really just an extremely TORTUOUS way of saying that back in *my* real world, I agree with Stacey about the belly dancers. "Yeah, I don't want to eat a big plate of lamb with half-naked ladies showing off the kind of six-pack abs I'll never achieve by eating big plates of lamb. And yes, will you please recruit the troops?"

Stacey's in charge of rounding up our friends, so it's my job to make the reservation. When I call, the hostess asks me if I want a regular table or if I want to sit on cushions on the floor. Naturally, I choose the floor.

We arrive around seven thirty to find that other than Gina, Stacey, Tracey, and me, the place is completely empty. At seven thirty. On a Thursday. We find this vaguely troubling.

I tell the hostess we have a reservation, and she looks all pensive for a moment, like she's not sure if she can squeeze us in. Perhaps they're expecting a tour bus of diners at any moment? Eventually she brings us to a spot in the front window. Our table stands about a foot off the ground and is made of some kind of hammered metal. There are a few layers of Persian rugs underneath, and it's surrounded by a dozen pillows in various shades of crimson.[225] We all stand there for a minute, quietly negotiating exactly who has the best knees and strongest back and is most able to

----

[224]Or possibly the result of having watched a *Cribs* rerun earlier in the day.

[225]This is where a certain fancy book-prize winner would take four pages to describe all the shades and would never, ever get to the *Real World* conversation.

climb up, over, around, and under to get into her place in the far corner. Tracey's back surgery was more recent than Gina's knee replacement, but somehow Tracey loses and gets stuck in the corner. Personally, I feel like I'm having hot flashes[226] and insist on the end, since there's better ventilation here.

Wanting to stay as authentic as possible, I order a glass of Turkish white wine, which tastes similar to a Sutter Home 2007 sauvignon blanc. Like, *remarkably* similar. *Suspiciously* similar. I'm not sure if this is a ruse or if shitty wine is an international phenomenon.

As Stacey's the only member of our party who's been to Turkey, we ask her to order for the table. Which isn't to say that I find this menu intimidating. I can totally navigate it myself. There's lamb, lamb, more lamb, and some chicken. Certainly I understand why there's no pork, and secretly I'm disappointed there's no turkey. I realize turkeys probably aren't indigenous to Turkey, and yet a part of me wishes I could say I had Turkish turkey.

Come on. It's funny.[227]

Regardless, I'm now a huge number-one-fan-with-a-big-foam-finger of Mediterranean food, and I'm learning that places like Turkey and Palestine and Israel have a ton of overlap in their cuisines, if not in ideology. They all pretty much feature the same kinds of dishes with slightly different labels, which makes me wonder if the whole Middle East schism isn't some ancient, elaborate "tastes great" versus "less filling" scenario gone terribly awry.

We get a big sampler platter of hummus, stuffed grape leaves, olives and feta, and tabouleh, which is a finely chopped salad of mint, parsley,

----

[226]I'm hoping it's just the extensions.

[227]To me, at least.

onion, tomato, and cracked wheat. I'm normally fussy about tabouleh because sometimes the wheat has the consistency of tiny rocks, and I feel like I'm eating sand.

We also get a plate of manti, a Turkish ravioli, filled with meat, tossed in tomato sauce, and drizzled with yogurt. Stacey said in Istanbul the manti were teeny—smaller than a dime—but these are the size of a quarter. Everyone at the table pronounces them a tad Chef Boyardee. Despite all my recent culinary education, that's still not necessarily a bad thing in my book.

The service is surprisingly slow considering we're the only ones here. Our dinner takes forever to arrive, and when it does, it's only adequate. The *idea* of the components appeals—the kebab format, the way the vegetables are grilled, the spice blends—but I'm unimpressed with the execution. It's still palatable, though, so I imagine if I were tasting well-made Turkish food in a restaurant that wasn't completely deserted, I'd go crazy for it.

The accommodations, however, are less than . . . accommodating.

"Is anyone else's ass sweating?" I ask.

"Those etiquette lessons are really paying off, eh, Jen?" Stacey teases me.

"Seriously, is anyone else getting boiling hot sitting on all these damn rugs?" I wonder.

"They're a little warm," Tracey agrees.

Gina chimes in, "I thought I was having a hot flash, too."

"I'm more concerned about how musty they are," Stacey counters. "Remember, Febreeze can be your friend."

"My knees are killing me," Gina admits. "I'm going to get up for a while." She extricates herself from our table and stands next to us in the archway.

"And I've lost all feeling in my back," Tracey adds.

Shaking herself to stop the pins and needles in her limbs, Gina observes, "This is probably why most restaurants opt for full-sized tables and chairs, rather than ottomans."

"Did you eat on the floor in Turkey?" I ask Stacey.

Stacey frowns a bit. "Not so much. We stayed at the Four Seasons. Mostly they just had regular tables."

"Listen, I'm sorry, guys, I picked a lousy place. And we're probably all too old to be sitting around cross-legged on the floor anyway," I apologize.

Tracey says, "Hey, it's nice to get together anyway. We'll just go somewhere different next time. Maybe we can do . . . what else is on your list?"

"Tons of stuff," I reply. "I have so much more world to eat. What are you thinking?"

Everyone starts talking at once. Tracey suggests, "How about Costa Rican?"

"Done it," I reply. "Dinner was great and the lizano salsa was surprisingly delicious. Totally didn't mind the spice. The thing is, when I called to order delivery, I realized I didn't have cash, so I asked if I could use my credit card. And they're all 'Oh, no, we don't take plastic. But you can write a check as long as you have your driver's license and social security number on it.' And I'm like, 'You're kidding. I haven't seen a restaurant that's accepted checks since college.'"

"They'd take a check?" Gina is shocked. "I haven't written a check for dinner since the eighties."

I bang my hand down on our metal table and the water in my glass sloshes over the side. "That's what I'm saying! Weird, right? Then I got all suspicious and thought, 'Those bastards are going to take my social and try to sell my identity down in Costa Rica.' So I went to the closet and fished through all my coat pockets and found enough cash to cover delivery and tip."

Stacey sighs. As the person who spends more time with me than anyone but my husband, she's well acquainted with my penchant for conspiracy theories. In Jennsylvania, every helicopter is black. "Jen, Costa Rica has a population that's ninty-six percent literate, their unemployment rate is half of ours, and they have some of the most gorgeous terrain in the world. I doubt anyone at *the burrito joint* wants to steal your identity."

Smugly, I reply, "I guess we'll never have to find out."

"Have you tried Indian?" Tracy asks.

"We had Indian together," Gina says. "Hey, lemme take a good look at you." She peers down at me. "Have your eyebrows grown back in yet?"

"They're getting there."

Stacey says, "What about Japanese?"

"Stacey, I've had Japanese *with you.*"

"Oh, yeah."

"We're all going to have to start taking that Geritol with memory boosters soon, aren't we?" I moan.

Stacey then proposes Lebanese, but given how underwhelmed everyone is with tonight's offerings, no one jumps on this suggestion, although she and I reconfirm our date to hit her favorite Lebanese place for lunch soon.

"What about Vietnamese?" Gina asks.

The rest of the group finds this to be a capital idea. And I agree, too, mostly because whatever the ladies at my nail shop have for lunch smells amazing.

"Then it's settled," Tracey confirms.

"So . . . ," I say, "that brings us to the most important question of the night. Who's watching *The Real World*?"

Tracey is shocked. "That's still ON? I thought it ended years ago."

And Stacey says, "I haven't watched it since they were in San Francisco."

I slump in my seat. "You people hurt my heart. This season kicks ass. Don't get me wrong; I'm only watching because Eudora Welty sucks."

This comment requires some tortuous backstory on my part.

I continue. "It's like the people they've chosen are caricatures of caricatures. They've moved so far away from the original concept of the show, it's an entirely different entity. Remember how once on *The Simpsons* Marge said, *'FOX turned into a hard-core porn network so gradually, I didn't even notice!'* Same thing. I mean, I bet these little bastards have never even heard of Eric Nies or *The Grind*. No one ever has a meaningful conversation or a decent fight for that matter. Remember when Pedro was in a rage because he couldn't live with Puck anymore, saying he compromised his health and sanity? That was riveting! The biggest drama these idiots ever contend with is whether or not someone's 'fake.' I mean, really? Fake? This is the end-all, be-all of insults now? Give me a fucking break. And there's this one guy on it who's supposed to be all punk rock, but when he got kicked off the show for being too big of a dumb ass to set an alarm clock, he was crying like a little bitch—"

Gina interrupts, "You mean Joey?"

My eyes light up. "You're watching? YAY!!"

"Yeah, but you know what's sad?" Gina says slowly, shaking her dark curls. "We were the target demographic when the damn series premiered, and now we're old enough to be these kids' parents."

No.

NO. That can't be right.

"Wait, what? No. These guys are, what, early twenties? I guess, yeah, Derek celebrated his twenty-first birthday a couple of weeks ago. Major drama. Boy troubles. Anyway, if he's twenty-one, that means I'd have been . . ." I furiously do the math. Fingers and toes may or may not be involved. "Oh, *God.* They don't know what *The Grind* is because they were three when it premiered. Which means I'd have been twenty-one when some of these kids were born. Which means I actually *could* be their parent."

I stare at the table in stunned silence.

I guess I was wrong.

Apparently there IS something in this world that sucks more than Eudora Welty.

We're having Lebanese today, and there's almost no difference between it and other kinds of Mediterranean cuisine, save for the liberal use of sumac, which is kind of a bumpy red, sour spice that Stacey had to assure me was not poison but it totally sounds poisonous but I guess they wouldn't be in business long if they made a habit of poisoning customers but other than the sumac everything was like every other Mediterranean place, which by the way totally encompasses the Middle East but no one actually says it's the Middle East, kind of like how the rugs are called Persian and not Iranian because that's not a selling point and anyway the hummus was like any other hummus and the falafel was like any other falafel and of course there was lamb because there's always lamb and the Middle East must have as many sheep as they do grains of sand as in there are so many that they cause traffic jams but instead of horns all you hear is "Baa! Baa!" because they're frigging everywhere kind of like Bank of America ATMs and it's probably a lot like in the movie *You Don't Mess with the Zohan* where Adam Sandler is always using hummus for everything like brushing his teeth and styling his hair only in real life everyone would be washing their glasses with lamb and waxing their cars with lamb and when something great happens, they're all "That's LAMB-tastic!" and I had Lebanese coffee, which is like Cuban coffee on crack, which is like regular coffee on crack, meaning it's like coffee to the second power and I had a whole pot of it because they put cardamom in it which made me exclaim, *"This must be what it was like to drink coffee with the three wise men!"* and then I interrupted myself and said, *"No, wait, this is what Jesus tastes like!"* and did I mention I drank a whole pot, which probably translates into about twenty regular cups of Joe and I told Stacey I'd turned into Cornholio and she didn't understand what I meant and I was all "How can there be a pop culture reference that I get and you don't since we're kind of the same person except for the politics, pets, and pearls?" and she said that when the show was on she was working full-time and going to grad school and married and also working part-time to make ends meet, so there wasn't a lot of room in her schedule to watch cartoons and now I kind of think I can fly.

Comin' down, man.

from the desk of ms. jennifer ann lancaster

Dear Karen,

I forgot to give you the number of where we're going to be in New York, so it's taped next to the phone in the kitchen.

Thanks again for being so flexible about us adding three kittens to the cat-sitting reservation. I think you'll find that they're loving and sweet and should be no problem whatsoever. Your check with the new total is attached. Please enjoy this bottle of wine on the counter, too.

Thanks,
Jen Lancaster

P.S. Out of curiosity, are your shots up-to-date?

C·H·A·P·T·E·R S·E·V·E·N·T·E·E·N

I Love New York 2

"We're here for our panel van, please."

Fletch and I have just flown into LaGuardia. The Hamptons are two hours away, and we'll be on our way as soon as we pick up our rental car. I thought a convertible at the beach would be really fun, so that's what I reserved. However, Fletch has an unbroken string of bad luck when it comes to rental cars and has never once gotten what he ordered. He's sure that there's no way we'll get a convertible, and instead we'll be stuck with the only vehicle left on the lot—a big white contractor panel van.

"Stop it," I hiss at him before turning my attention to the clerk. "Last name is Lancaster—we have a reservation." I hand over my credit card and driver's license while the clerk puts my information into the computer.

"Here we go, Miss Lancaster. I have a LeBaron convertible waiting for you."

"Ha!" I bark at Fletch. "I told you so!"

We complete the transaction and place our bags in the car, and we're ready to go. All we have to do is hook up the GPS.

Twenty minutes and one profoundly explicit string of profanity later, we're on the road. Fletch has chosen to drive because I'm too slow and too cautious, and I prefer to have both hands free in order to flip birds when needed. Yet I don't need to make obscene gestures at anyone, not even once. I'm deeply impressed by how much more polite New York drivers are than Chicago drivers. That's not a bet I'd have taken. At home, braking is for cowards and turn signals for the weak. George Wallace says anything going less than sixty miles per hour in Chicago is considered a house. But when other drivers here see a car trying to merge, they get out of the way, rather than considering the move a thrown gauntlet.

I don't know what to expect in the Hamptons. None of my friends has ever been there, since it's not a Midwestern thing. Depending on traffic, today's drive could take three hours. If you start the clock when we left our house this morning, by the time we get to our hotel, we'll have been traveling for more than nine hours. I guess Chicagoans would rather spend nine hours going somewhere else.[228]

The other weird thing about the Hamptons is there aren't any hotels, per se—you won't see a Hyatt or a Holiday Inn, and if you run into a Hilton, most likely she'll be walking Tinkerbell on the beach. New Yorkers have tried to explain the concept of the Hamptons to me—essentially, it's a tourist area that goes to considerable lengths to discourage tourism. People either own or rent houses up there, and the expectation is that

---

[228]Italy, maybe?

nonresidents should stay with friends. A few inns exist but are priced so stratospherically that no riffraff could possibly infiltrate.

Yet we're going anyway.

After we get to the inn and unpack, I insist we go to the ocean. We've got parking passes to five different beaches, and since the beach pass costs us a (refundable) seven-hundred-dollar deposit, I'm not about to let it go to waste.

Before we hit the waterfront, we drive around downtown East Hampton for a while to get our bearings. What looks like any typical sleepy little beach town proves deceptive upon closer examination. In place of all the cheesy T-shirt shacks and penny-candy places and ice-cream shops are satellite stores of Catherine Malandrino, Coach, Tiffany & Co., Michael Kors, and Gucci. To be fair, you can still buy candy here at Dylan's Candy Bar[229] but you'd better have more than a handful of pennies.

I have no plans to shop because I don't need any Theory or Alice + Olivia jeans.[230] Regardless, this is the quaintest Main Street I've ever seen. The sidewalks are so clean they're practically polished and almost every store is fronted by huge, blooming flowers. The Ralph Lauren store's halfway hidden by gigantic white bead-board troughs brimming with violet-blue hydrangeas, each blossom as big as my head.

I feel like I'm on another planet as no one on the street is shouting or swearing loud enough for children to hear. Mostly I just see deeply

....

[229]Owned by Ralph Lauren's daughter.

[230]Even if they did come in plus sizes.

tanned families, languidly strolling the boulevard under a canopy of ma-
ture trees. And they're all wearing madras plaid.

I already love this place.

We drive to Egypt Beach, passing the kind of mansions one only sees
in the movies. They really exist? And what, exactly, does one do with a
twenty-thousand-square-foot beach house? More important, how'd they
get it in the first place? That's what I want to know.

We pass places I've somehow already heard of, like Further Lane,
Lily Pond Road, and Montauk Highway. Right before we get to the
beach, I see the Maidstone Club. Not sure how this name has become a
part of my internal database, either. All I can figure is my subconscious
watches *Gossip Girl*, too.

The second we get to the beach, I throw off my shoes and make a
mad dash for the shoreline. I navigate around the beach grass and past
the fencing and over the pale sand, and there it is, just like I remembered
it. I maintain there's nothing more majestic than the Atlantic Ocean, particularly right now, as the sky's a dozen violent shades of gray and purple
with a pending storm.

The beach is practically deserted at this time of day, which makes
sense because the parking lot is tiny and permit only, plus each of the
mansions out here is spaced a good tenth of a mile apart.

I breathe in the salt air and revel at the feeling of soft, damp sand
between my toes. And I've soaked the cuffs of my capris in the surf before
I realize that Fletch isn't with me. Where the hell did he go? I scan
the beach to the east and west and don't see him. I wait a few more minutes, and when he doesn't appear, I trudge back up the incline to the car,
where I find him smoking.

"What are you doing?" I ask.

"I'm smoking," he replies.

"Are you coming down to the water?"

He shrugs. "I'm not finished smoking."

"Okay, so you're here at the mouth of not only one of America's most beautiful beaches, but also one of the most exclusive, and you're all *'Hey, look! Nature is one giant ashtray!'* Finish it up, don't you dare leave the butt on the ground, and let's go."

"Nah, I don't really want to go down to the beach."

This exasperates me. "Why not? I'm sorry, did we not just travel nine hours? And now you don't even want to take one look at the main attraction?"

He stubs out his cigarette and places it in a beach trash can. "I want to see the water, but I'm wearing Allen Edmund loafers. I don't want to get them sandy."

"I'm sorry, who are you, Simon Doonan? Giorgio Armani? Tell me, who wears Allen-fucking-Edmund loafers to the beach?"

"People who want to look nice," he quips.

And . . . I've now reached my breaking point. The stress of getting ready for this trip and trying to culture up enough so I don't feel foreign in my own skin and taking care of all the furry, ANGRY little patients in my house finally overwhelms me. Silently, I slip on my flip-flops and climb back into the car, pulling the door closed harder than necessary.

Fletch pokes his head in. "Hey, what's wrong?"

"NOTHING," I snap, eyes straight ahead.

"Your 'nothing' is always something. What's going on?"

"What's going on? What's going on is that I'm all freaked out that I'm going to make an ass of myself in front of all the authors I admire most in the world or accidentally commit some kind of politically motivated hate crime at the dinner. And you've been no help whatsoever.

You've been obstinate every step of the way. You argued with me about when we should leave and what we should rent and where we should stay and what you should wear, and it turns out I've totally made the right call on everything—"

Gently, Fletch interrupts, "Jen, I'm not wearing a seersucker suit and straw boater to your event."

"Why not?" I protest.

"Because I'm not the Great Gatsby."

"YOU WOULD HAVE LOOKED FANTASTIC! AND LIT-ERARY!"

"Yes, if we were going to Authors Night, 1924. 'Gretchen, you need to stop trying to make "fetch" happen.'" Well, great, how am I supposed to stay mad at anyone who delivers a perfectly timed *Mean Girls* quote? "Would it make you happy if I look at the water with you?"

"YES."

"Then I'll go."

"Thank you."

"I need to take my shoes off first."

Argh.

We stroll back down to the beach and Fletch spends the whole time humoring me, which I appreciate. I stick my feet back in the water— bracing!—and Fletch hangs along the shoreline, admiring the architec-ture behind us.

"I read that both Martha Stewart and Steven Spielberg have places out here. I wonder if one of those monster houses is theirs?" I muse. "How surreal would it be to just run into one of them out here?"

"Actually, that's not surreal, that's more of an odd coincidence. Sur-real would be if they were driving a birthday cake in the sky, and the whole thing started to melt."

I glower at him. "You realize I hate you a little bit today, right?"

"What? You're a writer and you're trying to improve yourself; I'm doing you a favor by helping you use vocabulary words correctly. You should thank me."

"No, I should *drown* you. FYI, you're being an enormous pill. Why can't you act like you're happy and thankful we're here?" Frustrated, I kick a wad of sand toward the water.

"I'm ecstatic to be here, actually. This is the most beautiful place I've ever seen. I already never want to leave." He leans in and gives me a big hug, pasting an enormous smile on his face. "See? I'm hap-hap-happy. I'm only teasing you because I'm in a great mood."

Mollified, I hug him back. "Hey, honey, do you want to sit and watch the surf roll in for a while? The storm clouds are magnificent and our dinner reservations aren't for a couple of hours."

"I can't. I'm wearing my Hugo Boss jeans. I don't want to get sand all over them."

I run my hand down my face and under my chin. "Honey? This? Right here? Is exactly why people think you're gay."

At dinner, Fletch can't decide on a wine, so I commandeer the list and ask a number of questions about particular grapes and geography. I finally choose a lovely Brunello di Montalcino, and when I taste it, it's like cashmere on my tongue.

The best part isn't just the drinking. It's when the sommelier compliments me, saying, "You have an extensive understanding of Italian wines."

Huh. When did *that* happen?

This morning at breakfast, Fletch is thumbing through a magazine called *Dan's Hamptons*. It's more of newspaper, really, full of typical local ads for stuff like Rolexes and private jets and multimillion-dollar real estate listings. I feel like Brenda Walsh on her first day at West Beverly High— cowed and intimidated by how different everything is from Minnesota, yet just a tiny bit exhilarated.

"Uh-oh, there's a crime wave going on up here, according to the police blotter," he ominously intones.

"What? You're kidding." For the first time in my life, I'm in a place safe enough that I don't feel like I have to lock the door before I even finish shutting it. I figure the worst thing that could happen up here would be a drive-by snubbing. But a crime wave? Really? I'm shocked.

"Yeah," he continues. "Apparently up in Montauk someone stole a couple of lobster pots. Also? A drunk guy hit a parked car and didn't leave his insurance information, a kayak was stolen, and a woman went to a bakery to return a pie, but I guess she'd eaten part of it. They wouldn't give her money back, so she threw the pie at the counter."

I snort. "Maybe the police should talk to the pie lady about the lobster pots. Sounds like she's a real recidivist. See? HA! You and your vocabulary words can bite me, Fletcher!"

Fletch closes the paper and looks thoughtful. "I wonder how many people were killed just now in Chicago while I read that article."

After breakfast, we spend the day on Georgica Beach, enjoying cloudless china blue skies. Fletch finally stopped being a pill at dinner last night, which is why he's settled into the chair next to me and not, you know, drowned.

One of us does not have the good sense to apply sunscreen to combat the blazing Hamptons sun. Surprisingly, it's not me. Fletch sunburns himself into a state best described as "radioactive," so after a few hours on the soft white sand, we grab our cooler full of cheese rinds and grape stems and head back to the inn. Before we get in the car, I'm pretty sure I see my literary idol, Jay McInerney, cooling down after a run on the beach. I don't chase after him. . . . whether it's out of a newfound respect for boundaries or because it's hard to get a foothold in flip-flops, I'm not sure.

As soon as we return to the room, we switch the television to FOX News while we get ready. Town meetings have gone on all week and a lot of these meetings have quickly headed south. Seems like after every break, Fox returns with new footage of old guys yelling at senators about nationalizing health care. If I weren't such a fan of reality TV, I'd find these shout-y encounters uncomfortable no matter how I leaned politically.[231]

Lots of broadcasters speculate whether the elderly are "plants" specifically sent to the town meetings to angry up the other constituents. "That old guy seems genuinely upset," I say, gesturing toward the screen as Fletch emerges from the bathroom draped in a towel toga. "Is our side deliberately trying to mess stuff up?"

He runs the white terry cloth over his hair. "Are you asking me if this

----

[231]Yet I appreciate living in a country where the ability to disagree with your government is an inalienable right. So there's that.

is part of the vast right-wing conspiracy? I doubt it. The emotion seems pretty authentic."

I sigh, eyes never leaving the screen. "I hope so. I hate to think people would deliberately gum up the works; it's disrespectful."

Fletch shrugs and continues to get ready. But as a nod to our worldview, he dresses in a gray athletic T-shirt with a silk screen of Ronald Reagan with the words "Old-School Conservative" on it. When he wears this shirt at home, he gets a ton of dirty looks, but up here, I imagine the crowd's a little more equally mixed. Seriously, all this plaid is like catnip for Republicans.

Once we're both showered and groomed, we head out to the rental car. And I don't even need to ask Fletch to put the top down; he's finally fully into the swing of this weekend. We drive from East Hampton down the length of the Montauk Highway to the lighthouse. The topography isn't as rocky and dramatic as parts of New England, but it overcompensates with all the giant bushes of blooming flowers. Plus, there's not a speck of garbage anywhere. In an effort to humor me, Fletch stops at every hilly, scenic lookout, too.[232]

The salt air's made us ravenous, so we pull into a little roadside crab shack about halfway between Montauk and East Hampton for a late lunch. We feast on the tempura-battered puffer fish appetizer. According to Wikipedia[233] puffer fish, also known as blowfish or fugu, is the second-most poisonous vertebrate in the world. The fish's skin and internal organs are totally toxic, and improper preparation can cause death by suffocation because the neurotoxins can paralyze the diaphragm.

What Wikipedia fails to mention is exactly how delectable puffer fish

....

[232]Mostly to smoke, but it's still nice.

[233]And that one episode of *The Simpsons.*

tastes with the restaurant's homemade tartar sauce—any risk incurred is totally worth it.

We follow up with enormous plates of creamy lobster salad, resplendent with chunks of meat as big as my thumb. Everything's beyond fresh—the bed of lush green lettuce appears to have been picked this morning, probably right after they hauled in the lobster pots. The salad's so huge I only make my way through about a third of it. I feel like I've officially satisfied any lobster craving I might have for the year with this meal.

There's nothing gourmet or exotic about my salad. There are no bacon lardons or Hawaiian gindai or yuzu jelly; there's just mayo and celery and salt and pepper, served with a plastic package of saltines. But despite the simplicity of the presentation and preparation, it's *perfect*.

After we went to Moto, we saw Anthony Bourdain feature it on *No Reservations*. He was just as impressed with Chef Cantu's food as we were. Yet in the next segment, he was writhing in ecstasy at some grotty old smoked fish served in a paper bag (and eaten in a car) out by the Ship and Sanitary Canal on Chicago's south side. I figured if Bourdain could appreciate the essence of whatever he was having, despite the circumstances of where it was served or the simplicity of ingredients, then who was I to feel any differently?

That's why we ended up here, sitting right next to the highway, at a rickety outdoor picnic table, drinking from a paper cup. Yet I couldn't be more enthralled with the whole meal if it had come with linen napkins, a tuxedo-clad maître d', and rows of silverware lining each side of my Wedgwood plate.

When we finally push our bloated bellies away from the table, we're presented with a three-figure check for our casual lunch. Thus I learn my most important lesson to date—when ordering lobster, always ask market price first.

After we finish exploring the farthermost tip of the island, we return to East Hampton to stroll through the picturesque downtown. I'd like to get a paperback to satisfy my tub-based reading needs, and Fletch wants some footwear. We run his errand first, which prompts my teasing him in the *"You know how I know you're gay? You bought deck shoes at Coach!"* variety for a solid twenty minutes.

About halfway down the main drag, we run across the most adorable independent bookseller. The shop is all wooden and warm with big display windows, and it looks like the kind of place where I'd get lost for hours. I'm delighted to see how crowded the store is, too. The staff rushes around with a sense of urgency, moving shelves here and there, making room for all the shoppers, and the whole scene feels chaotically comfortable. I finally select a book[234] and head to the cashier.

"I'm sorry," a harried young girl behind the counter tells me. "The registers are closed for the next fifteen minutes."

"Oh . . . okay," I say, before realizing it's kind of weird to have a packed store that isn't taking advantage of the captive customers. "Wait, is something going on?"

"Yes!" the girl gushes. "Howard Dean's going to be here in five minutes to discuss his book on health-care reform!"

I can feel my eyes bulge out of my head, and I turn to look at Fletch, standing in the middle of the Howard Dean crowd, thumbing through a gun magazine, his Ronald Reagan shirt drawing icy glares from all of those around him. He might as well have been erecting a cross in a public classroom or taking a leak on the *Roe versus Wade* case brief.

"Drop the magazine, we have to go!" I hiss.

"What, why?" he asks.

....

[234]Mostly because there's a cupcake on the cover.

"Because we're accidentally committing a hate crime!" I swat the magazine out of his hands and drag him out of the store by the wrist. "Move, move, move!" I hustle him out onto the sidewalk like I'm Jack Bauer, and I'm trying to keep his dumb ass from getting exploded. Once out, I pull him across the street and duck into the expensive candy store.

Fletch is confused but fairly pliant. "You really need a chocolate fix that badly?"

I peer on the happenings across the street through a window almost obscured by cartoon lollipops and stacks of multicolored sweets. I don't see anything, so I turn back to talk to him. "No, Howard Dean's about to give a talk about his book on health-care reform in there."

Fletch laughs so heartily that his head tilts back. "Ha! What are the odds? Why'd we have to leave? I bet that'd be *fun*."

"Yeah, and that's exactly why I yanked you out of there. I didn't want to be disrespectful at someone else's book signing. Terrible karma. Plus, even if you kept your mouth shut, with everything happening in the news, no one was going to believe you were there at that specific moment in that exact shirt because I can't take my Kindle in the tub."[235]

He picks up a paint bucket full of candy and looks at it quizzically. "Eh, I'm sure no one noticed."

"And I'm sure I saw pitchforks, lighted torches, and angry villagers. We had to go; it was the right thing to do."

What I fail to mention is, I was afraid my dinner host was in the crowd, and I don't want to get kicked out of Authors Night before it even happens.

---

[235]My friend Heather used to work with Howard Dean, and she says he has an amazing sense of humor. But I wasn't going to stick around and find out.

"Hey, look around," Fletch instructs.

"What am I looking for?" I glance up from my Kindle.[236]

"Tell me what you *don't* see."

"Um, I don't know. Monkeys? An office park? Martha Stewart flying a melting cake? What are you getting at?" What I do see is a mass expanse of shoreline ringed by mansions. Today we're camped on Main Beach, specifically because I wanted to be near a snack bar and none of the other East Hampton beaches have them. I mean, yes, I appreciate miles of stunning vistas and loads of privacy, but is any of it really worth it if I can't enjoy the scenery with a Diet Coke and an ice-cream sandwich?

"No one's on the phone. And no one has tattoos. Remember when we went to Oak Street Beach last year? It was like *Miami Ink* meets an iPhone commercial. But here? Everyone seems to be talking to the people they're with. It's like, families are actually being *families* together. Only a couple of people are attached to their electronic devices, and the few who aren't chatting are reading. It's almost"—he raises one eyebrow at me—"surreal."

There's an extended family camped out in front of us, maybe fifteen of them in all, with at least two sets of parents, a ton of children, and possibly a nanny sprinkled in. The whole time we've been here, they've been engaged in a group project. Two of the dads and most of the kids have been working on digging a crater in the beach. They're trying to dig deep

---

[236]I have a splash-proof cover, which makes it fine for the beach and pool, but not for the bathtub.

enough to hit water. They even brought real shovels, the kind I used to threaten hipsters with at my old house.

"This place is like taking a trip back to 1950," I say.

"It is," he agrees. "I like it."

We watch Project Hole until the family hits water about seven feet down. There's a mass amount of celebrating, but once everyone's congratulated one another, they all work together to fill in the crater. Then women collect some of the children and start hauling their gear back to their cars.

The family isn't loud and they're certainly polite, but they all work together so seamlessly that we can't help but pay attention. And this is why we both hear a dad detail weekend plans to one of the little boys.

"Hey, sport, I need your help bringing the rest of the chairs to the car. We're finished at the beach for today. When we get back to the house, you guys are going to jump into the pool to rinse all the sand off, then you'll get dressed because we're going to your dad's polo match. Tonight, we've got a private room at the restaurant for dinner, and tomorrow we'll hit the beach early. We're going to leave by two because we've chartered a boat, and we're going to go fishing and tubing. And then, once we're done, your dad and I are going to try to convince the moms to stay out here another couple of days."

And then the little boy in the SPF sun shirt says something that dissipates all the goodwill I'd built up toward them.

"It's so boring here; I don't want to stay! I want to go back to the city!"

I whisper to Fletch, "Do you think they might be willing to adopt us?"

"I have a stronger back and I'm much more efficient with a shovel. If they're taking anyone, they're taking me," he responds.

Eventually, the family clears out and we go back to our reading. I'm engrossed in my novel when I hear a voice next to me. "Excuse me, but is that the new Kindle DX?"

I glance up to the twentysomething kid standing beside me. "Yes. This one just came out a few weeks ago. You see how much bigger the screen is? It's more like reading a hardcover book than a paperback. Care to take a look?"

"You don't mind?"

"Not at all," I say, handing it over. I'd be willing to bet my, well, I guess my Kindle that he's not going to take off with it.

I show the kid all the features and demonstrate how to purchase a book, and then I show him where all my stuff's archived. He scans my library of titles. "Hey, Henry Miller and Margaret Atwood? You have good taste."

Sheepishly, I admit, "I'm hoping they balance out the Lauren Conrad."

He laughs and says, "Yeah, I saw that." Then he tells Fletch and me about how he'd talked to some girl at a party last night and she got all officious, saying she'd never once seen a reality television show. He sums up the encounter saying, "I figure she was lying or incredibly pretentious; in either case, no, thanks. I mean, come on, *The Hills? Everyone* watches reality television."

Oh, random beach guy, don't I know it.

I'm standing in the breakfast room of the inn, freaking the hell out. I'm having a huge crisis of confidence right now. Fletch, for lack of knowing what else to do, has taken me down here to fill up on freshly baked cookies before our car service arrives. (They have homemade key limeade but it doesn't pair well with white chocolate chip macadamia cookies, so I stick with wine.)

Hearing me panic and pace, the manager steps out of his office to offer assistance. Considering the level of service we've received here—beach chairs, umbrellas, coolers, six kinds of freshly baked cookies, et cetera, I'm sure he'd shoot me with a tranquilizing dart should I request one.[237]

"Can I do anything for you?" he asks.

"Do you know how to stop a panic attack?" I reply, while Fletch stands behind me mouthing *"drama queen"* and making drinky-drinky gestures.

"I've yet to figure that out," the manager admits. "If you find a way, please share. Seriously, though, what's happening?"

I explain about Authors Night and how I wheedled my way into coming and how even though I did everything I could to prepare, I still feel like I've shown up for the first day of seventh grade n-a-k-e-d.

"Are you an author?" he asks.

"Yes."

"Have you sold books?"

"Yeah, kind of a whole bunch."

"Then you belong there." The manager leans in conspiratorially to me. "Listen, years ago I used to be a TV writer. I wrote soap operas. Once back in the eighties, I was nominated for an Emmy, and I felt so unworthy."

Fletch has stopped mocking me and started listening. "What did you do?"

----

[237] I have love for the Mill House Inn.

"I went to the awards ceremony, and when they called my name as the winner, I tamped down any feelings I had of insecurity, I walked on that stage in front of Susan Lucci and everybody, and I said *thank you.* And it was one of the best moments of my life."

I exhale, suddenly feeling much better. "That's a really good story."

The manager shrugs. "I was a really good writer. Now it looks like your car is here, so you go walk in there like you own the joint. Remember, own it!"

We get in the car and arrive at Authors Night a few minutes before it starts. The event's being held in an enormous white tent, right behind the East Hampton library. Something like a hundred authors are participating, signing donated books, with all the proceeds going directly to the library. Patrons get to mingle and drink cocktails and meet any writer who catches their interest.

There are four quadrants of tables under the tent, and I make almost an entire lap around the space, looking for my spot. There are tons of names I recognize on the placards in front of the seats, and I cross my fingers that I'll be allowed to sit where I can watch them.

I come across one grouping of tables, and I practically swoon when I see who's stationed there—first up, Alec Baldwin, then Candace Bushnell, Jay McInerney, Barbara Walters, and then a couple down from them, the one who excites me most of all, Bethenny Frankel. On the other side of the table, I see spots for the Countess from *Real Housewives New York* and a bunch of *New York Times* bestsellers and my friend Stephanie Klein and . . . me? Wait, I'm with *them?*

Oh, my God, I'm at the "big table." I'm rock star adjacent! For the first time in my life, it's like I'm finally sitting with the adults at Thanksgiving! I can turn around and touch Bethenny or Barbara, because they're both *right behind me.* Suddenly I'm very, very grateful to the manager for helping me feel like I'm not one huge party crasher.

"Stephanie," I hiss behind the back of the author seated between us. "Do you see who we're sitting with? Do you see? Ohmigod, ohmigod, ohmigod!"

Stephanie's from New York and so doesn't go into superridiculous tourist mode when she encounters famous people. Actually, she's so cool and at ease with the situation, when she suggests I talk to some of my idols before it gets busy, I actually do.

I turn around and introduce myself to Bethenny, and she couldn't be nicer or less intimidating. She's stunning in person, and taller than you'd think. Plus, she's wearing a madras dress, yet I do not take this opportunity to explain that her fabric choice makes us besties. Score one for self-control!

Stephanie gets some shots of us together, and Bethenny and I discuss, for lack of a better or less pretentious term, our *craft.* Bethenny worked with a coauthor on her *Naturally Thin* book and tells me she wrote the first draft and then went over the final draft, but her coauthor did everything in between. "Don't you find that part so hard?" she asks me. "Does anyone work with you to write the middle of your books?"

"No," I giggle, giddy to be having a real conversation where—at least in the writing world—I'm kind of a peer. "I, um, write memoirs. I'm sort of obligated to write the whole thing myself since it's all about my life." We talk for another minute or so, and I'm psyched to discover the charm and humor she displayed on the show is genuine; her "reality" is actually real.

Then I meet Countess de Lesseps, and we converse briefly and at no point do I say anything idiotic. I don't try to touch her hair or remark on the smoothness of her hands or ask if she'll pretty please tell Jill Zarin I love her or anything. We're just two authors saying hello; it's awesome.

Once the event begins, I talk to authors who'd normally intimidate me, but between pep talks from Stephanie and the inn manager, I finally recognize that I have common ground with them.

As patrons drift by my table, we make pleasant small talk about all kinds of stuff, like writing and dining and wine and cheese. I chat with a woman about the show I attended at the Steppenwolf Theatre earlier this month and I have fun doing it. But our conversation isn't pretentious—it's just stuff I happen to enjoy now.

All too soon, the event comes to an end and I make it through with barely a faux pas, especially if you don't count Fletch going around taking pictures of celebrities' butts. ("But Baldwin wasn't wearing a belt!" he explains later when we review the shots on my computer. "And Barbara Walters had visible panty lines. Aren't you glad to know she's not into thongs?")

Right before we leave for the second part of the evening—the dreaded dinner—I talk to my icons. First, I see Candace Bushnell and thank her for inadvertently starting me on this project. She says she remembers me, but even if she doesn't, I still feel like I've come full circle from last spring when I didn't know my Baudelaire from a bowling ball.

I tell her, "Remember when you said your husband was with the American Ballet Theatre and everyone wants to sleep with him? Well, that's mine over there"—I gesture to Fletch, who's wandering around the periphery of the party looking for more wine—"the one who works for the phone company and no one wants to sleep with." But despite not being dressed in seersucker, he looks very handsome, and Candace chuckles.

Then I meet Jay McInerney, which is the biggest deal of all for me.

I've been reading him for twenty years and *Bright Lights, Big City* was the inspiration for the tongue-in-cheek title of my second book. I worship him as an author, and I've been in awe of his talent since my twenties. Which is why I assumed I'd end up blurting all the stupid thoughts at the forefront of my mind, like *"Hey, do you ever want to punch people when they tell you how much they loved* Less Than Zero[238] *and* American Psycho[239] *and do you think Michael J. Fox totally ruined your movie[240] and does anyone ever get up your ass about writing* Bright Lights *in the second person because, really, pretentious much? And how cool is it that being on* Gossip Girl *totally introduced you to an entirely new generation?"*

Instead, I steel my nerves, quiet my Shame Rattle, introduce myself, and say, "I'm honestly thrilled to meet you because I've been a fan since the eighties. Here's the thing—I've been working on a project and one of the phases of it is to read classic literature. I have to say in a hundred years, everyone's still going to know who you are. The way you write is every bit as important and poignant as the classics I've been covering. Think about *The Great Gatsby*—that book's still alive because Fitzgerald was able to take the Jazz Age, a very specific moment in time, and freeze it forever. And that's exactly what you did with *Bright Lights, Big City*. You captured what it was like to be in New York during a key moment of the eighties so no one will ever forget it. When people talk about the classics years from now, you're going to be part of that conversation."

He seems a bit surprised at my monologue and he's quiet for a second before responding thoughtfully. "Thank you, that's . . . a really great compliment and I'm quite flattered. Thank you."

....
[238]By Bret Easton Ellis.

[239]Also Bret Easton Ellis.

[240]Because he did.

He seems so genuine in his appreciation that I wonder if he didn't hear about *Gossip Girl* and *Less Than Zero* more than once tonight.

We pull up to a hulking home directly on the water. Some earlier Google-stalking tells me that the host has her own strip of private beach and this causes new waves of terror to flash through me. Although the evening has cooled, I'm sweating through my wrap. Despite the success of the event, the Sword of Dumb Ass is back and feels like it's dangling right over my head again.

We pass through giant boxwood hedges, traverse the crushed-shell circular drive, and arrive at the front door. Fletch squeezes my hand for luck before I ring the bell.

The door opens and my trial by fire begins.

Three hours later, I pass through the same door and I emerge . . . unscathed.

"You didn't get kicked out."

"Not only were we not kicked out, but we were fun and charming, and people seemed to like us. We were possibly the very best behaved guests there."[241]

....

[241]Except when Fletch snuck off to smoke.

"No way."

"Way."

I'm at lunch with Stacey, doing the whole post-Hamptons wrap-up. I've already described how great the authors' cocktail reception was, and Stacey was totally excited to hear that our favorite *Real Housewives* character is just as funny and snarky in person. I've moved on to describe the dinner portion of the evening.

"We get to the house and it's frigging enormous. It just goes on and on, and from where we stand in the entry hall, we can see a bunch of different wings spiraling off of it. I knew I'd be in this giant mansion by the sea, but until I saw it, I didn't have the full perspective."[242]

Driving up to that house, with my heart in my throat, I was ready to simply turn around and run. Fletch said we'd do whatever I wanted, but gently encouraged me to stick with it, as I'd already come this far.

"The host's the one who answers the door, only instead of looking like the enemy or something, she's this sweet, unassuming older lady who immediately makes us feel welcome. And as for the house, as soon as we get in it, we can see that every room is warm and full of books and family pictures, and it's homey, and even though it's massive, it's super-welcoming."

The host had kind eyes and soft gray hair, and she was wearing a tunic and some cute summer pants. Her outfit made me reassess the whole situation. I mean, the enemy can't possibly wear capris, right?

Stacey nods, drawing her feet in underneath her. I close my eyes for a second, trying to recall every detail. "We go out to this huge back room, surrounded by windows and there's water on three sides of us. Wish it

---

[242]Again, despite having checked it on both Google Earth and Google Street View.

had been lighter because I was dying to see the view. Anyway, we're seated with a bunch of well-heeled people, including this old guy who's next to me. We start talking and I tell him we're from Chicago. And he's all, 'Oh, I have a niece who lives by you.' And I say, 'Really? Where does she live?' I'm thinking maybe Lincoln Park or Andersonville or something. Then he goes, 'She's in Columbus, Ohio.'"

"Isn't that something like six hours away from here?" Stacey asks.

"It is. But I figure I'm talking to an old New Yorker who assumes that everything between there and LA is flyover country, and it's not worth having a geography fight. His arrogance is a little astounding, but it's more funny than anything. And then—then! While we're talking, he takes his finger, sticks it in his right nostril, and starts panning for gold, which kills me. I mean, how rich do you have to be not to care if you pick your nose in front of people?"

Stacey gives me a knowing nod. "That's called 'fuck you' money. If you don't like me picking my nose, then fuck you."

The old man pretty much puts the nail in the coffin on my theory that culture (and cash) equals class. And I realize the only way to accomplish my goal of being classier is to actively monitor my own behavior. I don't need outside learning. Yeah, having a solid background in theater and music and literature is nice, but if I want everyone to feel comfortable around me, I simply need to be conscious of being gracious, easy as that.

"Totally. So then the host sits down at our table, and I get tense. I figured I'd be safe if she weren't around, but she's directly across from me. The old couple next to me starts talking about visiting Cuba and how great it is and how Castro's been instrumental in providing health care for people, but before they can sing any more of his praises, I immediately asked about the Cuban food they ate."

Seriously, we were about to head down the health-care nationalization path, and I was pretty sure that Mrs. Media Matters and I would have different opinions. But that wasn't an appropriate situation in which to share those opinions, particularly unsolicited. Fortunately, I've learned enough in my Jenaissance not only to completely change the subject, but to do it with enough familiarity and panache that no one even notices.

"Did politics come up?" Stacey wants to know.

"Yes, they did in the context of the talk the general gave after we ate. What's ironic is Fletch and I were the ones who sat there like good little soldiers, but some of the rich old guys at the dinner kind of lit into the general about military strategy."

I hated hearing some of the questions a few guests asked, not just because of their incendiary tone, but because they didn't seem to treat the general with the respect he deserved. Yet their actions gave me such insight to all the times I've behaved similarly in the past.

"But overall," I declare, "we kicked ass. And we even had wine!"

A giggle inadvertently escapes from Stacey before she covers her mouth with her hand. "Wow, sorry; it's just wine usually works like truth serum on you. Or magic talking juice."

"I know! But I held it together. Frankly, I'm as surprised as anyone. Seriously, though, the biggest surprise of the night was the lady I was so worried about turned out to be completely, utterly lovely. There were plenty of opportunities for her to express dissenting opinions, but she never did. She made sure her guests felt welcome because the dinner wasn't about politics; it was about charity. The whole night I kept thinking I was a spy behind enemy lines, only to find out for the most part the enemy's not so different from us."

"I'm really proud of you." Stacey beams.

"Hey, you did an awful lot to help me get there. This was a group effort, so thank you."

"I'm so glad. By the way, how were the beasts?"

"The dogs had the time of their lives at the kennel, of course." These dogs also enjoy trips to the vet; they're strange.

"And the tiny devils?"

"Um . . . I suspect we're going to need a new cat sitter next time. I saw some blood on the carpet in the room where I was keeping them, and there's not a scratch on any of the Thundercats. But what's hilarious is the kittens were so freaked out to see a stranger in our house that they've totally been sucking up to us ever since we got home."

"Awesome. So, what's next?"

"You'll laugh when you hear this, but honestly, as soon as I get the book done? I'm going to work out so much!"

"Good for you!"

"Yeah, it's time. Plus, I'm going to continue with the Jenaissance. I don't feel like I'm done learning or growing yet. I mean, I want to see my first opera, live and in person. I don't *have* to; I *want* to. I've got a ton of cultural stuff already on tap with Joanna. And Fletch and I are going to keep taking cooking classes and going to wine seminars and trying new foods. Turns out we love having some shared hobbies. I mean, we've always been on the same page about society and politics and religion and everything, but in terms of interests, we never had that much in common, so we always ended up doing the lowest-common-denominator activity, which was watching television. Now we've got lots of stuff to do to get us out of the house."

When Fletch and I were on our way home from the Hamptons, we talked a lot about what we've both learned from this process. Oddly enough, the biggest lesson has come from Maisy getting sick. When she was diagnosed, we realized our time with her isn't unlimited like we'd blindly assumed. So it's up to us to make sure each of her days is happy. Maybe we can't change the course of her destiny, but we can make every minute with her count.

That's when it hit us—our own time on this earth is limited and we're getting older. If we can't come up with some kind of alchemy to stop the aging process, then we're obligated to make the most of what we have, and the best way to do that is expand the depth of our experiences. Do we want to spend the next thirty years on the couch, waiting to see who wins *America's Next Top Model* Cycle Forty-Five, or do we want to fill our lives with a million new experiences, even if sometimes they're unpredictable or scary or take effort?

Essentially, we realized we need to keep diving in.

And if we do, our lives won't be richer for being long; our lives will be richer for having *lived*.

In the course of this project, I read the original text of George Bernard Shaw's *Pygmalion*. In the play's introduction, Nicholas Grene writes that *Pygmalion* deals with two beliefs in conflict with each other: The first has to do with human beings having the capacity to re-create themselves, overcoming one's social or regional origin. The other contradicts this, as Shaw also maintained that no one could be so transformed that they weren't still essentially the person they were before their metamorphosis.

Or, to put it in reality-television terms, you can't edit in that which didn't happen.

Stacey laughs as I finish my Hampton tales and proclaims, "I guess your people like to say 'Mission accomplished' in cases like this. You danced at the Empire Ball, and now everyone's whispering and wondering if you aren't actually royalty. Well played, Miss Doolittle. Well played."

I should be basking in all my accomplishments over the past nine months, yet there's one thing I haven't told Stacey.

I clear my throat and begin. "Um, yeah . . . about that. My record isn't completely spotless. There was one small, barely worth mentioning incident in the Hamptons. You see, Alec Baldwin was about to leave the event and I wanted to get a picture with him."

Stacey stops me. "Ooh, is he dreamy in person?"

"*Pfft*, he was so dreamy that Fletch may have even considered switching teams.[243] Fletch and I kind of chased after him to see if we could get a shot taken together. But Alec was in a rush and had to go but he wanted to make sure he wasn't snubbing someone important by running off to his dinner. He looks at me—not rude or anything, just direct—and goes, *'I'm sorry, who are you?'*"

I run my hands through my newly extension-free hair and continue. "And somehow every single thing I've worked on for all these months totally flew out the window, and I looked him dead in the eye and said, '*New York Times* bestselling author, motherfucker.'"

Shame Rattle, Shame Rattle, Shame Rattle.

I sigh and continue. "I'm pretty sure he was so stunned, he held out his arm so we could pose for the picture together."

Stacey grins and pats me on the shoulder. "So there's that," she says.

I nod. "So there's that."

---

[243]Had Baldwin been wearing a belt, that is.

E·P·I·L·O·G·U·E

*L*ast Friday, Joanna and I attended a Stars of Lyric Opera performance in Millennium Park. Joanna stopped to buy us German food
for our picnic dinner because she wanted me to give her culture's cuisine
another shot. And you know what? Sauerbraten is way better than expected, and live opera is everything I ever dreamed it might be. Just
thinking of the performance still gives me goose bumps.

As for Fletch, he and I are loving our whole new, enhanced life together, and tonight we're dining at Alinea.

Later we'll eat scallops served on a pillow full of lavender air and a
tiny, perfect chunk of Wagyu beef presented with an ironic A1 powder,
but first we have to get past the osetra, also known as fish eggs.

Instead of serving his Black Sea caviar on a bed of ice with traditional toast points spread with butter, Chef Achatz has emulsified the
buttery toast into chilled, fluffed foam and covered it with a sprinkling of
the tiny black pearls.

Caviar has traditionally scared the bejesus out of me, and the few
times I've been offered it, I immediately rehomed the horrible little bastards to the edge of my plate or the inside of my napkin. I remember once

shaking my hand in revulsion as a black sturgeon egg clung to my index finger.

But today? Here? In this post-Jenaissance life?

I simply dive in.

Turns out I kind of love caviar.

Never saw that coming.

A·C·K·N·O·W·L·E·D·G·M·E·N·T·S

First and always, my biggest thanks go out to my readers. Because of you I have a job where I don't have to serve coffee anymore and that makes me incredibly happy. You guys rock and I'll do my best to return the favor.

A million thanks to everyone at NAL—Kara Welsh, Claire Zion, Craig Burke, Melissa Broder, Sharon Gamboa, and the rest of the ass-kicking teams in editorial, sales, art, publicity, marketing, travel, and production. I sincerely thank you for everything you do; I know how hard you all work. (And, Kara C., I miss you!)

For Kate Garrick and the rest of the crew at DeFiore, thank you for keeping this ship afloat in the stormy sea of my own neurosis. (I'm not easy but it's adorable that you all pretend I am.)

I need to thank my writer friends for all their support, particularly Danny Evans, Caprice Crane, Allison Winn Scotch, Karyn Bosnak, Tatiana Boncompagni, and Stephanie Klein. Thanks for being there! And many thanks to Melissa C. Morris—the world's a more gracious place for having you in it.

I feel very lucky to have had this project bring me closer to some of my best friends in the world. Mad love and pink drinks to Joanna, Gina,

Acknowledgments

Tracey, Angie, Carol, Wendy, Jen, Poppy, and Blackbird. Everything's a party when you guys are around!

Big, huge thanks go to Stacey Ballis, who is not only a frigging encyclopedia of high culture, but also, like, the funnest person I know. (Yeah, I quoted *Romy and Michelle*. What of it?) I could not have done this without you. Team Stennifer rules!

Many thanks to the folks at the East Hampton Library for letting me into the fancy party, thus giving me the best ending I could possibly imagine. If you have me back, I'll bring Baldwin a belt.

Endless love, devotion, and unbreakable promises to pick up dry cleaning go to Fletch. Technically this book was more fun for him than the ones in which we were broke or I was dieting, but still. I can be difficult during "writing season" and he remains steadfast. I love you so much I won't even tell everyone how you accidentally backed my new car into a burrito stand because you were ignoring the parking sensors. (Oh, wait.) And P.S., everyone realizes you're not gay.

Finally, an enormous round of thanks goes to everyone on my television who ever ate a bug, flipped a table, married a stranger, made out with a roommate, spit on a competitor, took a bubble bath with Flavor Flav, or had a bitch get beer in your weave. I might not be tuning in quite so frequently anymore, but I'll still be watching.